# Music Moments
## To Teach Academics

by Kerri Lynn Nichols

Artwork by
Robin Adalina Landsong

Dedicated to my husband, Scott, and my sons, Kyler and Sam, for their endless support, love, laughs and encouragement to continue with this project and to all of the teachers and students across the country who have contributed in some way to this project.

Illustrations and cover artwork by Robin Adalina Landsong.

Consulting Editor
Scott M. LaViollette

Associate Editors
Brent Holl, Karen Holl

Published by
Beatin' Path Publications, LLC
302 East College Street
Bridgewater, VA 22812

Music Moments to Teach Academics

© 2001 by Kerri Lynn Nichols. All rights reserved.
Published 2001. Third edition 2010. Fourth edition 2014.
Olympia, WA 98501

Order at www.beatinpathpublications.com
beatinpath@mac.com

**All rights reserved. No part of this book may be reproduced, in any form or by any means, without permission in writing from the publisher.**

Printed in the United States of America
ISBN: 978-0-9894773-1-4

# PREFACE

The writing of this book has been a long journey. Twenty years ago, when I began my college career, I had no idea where my educational pursuits would take me, but I knew my music would be the catalyst that would deliver me to my destination.

During my undergraduate years at Washington State University, I found it difficult to choose between Music Performance and Elementary Education, so I did what all type A perfectionists do: pursued degrees in both fields. Even at that time, I had a sincere interest in teaching in the regular classroom and was very excited about the prospect of integrating the arts to teach the curriculum, an idea that was not well-researched or implemented. Growing up with music, it seemed a natural for me.

Since that time, 17 years of teaching experience in the public and private sectors and two graduate degrees later, I have come to strongly believe in the power of learning through the arts as essential to preserving our heritage, culture and world peace and have become somewhat of an "activist" in the field. With the support of current research such as the theory of multiple intelligences (Howard Gardner) as well as new developments in the understanding of the brain and its functions, the practice of teaching through an integrated model is becoming a widespread phenomenon. Children who before were doomed to fail in the educational system are now given the opportunity to fulfill their intelligence and to see themselves as capable, creative and articulate beings.

This book was also written for educators. Through years of working with groups of teachers, my esteem for the incredible work these dedicated people have taken on has only grown. The ideas have come from creating experiences of learning with students and teachers of all ages and are intended as a starting place for you in your efforts to bring the gift of music into your pedagogy. All change begins with a thought - a challenge of looking at things from a different perspective. It is not necessarily an easier way of teaching, but a better one that empowers students, encourages teachers and creates a basis for which we can begin to build up our communities and each other. Take my ideas and develop your own, and remember the joy of learning.

I would like to sincerely thank Anne Green Gilbert for writing *Teaching The Three R's Through Movement Experiences* and for her inspiration, friendship and encouragement of this project.

*Kerri Lynn Nichols*

## TABLE OF CONTENTS

**Chapter One:** Introduction To Music Experiences..................................................1
- Music Is A Language...............................................................................1
- Inclusion.................................................................................................1
- What Is Music?.......................................................................................2
- Unconventional Sound Sources.............................................................4
- The Elements and Concepts of Dance....................................................7
- What Is Music?.......................................................................................8
- Why Children Learn Through Music.....................................................9
- Personal Music Reflection Inventory...................................................10
- The Elements and Concepts of Music..................................................11
- National Music Standards.....................................................................12
- Questions for Discussion......................................................................13

**Chapter Two:** Approaches To Integration............................................................14
- Three Approaches To Music Integration..............................................15
  - Supplemental..................................................................................15
  - Social..............................................................................................16
    - Building Community................................................................16
    - The Five A's of Audience.........................................................17
    - The Sandwich Principle............................................................17
    - Social Music Integration Links................................................18
  - Cognitive........................................................................................18
    - Music Moments.........................................................................18
      - Music Moment Criteria........................................................18
      - Subject Link..........................................................................19
      - Conceptual Link....................................................................19
    - BrainDance................................................................................20
    - BrainPlay...................................................................................21
    - BrainPlay Story: The Bakery....................................................23
    - Lesson Plan Format...................................................................25
      - Sample Lesson Plan..............................................................26
    - Day Plan Format.......................................................................27
      - Sample Day Plan #1..............................................................28
      - Sample Day Plan #2..............................................................29
    - Conceptual Lesson Plan: Weeklong Format............................30
      - Example Weeklong Format..................................................31
    - Lesson Plan Format (Template)................................................32
    - Day Plan Format (Template).....................................................34
    - Conceptual Lesson Plan: Weeklong (Template)......................36

**Chapter Three:** Language Arts and Music............................................................38
- The Concepts of Language Arts...........................................................39
- Music Moments....................................................................................40

| | | |
|---|---|---|
| Chapter Four: | Mathematics and Music.................................................................................68 | |
| | The Concepts of Mathematics.....................................................69 | |
| | Music Moments...........................................................................70 | |
| Chapter Five: | Science and Music......................................................................................104 | |
| | The Concepts of Science...........................................................105 | |
| | Music Moments.........................................................................106 | |
| Chapter Six: | Social Studies and Music............................................................................128 | |
| | The Concepts of Social Studies.................................................129 | |
| | Music Moments.........................................................................131 | |
| Chapter Seven | Visual Arts and Music.................................................................................142 | |
| | The Concepts of Visual Arts......................................................143 | |
| | Music Moments.........................................................................144 | |
| Chapter Eight: | Wellness and Music....................................................................................150 | |
| | The Concepts of Wellness.........................................................151 | |
| | Music Moments.........................................................................152 | |
| Chapter Nine: | Pedagogy: Tips For Success.......................................................................168 | |
| Chapter Ten: | Resources....................................................................................................174 | |
| | Materials....................................................................................175 | |
| | Musical Name Games................................................................178 | |
| | Vocal Warm-Ups.......................................................................180 | |
| | Familiar Tunes...........................................................................181 | |
| | Forms and Structures For Music Making..................................182 | |
| | Sample Block Charts.................................................................184 | |
| | Simple Rhythmic Notation........................................................185 | |
| | The Melody Chart......................................................................186 | |
| | Glossary of Musical Terms........................................................187 | |
| | General Discography.................................................................193 | |
| | Conceptual Discography...........................................................201 | |
| | Bibliography..............................................................................238 | |
| | Websites....................................................................................246 | |
| | Videography/DVD....................................................................247 | |
| | Rhythmic Notation Paper..........................................................250 | |
| | Staff Paper.................................................................................252 | |

# Chapter One:
# Introduction To Music Experiences

*Music Moments To Teach Academics: Introduction to Music Experiences*

## MUSIC IS A LANGUAGE

Music is a language common to all the people of the earth. It can express thoughts and emotions where words fall short. It is a form of communication that can be traced back to the earliest times of man and has only grown in depth and diversity over the ages. Through music, our heritage is preserved and passed on from generation to generation. Music can celebrate the joy of individuality while building people together in a community. Throughout the ages, music has been associated with healing, rituals, gatherings, spirituality, history, mathematics, science, social studies and much more and still is today.

A great deal of time is spent in our educational systems developing verbal and visual skills, while our aural vocabulary, to some extent, is virtually unexplored. Children receive little or no training in listening skills and yet this ability or disability will affect their success in many areas. As a focus on standardized tests has returned, many music programs are being cut out as frills, but are they?

Recent research supports music as an intelligence or a way of knowing, both as a separate discipline and to support learning in other disciplines through integration (see Bibliography). Howard Gardner has stated in his theory of multiple intelligences that all people have musical/rhythmic intelligence that can be nurtured and developed to enhance other intelligences. By experiencing music to learn, children are challenged to use divergent, creative thinking to solve problems and answer questions. They are able to stretch their abilities and are supported in learning via exploration. Music activities motivate children to learn by nurturing self-esteem and creating a group excitement and energy towards the learning. When music experiences are inclusive, they provide a model for cooperative learning instead of competition, which tends to exclude and discourage many students. Music is also linked to increased memory function, where students can retain up to 90% of the material learned with fewer review sessions. Current studies regarding brain research also point to musicking (actively creating or engaging in music) as a means of developing new synapses between neurons, right and left brain integration, enhanced sensory integration and building multiple brain functions (cognitive, emotional and motor abilities).

## INCLUSION

It is important to emphasize that the model for participating in music experiences in this book is one of inclusion. Music belongs to every person and each of us has musical ability. It is our heritage, our birthright. This is a difficult concept to accept in modern American society, which promotes competition over a collective approach: those who are talented perform, those who are not will watch and listen only. This view of music is not widely held by the rest of the world. In many cultures, there is no word for "art." Music plays an important role in the daily life of the community, where all contribute and participate. It creates a common language and format for sharing stories, passing on traditions and history, commemorating important events, celebrating, accompanying work in the field or gathering people together towards a shared goal. What brain research is now confirming, the world's oldest cultures have known for centuries: Music is essential to fulfill humankind's life potential. Our brains are biologically wired for music.

Many may have had negative experiences with music early in life that have shaped a negative response to it today. Some may have been told by a well-meaning music teacher or parent, "Don't sing. . .just mouth the words." This is unfortunately a common story, however I have witnessed many of these people moving beyond these experiences and opening themselves to the possibility and power of music to enhance learning and life with extraordinary results. And now these same people are passing on their new growth and discoveries to their children, students, parents and communities. If you can breathe, if you can talk, if you can move - you can make music!

## WHAT IS MUSIC?

**Music is singing.** The voice is our first, natural instrument. Housed in the body, all of life's experiences can be expressed not only through words but also sounds: joy, anger, grief, excitement, stress, fear, laughter. The way in which we acquire language is also the way we develop our musical abilities, one small sound or word at a time.

Many people feel that they are "tone deaf"; that they can not match or reproduce pitches to their liking. Current research has shown that tone deafness is a misnomer and that these pitch-matching difficulties may be a result of hearing differently. Just as no two people taste food or see color exactly alike, the same can be true for hearing musical tones and sounds. What one needs are daily opportunities to sing and sing with others to refine the ear's ability to hear pitches. Everyone can learn how to sing well; it is simply a matter of experience and practice, just like math, reading and writing. Every person has a unique and precious voice that will serve them for eighty or ninety years; there are no two exactly alike. Again, the focus is on developing your own vocal potential without comparing yourself to others. Nurturing a positive attitude of acceptance with your students is essential and this begins with accepting your own voice. It helps to define what the goal of our singing is and children will usually buy into anything that is fun and helps them to be smarter, healthier and more successful. We need to sing with our students daily, focusing on age-appropriate songs that empower students to learn (see Bibliography for suggestions).

Many children in our country no longer sing as a means of play, communication, and self-entertainment. Some of this may be attributed to a preference for TV, computer games and other forms of passive entertainment. This should be of great concern to our society as our music, folksiness and popular culture pass on our history and reaffirm our connection to each other.

*Music Moments To Teach Academics: Introduction to Music Experiences*

Singing is a natural, childhood phenomenon, common to all cultures of the world. When children are singing they are getting more oxygen to the brain, resonating the cells in their body (long associated in the Far East with health and healing) and energizing their minds and creativity.

There are four forms of vocal use that will be discussed in this book in reference to music: *speaking, singing, whispering* and *shouting*. These four voices form the basis for a variety of our integrative experiences in the classroom. Using the voice for learning is economical: it is cheap, everyone has one and uses it every day and it is fun! In addition to these four voices, we can also engage in the following sounds: whistling, coughing, sneezing, laughing, tongue clicks, vowels, consonants, rolled tongue and "nature" sounds.

To create an environment for successful singing and vocal experiences with your students, keep the following in mind:

1. *Develop a daily, positive attitude towards singing. This starts with YOU! The students will follow your lead - an open, excited heart is more important than years of vocal training. Prepare students to look forward to this time. Don't focus on "mistakes." Instead, help your students keep the group goals in mind.*

2. *Choose good songs that have stood the test of time and empower/teach students. Begin with something simple that you feel confident leading or use a quality recording to give you a little "support."*

3. *For best success in singing, teach students to breathe deeply into the diaphragm (belly) and open their mouths the width of two fingers between the upper and lower teeth (this opens the throat). Stand or sit up tall, but relaxation is the key!*

4. *Keep a notebook of the songs the class sings and jot a few notes down next to each regarding favorites. A cappella singing (without instruments) is great and preferable to singing with a recording.*

5. *Singing makes a great ritual for several classroom activities: opening, closing, cleanup, transitions and celebrations.*

**Music is playing and making instruments**. We begin instrumental exploration by using *body percussion* (stomping, clapping, patting and snapping). Again, this is accessible to everyone and has the added benefit of providing tactile-sensory stimulus. With your students, experiment with how many different stomping, clapping, patting and snapping sounds they can make. Once the students are comfortable and adept at working with body percussion, they will be ready to explore other sounds, beginning with their immediate environment (the classroom). Students enjoy exploring the classroom, their homes (particularly the kitchen and garage) and the natural world to create instruments we call *found sounds*. They enjoy playing in the rhythm or drum circle (see Bibliography).

It is important in all of these musical experiences to emphasize the magic of play. Play is an essential part of developing creativity with any group of learners, and yet play is discarded by most of our educational institutions beyond the elementary level. We know from research that learning and brain growth continue into our elderly years and that this stage of life can actually be a return to the childlike qualities of youth. Play is where students can cast away preconceived rules and stereotypes and think "outside the box." It is essential that children are able to experience life through the laughter, energy and spontaneity of play, and music is the perfect catalyst. Through playing with sounds and the elements of music, students are encouraged to move beyond the knowledge and application levels of thinking and into analyzing and synthesizing. In these explorations, the children become aware of what they are learning and develop a new way of knowing; they are able to see multiple possibilities and find their unique voice to express themselves. The element of play also broadens their perspective beyond "right and wrong" answers. Games are used in this book to engage and enhance learning for students of all ages as well as free exploration of sounds and music resources. A good phrase to use with students is "When in doubt. . .improvise!" This not only gives them the freedom to explore divergent solutions, it builds their self-confidence in making decisions and trusting their inner knowledge. This phrase also applies to life!

Students love to make their own instruments. These can be recreations of existing instruments or *avant garde* style. There are several good texts available about instrument construction (see Bibliography), but the children enjoy creating their own. This process is an excellent study for the science of sound and spatial awareness. The instruments can then be used for other music integration experiences in the classroom. If you have a budget to work from, you can purchase a few key percussion instruments and supplement homemade items.

## UNCONVENTIONAL SOUND SOURCES (Found Sounds)

### Outdoor Materials

| | | | | |
|---|---|---|---|---|
| dirt | pebbles | rocks | leaves | grass |
| snow & ice | rain | twigs & sticks | branches | pine cones |
| nutshells | water | river stones | wind | corn husks |
| gourds | shells | sand | reeds | hollow logs |
| willow switches | gravel | lightning | thunder | eucalyptus pods |

*Music Moments To Teach Academics: Introduction to Music Experiences*

## Indoor Materials

| Paper | Rubber | Wood | Metal |
|---|---|---|---|
| construction paper | bands | ruler | kitchen utensils |
| wax paper | balloons | spatula | sheet metal |
| tissue paper | hose | yard stick | saws |
| newspaper | balls | bowls | tools |
| lightweight cardboard | inner tubes | bamboo sticks | cans |
| brown paper bags | tires | tongue depressors | wire |
| stationery paper | toys | pencils | pie tins |
| sandpaper | | blocks | pails |
| napkins | **Glass** | whistles | baking pans |
| magazines | | toys | cookie sheets |
| paper balls | soda bottles | tables | pipes |
| cardboard boxes | jugs | chairs | strips |
| old books | toys | clothespins | whistles |
| egg cartons | glasses | poles | toys |
| cardboard cylinders | jars | popsicle sticks | washtub |
| carpet cylinders | | brooms | nails |
| corrugated cardboard | **Plastic** | kitchen utensils | screws |
| straws | | containers | washers |
| milk containers | funnels | crates | bottle caps |
| paper maché | water jugs | dowels | paper clips |
| cigar boxes | ruler | | scissors |
| cups | straws | **Food** | bolts |
| detergent boxes | food containers | | foils |
| toilet paper rolls | bottles | seeds | trash cans |
| | sprayers | kernels | springs |
| **Other** | toys | rice | machines |
| | brushes | coffee beans | dustpans |
| string | buttons | sugar | pop cans |
| rope | combs | cereal flakes | car parts |
| flower pots | old records | condiments | |
| chamois | cups | grains | |
| calfskin | boxes | macaroni | |
| | tools | coconut shells | |
| | garden tubs | beans (uncooked) | |
| | shampoo bottles | nuts (in the shell) | |

*Music is listening*. We need to provide our students with opportunities to hone their listening skills. Many times, this ability is expected in the classroom but not cultivated. While music, in general, activates all areas of the brain to varying degrees, the process by which we "hear" sound is quite complex, integrating several brain systems to achieve a common goal. Research has shown that the musical elements of rhythm, melody, timbre and texture activate specific areas of the brain, both in the right *and* left hemispheres. Students can greatly improve their *aural vocabulary* by working with the concepts of music, particularly with singing and playing instruments daily. The development of this vocabulary builds a greater opportunity for educational success by increasing the percentage of what the child can hear and process. Hearing challenges can be identified early and corrected before a student is discouraged.

While every music experience can be a lesson in listening, there are specific explorations which help to develop these skills in depth and they are easily integrated within the curricula of the classroom. Sound stories, mapping and looping are examples of listening experiences that require multitasking, a skill wherein the brain can focus on two or more tasks simultaneously. Through integrating music into the curriculum, students can practice listening and following directions via modes other than speech. They learn alternative methods of communication through patterns of movement and sound, but not necessarily words. Listening actively, students become receptors of information from outside sources and are able to interact with that information to formulate a response. This skill is essential not only to success in school but in life as well.

*Music is creating*. The act of playing, improvising and making up stories, songs and chants comes naturally to children. In their early years, they are not aware of the complexities of what is occurring in the brain to produce such an endeavor. Our goal, as educators, is for students to begin to create their own learning, to personalize and expand on the many concepts explored in the classroom and find connections between these concepts and life. Music experiences encourage creative and divergent thinking, which is essential to mathematics and science. Students working through music are motivated to explore, question and develop several options to solving a given problem. This taxonomy of brain function is not merely a memorization exercise, but requires a personal engagement with the materials to create something new that can be shared with others.

Experiences in music creation that enhance academic learning include games, improvisation ("making it up as we go"), writing simple chants and songs, working with partners and small groups, developing soundscapes and sound stories, mathematical drum improvisation, experiments with sound science, creating folk dances and movement experiences, writing lyrics, chance music, orchestrating the alphabet and many more.

*Music is dancing*. It is impossible to discuss music without discussing dance. These two languages have been linked since the beginning of time. Movement is the key to learning and music is most efficiently learned through the process of movement. The majority of the music experiences in this book will focus on actively (physically) engaging students in the learning (body to mind link) in order to facilitate multiple brain system integration. Children run, jump, spin, hop, walk and skip as an essential part of each day. These "dances" feed the instinctive, social/emotional and thinking brains which must work together to achieve a balance in life. Movement also serves as a catalyst for body/muscle memory while regulating emotions, behavior and intellectual thought.

The creative movement concepts and the BrainDance presented here are based on the lifelong work of Anne Green Gilbert (see Bibliography). These concepts provide a foundation for delivery of the music concepts with success. As you work with the activities in this book, you will notice that your students are moving more. Remember that this is a direct indication that learning is occurring! Here are the basic movement concepts we will refer to:

## ELEMENTS AND CONCEPTS OF DANCE*

*SPACE*    place (self and general)
           size (small, medium, large)
           level (low, middle, high)
           direction (up, down, right, left, forward, backward)
           pathway (straight, curved, zig zag)
           focus (single and multi)

*TIME*     pace (slow, medium, fast)
           rhythm (pulse, pattern, grouping, breath)

*FORCE*  energy (sharp and smooth)
           weight (strong, light, heavy, weak)
           flow (free and bound)

*BODY*    parts (head, neck, torso, arms, legs, etc.)
           shapes (round, straight, angular, symmetrical/asymmetrical)
           relationships (mirror/shadow, over/under, opposites)
           balance (on and off)

*MOVEMENT*  locomotor (walk, run, skip, gallop, slide, etc.)
           non-locomotor (swing, sway, bounce, rock, twist, stretch, etc.)

*** from *Creative Dance For All Ages*, by Anne Green Gilbert. Used with permission.**

This vocabulary also provides students with a means of creating their own dances to varying styles of music. One style of dance that will be emphasized is that of *folk dancing*. Folk dancing is the heartbeat of music education. Developed as a dance of the people, the folk, it is a tradition of community sharing, unity and storytelling, rather than a performance art. Many of these dances are done in a circle to emphasize personal connection within the group dynamic. Folk dancing is a powerful way to share and experience world cultures. By learning, analyzing and creating their own folk dances, students are fully engaged in mathematical concepts such as sequencing, spatial awareness, formations and computations. Facilitated through movement, the learning is meaningful and memorable, creating a personal and physical connection between mind, body and experience. Music and dance bring people together. Folk dancing consistently with your students can completely change and improve the classroom climate and way they work cooperatively. Students who before functioned on the outside of the group, perhaps through disruptive behavior, often become positive leaders when movement is incorporated into the educational setting. Creative dance and folk dance are great equalizers!

*Music is Art*. As you begin to define music for yourself and your students, consider the following:

## WHAT IS MUSIC?

### Music is science.
It is an exact, specific language. It demands exact acoustics and the sounds can be analyzed and modified through experimentation. The musical score is a chart, a graph which indicates frequencies, intensities, volume changes, melody and harmony with the defining control of time.

### Music is mathematics.
It is rhythmically based on the subdivisions of time into fractions which must be performed instantly, not worked out on paper. It is logical and precise and processes in the brain identically to mathematics. It is sequences, patterns, intervals, symbols, formations, shapes, computations and tessellations.

### Music is language.
It is communication, a specific, nonverbal language. Music notation is a highly developed kind of shorthand that uses symbols to represent ideas. The semantics of music are the most complete and universal language, going beyond words and evidenced in all human cultures.

### Music is history.
Music reflects the environment and times of its creators, often even the country, culture or racial feeling. It is steeped in tradition; a storyteller that connects the past to the present and future. It is a living, breathing record of time through human interaction and response.

*Music Moments To Teach Academics: Introduction to Music Experiences*

**Music is physical education.**
It requires coordination of fingers, hands, arms, lips, facial muscles, breath, torso, spine, shoulders, legs and is, therefore, a full-body experience. In addition, it develops extraordinary control of the diaphragm, back, stomach and chest muscles. The brain responds instantly to the sound the ears hear and the mind interprets. Music activates all parts of the brain which in turn creates a response in the body.

**Music is reading.**
Music provides practice in reading and tracking horizontally and vertically, through use of scores and lyric sheets. It is verbally engaging, using words for singing, learning rhythm and discussing aesthetics. It is visual and verbal.

**Music is all of these things, but most of all, Music is Art.**
It allows a human being to take all of these technical concepts and techniques and use them to create powerful emotion. Music is an expression of our perception and meaning of life: purpose, feeling, choice, struggle, and triumph!

## *WHY CHILDREN LEARN THROUGH MUSIC MAKING*

**Music activates multiple brain systems.**

**Music enhances the learning environment.**

**Music generates self-esteem, motivation and positive emotional responses.**

**Music engages a variety of learning styles.**

**Music integrates multiple human intelligences.**

**Music is a communal experience, while celebrating individuality.**

**Music is processed and recreated through the body.**

**Music is intricately linked to the memory system.**

**Music is a common language to all people.**

**Music is motivating, stimulating and energizing.**

*Music Moments To Teach Academics: Introduction to Music Experiences*

Take a few minutes to think about and respond to the following questions about your personal music experience history. Journaling will provide you with quality information about your attitude about music and your comfort level for using it in the classroom to enhance learning.

### *PERSONAL MUSIC REFLECTION INVENTORY*

1. *What is music to you? Write down all of the words you associate with music.*

2. *What is your music background/experience to date? What music skills do you have? What would you like to be able to do?*

3. *How comfortable are you to teach music and use music in your teaching?*

   *comfortable*                                                                 *terrified*

       1    2    3    4    5    6    7    8    9    10

4. *What music or musicians have influenced your attitude/appreciation for music? Positively? Negatively?*

5. *How do you feel about your own singing? About singing with your students?*

6. *As you begin integrating music into your teaching, list "aha" moments and responses to musical experiences in and outside of the classroom. Keep a journal and read back through it each week.*

*Music Moments To Teach Academics: Introduction to Music Experiences*

## THE ELEMENTS AND CONCEPTS OF MUSIC

The following elements and concepts of music are indeed the building blocks of the activities in this book. By understanding these concepts, you will have a broader base from which to develop new integrative experiences in the classroom with your students. These terms are described in the simplest, most common language possible. Be sure to check out the Glossary for definitions of music vocabulary.

### ELEMENTS AND CONCEPTS OF MUSIC*

*RHYTHM*
- pulse (steady beat)
- grouping (groups of two or three pulses)
- pattern (pulses of differing paces and rests)

*MELODY*
- pitch (low, middle, high)
- scale (a pitch or note ladder)
- interval (the space between two pitches)

*FORM*
- motive (a sequence of three or four pitches)
- phrase (a rhythmic or melodic "sentence")
- repeat (same)
- contrast (different)

*EXPRESSION*
- pace (slow, medium, fast)
- dynamics (soft, medium, loud)
- articulate (accents, staccato, legato)
- interpret (style, culture, aesthetic, period)

*TIMBRE*
- body (snap, clap, pat, stomp, etc.)
- voice (sing, speak, whisper, shout)
- percussion (woods, metals, drums, shakers)
- instruments (strings and winds)

*TEXTURE*
- combinations (solo, duet, trio, quartet, etc.)
- harmony (differing pitches played or sung together)
- accompaniment (part that supports the main part)

\* from *Music for Dancers*, by Kerri Lynn Nichols. Used with permission.

As you become familiar with the music concepts, and guide your students through explorations of the concepts, together you will be able to create activities that correlate to your curricula far beyond the ones presented in this book. The examples in the following chapters are forms, that is, structures that you can use to develop music moment experiences that specifically relate to your teaching assignment. Consider each idea as a seed for extensions; feel free to adapt, change, revise and build on the suggested activities to refine your own approach.

In 1994, the Consortium of National Arts Education Associations in conjunction with the National Committee for Standards in the Arts and Music Educators National Conference (MENC) prepared The National Standards for Arts Education under a grant from the U.S. Department of Education, the National Endowment for the Arts, and the National Endowment for the Humanities. Here are the standards for what every student (K-12) should be able to do in music:

## NATIONAL MUSIC STANDARDS

*Singing alone and with others, a varied repertoire*

*Performing on instruments, alone and with others*

*Improvising melodies, variations and accompaniments*

*Composing and arranging music within specific guidelines*

*Reading and notating music*

*Listening to, analyzing and describing music*

*Evaluating music and music performances*

*Understanding relationships between music, the other arts and disciplines outside the arts*

*Experiencing music in relation to history and culture*

While many other countries, including Japan, Hungary and the Netherlands far exceed these standards, very few American children will even master one of these, usually based on economic status of the family and community, school district and national priorities and a lack of information about the critical necessity of music education in our schools for the well-being of our youth and society.

*Music Moments To Teach Academics: Introduction to Music Experiences*

The Music Standards are a great starting point for educational reform, but it will take a grass roots effort from teachers, parents and community leaders to effect quality, lasting change. The children will gain the maximum benefits from music training only when it begins in the early years, is available to all and continues throughout the students' educational lifetime.

As you begin your coursework, here are some questions to begin with for discussion. Share your thoughts with the class and revisit these questions as you progress through your experiences with music integration and study of the current research in the field.

1. What are the greatest challenges facing students today? How can music address those challenges?

2. What are the greatest challenges facing educators today? How does music address those challenges?

3. What are the key goals of the educational system? Write *your* vision in a one sentence statement.

4. What place does music currently hold in the schools in your area? How does it serve the needs of the students and community? Do all students have equal access?

5. Do you believe music is an essential tool for learning and teaching? Why or why not? Aside from performing groups, can you share a memory where you learned through a musical experience (excluding the Alphabet Song)?

6. List other questions or thoughts your group may have regarding these topics to share with the class.

_____
_____
_____
_____
_____
_____
_____
_____
_____
_____
_____
_____
_____
_____

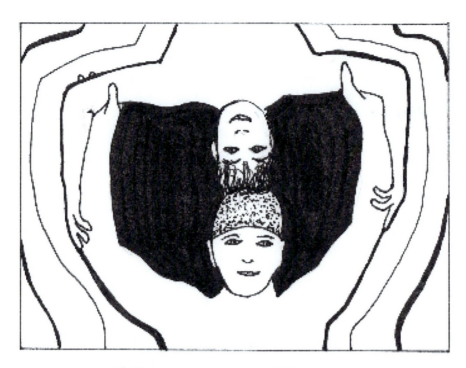

# Chapter Two:
## *Approaches To Integration*

*Music Moments To Teach Academics: Approaches To Integration*

## THREE APPROACHES TO MUSIC INTEGRATION

Music integration can be approached in a variety of ways. From background music to active music making, each has its strengths and connections to learning. While music making and creating are by far the most integrative in regards to brain systems, it is important to begin where you feel comfortable and confident. This may simply mean playing appropriate background music during various classroom activities as a start. Once you have a few successes to build upon, you can challenge yourself and your students to take a few risks and participate in more active experiences with music. Be prepared to be surprised by your musical abilities and those of your students! Remember, you do not need years of music training to create interesting and exciting music moments. An open mind and a good sense of humor will go a long way towards facilitating enhanced learning through music in your classroom.

It is important to note that the common thread that runs through each of these three approaches is the aesthetic nature of music. As students participate in music activities, they develop skills in recognizing and appreciating beauty and can identify and express their own feelings and emotions with a refined sense of self. This allows them to recognize these same qualities in others, and in the local and global communities. Through music experiences, students gain understanding of what makes us uniquely human and the artistic vocabulary to articulate it.

## SUPPLEMENTAL

This mode of integration includes playing background music to support the learning environment or atmosphere. Examples of academic activities that this approach would be used with are "silent" reading, test taking, journal reflection, study skills, focus or concentration work, visualization and other kinds of seat work. Music can also be used to support transitions, like clean-up time, preparation for recess, beginnings and endings of class or changing subjects. Playing West African music softly in the background while reading a story from Ghana would be a great example of the supplemental mode of integration. While studying deep ocean life, taped whalesong is playing in the classroom. In this approach, the music serves to support learning in another subject at a surface level. This is the least active model for integration, but its value is in creating an educational tone that works with the emotional brain and nervous system. Research has identified specific kinds of music to be particularly supportive for certain activities (e.g., The Mozart Effect, see Bibliography), although it is somewhat controversial in educational circles. What we do know, from current brain scans (PET), is that many areas in the brain are activated simply by listening to familiar and unfamiliar music and that different styles of music are processed uniquely in the brain to create varying responses.

This is why a particular kind of music is playing when you are shopping in the grocery store, waiting on hold on the telephone or watching a commercial on television; music creates a physical response in our minds and bodies. Since music influences several brain and body systems, it makes good sense to apply this information to the educational setting. Think about all of the places you hear music in any given day and notate the type of music and your responses in your journal.

## SOCIAL

In this mode of integration, music is experienced for its social benefits and its ability to enhance the community and cooperation of the classroom. Music creates a venue for the students to work on life skills, such as teamwork, respect, work ethic, contribution, responsibility and inclusion. Music brings diverse people together through a common language and nurtures a powerful learning dynamic called *synergy*, where the combined efforts of the group are greater than each individual's efforts. Carefully selected music experiences act as a laboratory for personality training and character development. These concepts are part of the unwritten curriculum in our schools, expected by society and essential for student educational success. Music allows us to prepare our children to be a part of the work force and to have a voice and a hand in shaping changes for the future.

Here are a few techniques to use with your students as you begin to build the community environment in your classroom:

1. Each day, allow students to process through the following modes: self work, partners, small groups, large group. The group can extend the work beyond the classroom and into the greater community.

2. Know every name in class and look at each face every day. Play a name game each day to make sure students know all of the names in class. This is the first way we show respect for each other.

3. Use rights and responsibilities instead of rules. Let the students brainstorm what rights they would like to enjoy in the classroom (to learn, to be assisted, to be respected, etc.) and what responsibilities they must accept to ensure those rights.

4. Use circles often in group work. Circles are symbolic in every culture on earth. They represent unity, equality and wholeness. Use circles for sharing ideas, thoughts and feelings in class. No one is allowed to interrupt and every student has a chance to speak and be heard. Students can successfully use circles in their small group work to make sure that each person's idea will be given consideration. This technique dispels problems with attitude and cooperation that may occur in the group learning process.

5. Use a conceptual approach in your teaching. When one concept runs through the entire lesson, the group has a united focus and students are empowered to create their own learning beyond your classroom. Try to be such a good teacher that you make yourself obsolete!

6. Create a learning space where every student is respected, valued and supported. Base the class on opportunity instead of "talent," modeling inclusion for the students. Encourage students to take ownership of the classroom space, displaying artwork, assigning jobs and taking care of the room so that they look forward to coming to class.

7. Use music in rituals and celebrations. Rituals are short rites or activities that are repeated by the group. Some examples are the BrainDance, opening and closing day songs, name games, breath work and relaxation and welcoming new students into the group. Students enjoy celebrations as a way to commemorate group or individual accomplishments and shared goals.

8. Teach students and parents the Five A's of Audience: *attend, allow, appreciate, applaud, affirm*. *Attend* is to give a person or group your full attention including eye contact, body position and mind; *allow* means to give a person or group space to make mistakes and to achieve new successes; *appreciate* is an inner attitude of respect, empathy and gratitude towards what a person or group has shared; *applaud* is the outer expression of our appreciation. *Affirm* is to make genuinely constructive comments which strengthen the cohesiveness of the learning team.

9. The Sandwich Principle is a technique that allows students to accept constructive criticism. When giving feedback, share something positive, a suggestion for change, and then another positive comment.

10. At all grade levels, encourage a learning atmosphere of play, exploration and fun. Students learn more when they enjoy what they are doing. Find creative ways to deliver the curriculum through games that engage the students' minds, hearts and bodies while employing humor and laughter. The games can be used to introduce concepts, explore ideas and review material. Students of all ages are skilled at creating learning games, so draw from their ideas.

> "Tell me, I forget. Show me, I remember. Involve me, I understand." - Chinese Proverb

*Music Moments To Teach Academics: Approaches To Integration*

## SOCIAL MUSIC INTEGRATION LINKS

| | |
|---|---|
| language (communication) | music as a separate discipline |
| musicking (active music-making) | inclusion |
| defining group roles | expression of feelings and ideas |
| metaphor for life skills | unity or united focus |
| community building | rituals and celebrations |
| independence and interdependence | social structures (order/rules) |
| culture definition and appreciation | ethic platform |
| communal ownership | empowerment |
| spiritual or religious connection | physical and emotional healing |
| representation and result of history | sound space or pollution |
| emphasis for change | consumerism |
| entertainment | play and enjoyment |
| aesthetics | life skills development |
| individual and collective | diversification |

## COGNITIVE

The final approach to music integration that we will discuss, and perhaps the most directly linked with your curriculum, is the cognitive approach. In this mode, music experiences and concepts are connected with concepts from the general curriculum in order to enhance cognition: memory, basic knowledge base, application, synthesis, evaluation, problem solving and other cognitive processes. Music integration can be implemented through a *subject* or *conceptual* link, via *music moments*.

## MUSIC MOMENTS

A *music moment* is generally a short music experience or activity focused on teaching an academic concept. It allows students to actively engage with the materials and concepts of music that relate to a specific academic idea or skill.

## MUSIC MOMENT CRITERIA:

1. *Everyone participates.*
2. *Active student involvement and input.*
3. *Purpose is clear; academic concept presented.*
4. *Demonstration and clear directions provided.*
5. *Brief.*
6. *Music concept, skill or subject linked to academic concept.*
7. *FUN!*

## Subject Link

The most common and simplest music moments are those that are connected to the curriculum by subject.

*Example:* A class that is studying one aspect of the Vietnam war: soldiers leaving this country to fight and die overseas

*Music Moment:* The class sings "Where Have All The Flowers Gone?" by American folk singer Pete Seeger. The class then reflects on the lyrics and a discussion follows.

## Conceptual Link

A more difficult, but cognitively challenging approach to music moments is to connec music with the curriculum by concept.

*Example #1: Academic Concept:* Counting (to 20)

*Music Concept:* Pulse

*Music Moment:* While patting a steady pulse on the lap, students count the numbers out loud, either from memory or as the teacher points to them on the board. Try pulses of different speeds to challenge the students. Sit in a circle. As students pat a common pulse on their laps, one student at a time says the next number out loud. How else can we learn counting with pulse?

*Example #2: Academic Concept:* Punctuation

*Music Concepts* — Timbre: percussion, voice, body
Expression: dynamics, articulations

*Music Moment* (see chart)

| Process | | Instrument | Explore different ways to: |
|---|---|---|---|
| Period | . | Hand Drum | a. use your voice to "draw symbols" |
| Excl. Point | ! | Slide Whistle/WB | b. use energy to express symbols |
| Comma | , | Cabasa | c. read text, insert sounds |
| Quot. Marks | " " | Maracas | d. show flashcard/make soun |
| Colon | : | Tic Toc Block | e. use claps, snaps, pats, stomps |
| Semi-colon | ; | Agogo Bell | f. sing a sentence, punctuate |
| Quest. Mark | ? | Triangle | g. punctuate same sentence diff. |
| | | | h. silent read, play only punctuation |

*Music Moments To Teach Academics: Approaches To Integration*

The *Music Moments* examples in the following chapters of this book will usually be conceptually linked as this is the deepest form of integration and the most stimulating in terms of the brain and cognition. Once you begin using music in your classroom to enhance learning, your creativity will be brought to the forefront and you and your students will easily be able to design and implement new *Music Moments* that are tailored to the specific needs of the class.

## BRAINDANCE

Another important facet to discuss as a part of the cognitive approach to music integration is that of the eight fundamental patterns of movement that directly correlate to the healthy development of the brain, beginning from the time we are in the womb and continuing throughout our lives. Blending ideas from the work of Rudolf Laban, Irmgard Bartenieff, Florence Scott (founder of Neurological Re-organization Theory), Bette Lamont, Carla Hannaford and Eric Jensen, world renowned movement educator Anne Green Gilbert has formulated the eight fundamental movement patterns into a coherent sequence which she calls the BrainDance. In four minutes, students can process through these patterns in a fun way to increase focus, attention span, spatial awareness, reading and studying skills and emotional well-being. It is particularly useful before tests or presentations, between classes, during computer work or TV commercials and as a wake-up or calm-down. It increases brain integration, recuperation and oxygenation. As you are beginning to work with *Music Moments* in your classroom, make an effort to include these patterns as much as possible in the activities you present to your students. It is great for adults, too!

### BrainDance®

| | |
|---|---|
| *Breath* | Deeply inhale through the nose and into the body fully; exhale completely through the mouth. Repeat several times. |
| *Tactile* | Four series of sensory touches to the body, starting with the arms, torso, legs, back, head, neck and face. 1) squeeze strongly, 2) tap lightly, 3) slap sharply and 4) brush smoothly. |
| *Core-Distal* | Movements contracting around the center (navel) of body; movements expanding away from the center. |
| *Head-Tail* | Movements bringing the head & tail close together and then reaching away from each other: forward, backward, right and left. Undulate the spine. Explore different planes. |
| *Upper-Lower* | Upper body (expressive) moving as a unit; lower body (supportive) moving as a unit. Switch roles (upper = supportive; lower = expressive). |

*Body Sides* — Right body side moving as a unit, left side still. Left body side moving as a unit, right side still. Move eyes right to left and left to right (follow thumb) to develop horizontal eye tracking.

*Cross-lateral* — Arms and legs crossing over the midpoint of the body to create diagonal connections (right hand to left foot). These movements are both in front of and behind the body. Move eyes up and down and down and up to develop vertical eye tracking.

*Vestibular* — Turning, spinning, rolling, hopping, jumping, swinging, bouncing or rocking for 15 seconds in one direction. Stop and reverse directions.

*Breath* — Repeat first pattern to complete the BrainDance.

**BrainDance ©2000 Anne Green Gilbert. Used with permission.**

## BRAINPLAY

BrainPlay is a series of music games, songs, stories and activities that integrate the concepts of music with the eight fundamental connections of the BrainDance. As you become familiar with these patterns and the elements of music, you will find opportunities to integrate them into your curriculum to support the success and achievements of your students. Here are a few examples of BrainPlay:

| | |
|---|---|
| *Breath* | chanting, singing, playing recorder, making vocal sounds, folk dancing |
| *Tactile* | body percussion (claps, snaps, pats, stomps) and use of different props |
| *Core-Distal* | closed/open vocal sounds with corresponding movements (e.g., inner humming to opera singing on "Ah"), crescendo and decrescendo |
| *Head-Tail* | use eight pulses to melt down forward; eight pulses to rise up tall; eight pulses to melt and rise to each side; ascending and descending scales |
| *Upper-Lower* | walk a steady pulse while playing a different pattern on a small percussion instrument with both hands (woodblock); conducting and performing |
| *Body Sides* | hold a hand drum in your right hand and bounce it off your right knee; repeat on the left side |
| *Cross Lateral* | rhythm stick activities on floor, body and in the air that use cross-lateral patterning; playing xylophones and recorders, partner singing games |

*Vestibular*     practice waltzing, swinging, turning and swaying to music in 3/4 meter (strong light light)

BrainPlay also employs the patterns to create name games and partner games with chants and songs:

```
What's  in a name?   What's  in a name?  If you think of  it, there's a game in your name!
  B      C R C         B      C L C       B     C  H       C    B    C    T
```

KEY:  B = pat both legs          C = clap your own hands together
      R = pat partner's R hand   L = pat partner's L hand
      H = "high 10" your partner T = turn the "high 10" around

*Fundamental Movement Patterns used: tactile, cross-lateral, upper, breath*

**Variations: With your partner, simplify the pattern or create different ones using the same or new motions. Share these with your classmates.*

## THE BRAINDANCE PATTERNS
(Piggyback song by Kerri Lynn Nichols to the tune of "The Hokey Pokey")

You take a big breath in, you let a big breath out,
You take a big breath in and you let a big one out.
You do the braindance patterns and you give a little shout!
That's what it's all about! (clap clap)

You squeeze your body here, you tap your body there,
You pat your body here and you brush a little there.
You do the braindance patterns and you give yourself some care!
That's what it's all about! (clap clap)

You shrink your body in, you grow your body out,
You shrink your body in and you grow your body out.
You do the braindance patterns and you give a little shout!
That's what it's all about! (clap clap)

You curl your spine in front, you curl your spine in back,
You curl your spine to the sides, then you place it in a stack.
You do the braindance patterns and soon you'll get the knack!
That's what it's all about! (clap clap)

You move your upper here, you move your upper there,
You move your lower here and you move it everywhere.
You do the braindance patterns and you give yourself some care!
That's what it's all about! (clap clap)

You move your right side up, you move your right side down,
You move your left side up and you move it all around.
You do the braindance patterns and you make a little sound!
That's what it's all about! (clap clap)

You touch your right hand here with your left foot there,
You touch your left hand here with your right foot over there.
You do the braindance patterns and you give yourself some care!
That's what it's all about! (clap clap)

You bounce your body left, you swing your body right,
You turn your body left and you spin your body right.
You do the braindance patterns in the morning and at night!
That's what it's all about! (clap clap)

You do the braindance patterns, you do the braindance patterns!
You do the braindance patterns and you're sure to do alright!
That's what it's all about! (clap clap)


## BRAINPLAY STORY: THE BAKERY

*Breath*  Let's all go on a journey down the street to the bakery (class walks around the room in free space). Mmmm - smell all those wonderful things baking! Smell the hot, fresh bread (deep belly breath in) - Ahhh! (exhale breath fully). Smell the . . . (students can give their ideas; repeat the breath process four more times). Oh, it is so wonderful! What do we see in the bakery?

*Tactile*  Let's see what the baker is doing in the kitchen. First, she kneads the dough (squeeze the body following the tactile progression). Then, she sprinkles some cinnamon on the dough (tap lightly). Next, the baker pats the dough flat (slap sharply). Oh no! The baker is covered with flour! She will have to brush it all off (brush smoothly).

    CHANTS:    *"Knead, knead, knead the dough."*
                         *"Sprinkling the cinnamon."*
                         *"Pat, pat, pat it flat!"*
                         *"Brushing off the flour!"*

*Core-Distal*  The baker folds and squishes the dough into a small, round ball and leaves it on the warm counter to rise (coil body around center). Look! It is growing, growing, growing - SMACK! The baker squishes it down again (repeat grow/shrink sequence four times).

    CHANT:    *"Rising, rising, rising, SMACK! Shrinking, I'm shrinking!"*

*Head-Tail*      At another table, the baker's assistant in making crescent rolls and cinnamon buns, carefully coiling one end of the dough to the other (head to tail rolls and stretches in different directions). She coils it this way and that way, and this way and that way.

         CHANT:     *"Crescent rolls and cinnamon buns!"*

*Upper-Lower*    Here comes the baker. She sees the terrible mess being made in the kitchen and says, "Let's remember to clean up as we go!" All the people start to clean the kitchen furiously (upper body movements to clean the kitchen) and leave no spot untouched. They clean the ceiling, the walls, the floor and the cupboards (students give other ideas). To make sure, they clean it a second time (lower body movements to clean the kitchen).

         CHANT:     *"Clean as you go, clean as you go;*
                            *Don't forget to clean as you go!"*

*Body Sides*     Everyone in the kitchen goes back to work. One group is getting ready to bake some fruit pies. What kinds of pies are there? Mmm. Apple and raisin and berry and peach pies! To make the top crust, the baker's assistants cut the rolled dough into long strips ("cut" with right body side, knee and elbow together and apart, together and apart; repeat with the left side of the body).

         CHANT:     *"Snip, snip, snip, snip; now we cut the dough in strips!"*

*Cross-Lateral*   At the next table, they lay the strips in a criss-cross pattern across each lovely pie (do cross-lateral movements with arms and legs).

         CHANT:     *"Criss-cross, cross-criss; making pie crust just like this!"*

*Vestibular*     The final touch on the pie crust is to brush it with a beaten egg. The recipe says, "Beat the egg 15 times in each direction." So the baker follows the recipe exactly, beating the egg 15 times in one direction (body turning right for 15 seconds with arms up and counting out loud) and 15 times in the other direction (body turning left for 15 seconds with arms up and counting out loud). Yes, that is just right! She brushes the crust with the beaten egg and places it in the oven to bake.

         CHANT:     *"Beat the eggs once and twice.*
                            *Beat them till they're smooth and nice!"*

*Breath*  Well, the bakery will be closing soon and we will need to go. But before we do, let's steal a few more deep breaths of the delicious smells coming from the kitchen. Mmmm - Ahhh! Goodbye, Baker! Goodbye, assistants! Goodbye, crescent rolls and cinnamon buns! Goodbye, breads and pies! We will see you again soon!

*The End*

It is fun to take this story and turn it into a musical-play. You can choose or create songs to go with the text and add instruments to make the sounds of the bakery. The students can write short poems about different foods or recipes to be spoken or sung at various places in the story. You can develop a scene at the beginning where each student is a different character or object in the bakery and make up rhythms that go with each character or object. Once the students know the eight patterns and the symbols, they can write their own stories about a variety of topics: undersea, outer space or the city. The possibilities are endless!

## LESSON PLAN FORMAT

Another approach to integrating music into the curriculum, or teaching it as a separate discipline is to use the *lesson plan format*. This sequential, progressive format was adapted from Anne Green Gilbert in her book *Creative Dance For All Ages*. This is a conceptual approach to teaching, that is, one concept (academic or musical) is the connecting thread through the five parts of the plan. These five steps allow students to progress from the teacher-directed/knowledge stage to the student-generated/synthesis learning that occurs in the creating section of the lesson. Students are able to explore one concept in depth through a virtual kaleidoscope of experiences.

### LESSON PLAN FORMAT

*Imitate*        (copy teacher)
             Introduce the Concept
             Hear, See, Say and Do the concept
             Quick warm-up for voice/mind/body using the concept
             Brief description

*Explore*        (teacher-directed play)
             Games and explorations that use the concept playfully
             Experiences that have guidelines and experimentation
             Question/answer forms, vocabulary games, chanting

*Music Moments To Teach Academics: Approaches To Integration*

*Develop Skills*
(teacher guides practice of skills)
The body of the lesson
The "teaching" part of the lesson using the concept
Skill development and practice
New information presented about the concept
Combining skills or ideas in reference to the concept

*Create*
(student-directed, teacher-supported)
Using the concept, the students create something new
Writing, presentations, songs, dances
Working in small groups or individually
Creating something that can be shared with others
Improvising using the concept

*Reflect*
(final group closure, teacher-guided)
Share creations from previous step with the class
Students give feedback to each other for group work
Discussions, reflections, impressions shared in a circle
Review concept and relate to life skills
Written, taped or recorded pieces to be turned in
Final focusing or transition activity for brain recuperation
Five A's of Audience: attend, allow, appreciate, applaud, affirm

## SAMPLE LESSON PLAN

*Imitate*     Concept:     Haiku

Hear, See, Say and Do the Concept:
Write the word "haiku" on the board. Point to it and say it; have the students echo you back as they look at the word. Make two sounds as you say the word (e.g., hai-ku, pat-clap). Ask the students to join you. Write the word "haiku" in the air with your finger; the students copy you.

     Warm-Up:     Write a haiku poem on the board. Have the students make shapes and movements to express the poem as they say it.

     Description:     Briefly describe the form and nature of haiku poetry. Some haiku originates in Japan and has a syllabic rhythm of five for the first line, seven for the second line and five for the third line. Haiku poems are often about two aspects of nature or images in juxtaposition.

*Explore*     Use pulse and pattern to play with the concept of five/seven/five. Divide the class into two groups: clappers and snappers, or wood instruments and metal instruments, or pencil tappers and desk slappers. The first group claps five pulses with one pause, the second group snaps seven pulses with one pause, and the first group claps five pulses with one pause again. The patterns would look like this:

*Music Moments To Teach Academics: Approaches To Integration*

|         |   |   |   |   |   |         |   |         |
|---------|---|---|---|---|---|---------|---|---------|
| *Clap:* 1 | 2 | 3 | 4 | 5 | *(pause)* |   |         |
| *Snap:* 1 | 2 | 3 | 4 | 5 | 6 | 7 | *(pause)* |
| *Clap:* 1 | 2 | 3 | 4 | 5 | *(pause)* |   |         |

Try the pulse pattern faster or slower and louder or softer. Let the two groups switch roles. If using body percussion sounds, each student could perform the entire pattern. Take the haiku you wrote on the board and say the words/syllables as you play the pulses.

*Develop Skills*   Talk about how you would start to write a haiku. Write a new haiku on the board as a class. Start by brainstorming in the following categories: subjects (nature or other), related nouns and verbs, and descriptive words. Have students make the sounds of the words as they decide which ones to put in the poem together. Use the concepts of expression (pace, dynamics, articulate and interpret) vocally as they read the poem together (choral reading). Add sound effects/instrument sounds at appropriate places.

*Create*   Divide the class into groups of five or six students. Each group can write an original haiku (or you can do this individually). After the group finishes their poem, they can create a song by making up a tune for the words or use movement and sounds to present their haiku.

*Reflect*   Review the Five A's Of Audience with your students. Each group shares their haiku with the class. The group gives feedback via the Sandwich Principle. Review characteristics of haiku.

## DAY PLAN FORMAT

The *day plan* differs from the lesson plan previously described in two ways:

1. It is not conceptually focused, that is, one concept does not run through the entire plan.

2. It is not progressive. One experience does not build upon the previous one in a sequential manner.

The day plan is an excellent choice for elementary and secondary teachers. At the elementary level, several subjects are taught within the day for short periods of time. In the day plan, music moments are inserted easily into each subject's time period. Music moments can also be used for transitions between many subjects and activities. In the same way, secondary teachers can use the day plan to add music into their curriculum and to keep the learning fun and energized for the older students. With longer class periods, music openings and closings provide a great opportunity for brain recuperation and focus. At both levels, music can be integrated by subject or concept.

*SAMPLE DAY PLAN #1: Grade: Kindergarten, half day schedule*

| *Time/Subject* | *Academic Concept/Activity* | *Music Moment* |
|---|---|---|
| 8:55-9:15 Opening | Student recognition Community | "Welcome, Welcome" song by A. Gillespie; Choral reading of flag salute; BrainDance to Nursery Rhymes |
| 9:15-9:45 Reading | Read "The Snowy Day" by Ezra Jack Keats | Create a Snowy Day sound story. |
| 9:45-10:15 | Recognizing spaces between words | Teacher writes a few sentences on the chalkboard. As she points to a word/space etc., the students use two different voice sounds to indicate words or spaces, e.g., pop, zzz, pop, zzz, pop. . . (idea from Kathi Naffah, Denver, CO). |
| 10:15-10:30 Recess | Transition activity | Make up words for a clean-up song to "London Bridge"., e.g., "Now we put our things away. . ." (K. Nichols). |
| 10:30-11:00 Math | Progression of numbers, 1-10 | Sing "This Old Man" with the class. After the first line, "This old man, he played one", have the class clap their hands once. Repeat with other verses, adding a clap each time (source: Traditional song). |
| 11:00-11:30 Activity Time | Science of sound explorations | Collect two groups of sound objects: woods and metals. These can be small percussion instruments or found sounds. Allow the students to look at and touch the objects, deciding what each is made of. Divide the class in two, one group with the woods, the other with the metals. Take turns playing them in different ways. Then, discuss the difference in the sound (e.g., metals = long and ringing; woods = short and sharp). |

*Music Moments To Teach Academics: Approaches To Integration*

| 11:30-11:35 Closing Circle | Group affirmations | Sing a goodbye song that you can include student names in. |

---

### SAMPLE DAY PLAN #2: HIGH SCHOOL

| Subject | Academic Concept | Music Moment |
|---|---|---|
| Advisory | Learning Preparation | Rhythmic Body Percussion Jives: 1-3-5-7-9 |
| English | Five Paragraph Essay Form | Form: repeat and contrast A1  B  C  D  A2 Have students also examine the form within each paragraph. |
| Physical Ed./Health | Heart and Lung Health | Use movement, sound and voices to show the following MM's in Chapter Eight: page 149, #'s 1, 2, 10, 11. |
| Geometry | The Pythagorean Theorem A2 + B2 = C2 | Piggyback Song: In groups, students review what they've learned about the PT and write lyrics to a known tune. |
| Lunch/Break | Self-care | Teacher does BrainDance to relaxation music to rejuvenate. |
| Physics | Momentum | Chant: *"Mass times velocity equals momentum!"* Bounce balls of differing sizes to beats of varying paces. For contrast, small groups can rap a rhyme giving another example of the mysteries of momentum. |
| Literature | Conventions in poetry (evaluating meaning through sound and structures) | Explore several examples of poetry in terms of rhythm, repetition, meter and rhyme. |
| US History | Review of significant events of the Civil War period | Famous Figure Chants. See Chapter 6, page 130, #4. |
| Visual Art | Technique: "Dripping" (also known as pouring": Pollack | Integrating rhythm to create art *"Jackson Pollack Jazz"* CD |

## CONCEPTUAL LESSON PLAN: WEEKLONG FORMAT

On the following page, you will find an example of a conceptual lesson plan laid out in a week long format. For elementary and some secondary teachers, it may work better with the given time schedule to integrate the conceptual lesson plan format over the course of a week. This combines the continuity of the conceptual lesson plan with the flexibility of the day plan. In the example, each content area represents the five-part lesson plan, beginning with *Imitation* on Monday and concluding with the *Reflection* on Friday. This format can be adapted for a variety of grade levels and subjects.

While there is a music moment listed daily for each subject, the duration of these music moments varies greatly. The students may engage in a one-minute music/math experience and spend the rest of the math time working with pencil and paper. Another day, they may be engaging in a creating activity with a small group, and the music "moment" will take the entire math period. The important thing to focus on is the *quality of the process by which students are guiding their own learning experience.* When the process is strong, the outcomes are exceptional.

## CONCLUSION

Whether you choose the lesson plan format, the day plan, or to simply integrate a music moment here and there, you will begin to notice significant changes in the atmosphere and energy of your students, classroom and even within yourself. One small change will create a ripple effect across the surface of your teaching and their learning. Take your time and begin with those activities that you feel comfortable with, while challenging yourself and your students each week with new ideas. Use the music moments presented here as a springboard into your own creative teaching and to renew the joy and excitement you can provide for your students on a daily basis. Remember, every person has musical ability. Take the first step bravely and happy musicking!

CONCEPTUAL LESSON PLAN: WEEKLONG FORMAT (Example)

| | Monday (Imitation) | Tuesday (Exploration) | Wednesday (Developing Skills) | Thursday (Creating) | Friday (Reflection) |
|---|---|---|---|---|---|
| READING<br><br>Concept: Comprehension | Create a one line chant to a pulse that the students can repeat to memorize the definition of comprehension. | *Vocabulary Game Music for Dancers #1*: A section) show a verb from the story; B section) show a noun | *Zipper Song*: Teach the Princess Song or other folk song that tells a story. Practice until the melody is known. | *Lyric Writing* – Use the tune and form of the song from Wed. to summarize a basal reader story in sequence. | *Review: Vocabulary Game, Basal Zipper Song, BrainDance, Circle Story Sharing* |
| MATH<br><br>Concept: Multiples of four | *Keith Terry Body Percussion* (see Resources). Use body percussion number system to chant multiples of four. | Use *Music for Dancers #2*. A) clap on the strong pulse for each multiple of 4. B) walk 16 counts while chanting the same. | *Folk Dance: Yankee Doodle* – Use this tune or another folk dance in 4/4 meter. Teach the traditional steps to the class. | *Yankee Doodle* Divide the class into groups. Each choreographs 4 sets of 4 pulses to the same music. | *Share new dance choreography.* Call out multiples of four after each set. Teach the new dances to each other. |
| SPELLING<br><br>Concept: Words ending with silent "e" | *Speak & Whisper* Write a spelling word on the board. Spell using call and response; whisper for silent "e". | *Silent E Game*. Play the game in Ch. 3, pg. 48, #31. Ask students for their ideas for variations. | *Spell Variations*, Ch. 3, pg. 45, #2. Vary by playing a triangle on "e"; sing letters and whisper on "e". Other ideas. | *Spelling Is Neat* – Ch. 3, pg. 47, #19. Groups spell their word to show "e" differently than the other letters. | *Final Sharing of "Spelling Is Neat"*, *BrainDance* while chanting spelling words; spelling test (w/ ambient music) |
| WRITING<br><br>Concept: Story Development | *Story Development* Follow instructions in Ch. 6, pg. 133, #4. Use setting, characters and plot for three facts. | *Beginning To End* MFD #4. Pick a known tale and use movement to show beginning, middle, end and a choice. | *Story Starters* – Ch. 3, pg. 66, #8. List characters, setting and plot for each selection. Write the storyline as a class. | *What Happened?* Ch. 3, pg. 66, #9. Follow the form of the piece to develop your own story in a small group. | *Narrate stories to the music.*<br>*Create illustrations.*<br>*Compare and contrast stories.* |

# CONCEPTUAL LESSON PLAN

**Concept:**  **Class/Period:**

**Imitation:**
    BrainDance:
    Hear, See, Say & Do:

**Exploration:**

**Developing Skills:**

**Creating:**

**Reflection:**

**NOTES:**

Permission granted to photocopy.

# DAY PLAN

| Time/Subject | Academic Concept | Music Moment |
|---|---|---|
|  |  |  |
|  |  |  |
|  |  |  |
|  |  |  |
|  |  |  |
|  |  |  |

Permission granted to photocopy.

CONCEPTUAL LESSON PLAN: WEEKLONG FORMAT

|  | **Monday** *(Imitate)* | **Tuesday** *(Explore)* | **Wednesday** *(Develop Skills)* | **Thursday** *(Create)* | **Friday** *(Reflect)* |
|---|---|---|---|---|---|
| Concept: |  |  |  |  |  |
| Concept: |  |  |  |  |  |
| Concept: |  |  |  |  |  |
| Concept: |  |  |  |  |  |
| Concept: |  |  |  |  |  |

Permission granted to photocopy.

# Chapter Three:
## Language Arts and Music

*Music Moments To Teach Academics: Language Arts and Music*

## LANGUAGE ARTS CONCEPTS AND CONTENT

| | | |
|---|---|---|
| *alphabet* | *consonants* | *vowels* |
| upper/lower case | diphthongs | long and short vowels |
| silent e | vocabulary | nouns |
| verbs | pronouns | articles |
| adverbs | adjectives | gerunds |
| verb tense | *spelling* | read left to right |
| word shapes | prefix/suffix | hyperbole |
| punctuation | contractions | abbreviations |
| root words | pictures (symbols) | penmanship |
| cursive writing | printing | pacing |
| word origins | predicting | definitions |
| oral reading | silent reading | comprehension |
| subject/predicate | syntax | prosody |
| sentence structure | homonyms | antonyms |
| synonyms | syllables | proper nouns (names) |
| word recognition | meaning skills | text comprehension |
| phonetic principles | sounding out | initial letters |
| common letter patterns | whole words | *rhymes* |
| compound words | accents (emphasis) | imperatives |
| interjections | prose | *story* |
| theme | development | conflict |
| climax | resolution | characters |
| setting | plot | perspective |
| sequence | plays | tragedy |
| comedy | drama | period |
| alliteration | onomatopoeia | *poetry* |
| haiku | limericks | diamante |
| cinquain | simile | metaphor |
| subjective | objective | mood |
| acrostics | alphabet poems | pantoums |
| sonnet | villanelle | fables |
| fairy tales | myths | legends |
| folk tales | fiction | non-fiction |
| sequence | genre | biography |
| autobiography | literal | figurative |
| abstract | irony | exaggeration |
| narrative | descriptive | compare and contrast |
| fact vs. opinion | oral reading | slang |
| humor | dialogue | tension |
| writing structures | writing organizers | persuasive devices |
| stereotype or bias | style | essay form |
| connotation/denotation | outlines/webbing | non-verbal communication |

*Music Moments To Teach Academics: Language Arts and Music*

## The Alphabet

1. Speak/whisper/sing the *Alphabet Song*: (to the tune of *Twinkle, Twinkle, Little Star)*; then, try singing the *Alphabet Song* backwards (a great brain game!).

    *A B C D E F G, H I J K L M N O P, Q R S T U V, W X Y and Z,*
    *Now I know my ABC's, next time won't you sing with me?*

2. Chant the alphabet using a steady pulse. Change the pitch of your speaking voice between high and low for each letter (A = high, B = low, C = high, etc.).

3. Chant the consonants out loud; chant the vowels in a whisper; reverse.

4. Chant the alphabet using a fast-fast-slow pattern for groups of three letters.

    ♫♩ ♫♩ ♫♩ ♫♩ ♫♩ ♫♩ ♫♩ ♫♩ ♫♩

    A B C,　DE F,　GH I,　JK L,　MN O,　PQ R,　ST U,　VW X,　Y & Z.!

5. Sing the alphabet using the pitches so and mi (five-three) motive.

    |   A   |   C   |   E   |   G, etc. |
    |   B   |   D   |   F   |           |

6. Chant the alphabet with a steady pulse. Each person claps or plays an instrument on the first letter of their first name.

7. Inner hear the alphabet pulse chant in your head. When we get to the first letter of your first name, say that letter out loud.

8. Walk around the room and chant the letters of the alphabet on a pulse in groups of two (loud/soft, strong/light, accented/unaccented).

    **A**　B　**C**　D　**E**　F　**G**　H,　etc.

9. Walk around the room and chant the letters of the alphabet on a pulse in groups of three (loud/soft/soft, strong/light/light).

    **A**　B　C,　**D**　E　F,　**G**　H　I, etc.

10. Chant the letters using different rhythmic patterns and/or rests (pauses).

    A  B  CD  E  F  G  HI  J  K  L  MN OP  Q

11. Create a rhythmic chant for the vowels.

    ♩   ♩   ♫   ♩   ♫   ♫   ♫   ♩

    A   E   I O   U,   sometimes   Y and   W!

12. Sing or speak the alphabet starting low and gradually raising the pitch of your voice; repeat, starting high and lowering the pitch of your voice.

13. Trace the shape of a letter with your finger in the air as you change the pitch of your voice (V = start high, slide voice down and back up).

14. Sing or speak the "ee" sound as you trace the letter E with your finger; repeat with the other vowels and their sounds.

15. Create a vocal percussion piece using different consonant sounds from the alphabet. Make up a second part using pulse or a different pattern.

    T-T-T-T   K   K   S-S   P   S-S   D

16. Explore the consonants and vowels with the four different voices: sing, speak, whisper and shout. Which vowels engage our vocal chords? Which consonants? Which consonants do not engage our vocal chords?

17. Talk about the musical alphabet (A B C D E F G). Play these notes on an instrument like the piano or a xylophone. Sing the notes as you say the letters.

18. Choose a group of seven or eight letters and sing them on the notes of the scale.

    do-re-mi-fa-so-la-ti-do   or   1-2-3-4-5-6-7-8

19. Sing or chant the letters of the alphabet in an alternating pattern. You can use different pitches to designate your placement in the sequence.

    | Letters: | A | C | B | D | C | E | D | G |
    |---|---|---|---|---|---|---|---|---|
    | Pitch: | 1 | 3 | 2 | 4 | 3 | 5 | 4 | 6 |

20. Practice saying the alphabet in phrases for one breath.

    A B C D E F G (breath)   H I J K L M N O P (breath)
    Q R S T U V (breath)   W X Y and Z (breath)

21. Practice groups of letters via call/response (echo) process.
    Teacher:   A B C   Class: A B C, etc.

22. Alternate phrases shown in exercise #20 via call/response (QA) process.
    Teacher: A B C D E F G (breath)    Class: H I J K L M N O P (breath), etc.

23. Practice the alphabet in a round (canon). Divide the class in two groups. First group begins; second group begins when the first group finishes the first phrase. Teacher keeps a steady pulse to maintain synchronicity.

    Group #1:    A B C D E F G (breath) H I J K L M N O P (breath)
    Group #2:        (waits)        A B C D E F G (breath)

24. Can you say the capital "A" loudly? Can you say the lower case "a" softly? Repeat for other letters.

25. Can you sing or speak the alphabet slowly? Fast? Can you start slowly and get faster? Can you start fast and get slower?

26. Speak the vowels using a legato (smooth, connected) voice and phrase; speak the consonants using a staccato (broken, separate) voice and phrase.

27. Write the alphabet on the board. Place a fermata over certain consonants or vowels and hold those sounds when you get to them; repeat the exercise using other music symbols such as accents (>).

28. Use body percussion to explore the letters of the alphabet. Chant the alphabet while patting the consonants and clapping the vowels.

29. Can you clap the rhythmic patterns of the *Alphabet Song* as you sing the letters in your head?

30. Divide the class into two groups with instruments: drums and woods. As the class chants the alphabet, those with woods play on each consonant pulse while the drums play on each vowel. Repeat the exercise, changing groups.

31. Use an additive form game to practice the letters of the alphabet. Say the first letter, then the first two, three and so on.

    A, AB, ABC, ABCD, ABCDE, ABCDEF, ABCDEFG, etc.

32. Each student chooses two or three letters that they will stand up and shout/sing/speak. As the class chants the alphabet on a pulse, some letters will be silent, others will have groups of students in unison or solos.

*Music Moments To Teach Academics: Language Arts and Music*

33. Use consonant sounds to create a rhythm; use vowel sounds to create a melody (song).

34. In a group, create a machine with your bodies and voices that uses only consonant or vowel sounds. Compose a beginning, middle and ending.

    Beginning - machine is created, turned on or starts in some way
    Middle - the machine is working to accomplish something
    Ending - the machine breaks down, is turned off or goes awry

35. Music: *Music for Creative Dance, V. 2, #5 Pizz-Ah! E. Chappelle*. This music has 28 short sections. On the first and last sections, practice writing the first letter of your first name. On sections 2-27, practice writing one letter of the alphabet for each section. My name is Kerri, so I would:

    | Section 1: | Practice K's | Section 2: | Practice A's |
    | Section 3-27: | Practice B through Z | Section 28: | Practice K's again |

36. Music: *Music for Dancers #1, "Pulsation."* At the beginning of the music, one student makes a shape in the middle of the space and makes the sound of one letter in the alphabet; the next student makes a shape attached to the first student and makes the sound of a different letter in the alphabet. Continue until all of the letters have been sounded and start over.

37. Sing a familiar tune (*Twinkle Twinkle, Hot Cross Buns*, etc.) on any vowel. Practice tracing or writing the vowel as you sing.

38. Use consonants and vowels to warm-up the voice and focus the mind for class activities. Which animals make which vowel sounds? Which animals make which consonant sounds? Can you make these sounds?

39. What letters from the alphabet can you use to copy the sound of an instrument with your voice?

    bell - rrrringggg          woodblock - tongue click, cluck
    drum - boooommm      shakers - ts ts ts, ch ch ch, or ss shh

## Reading Readiness

1. Sing *Twinkle, Twinkle* and draw "rainbows" (phrases) from left to right in the air or on paper for each phrase as you are singing.

    *Twinkle, twinkle, little star,   how I wonder what you are?*
    *Up above the world so high,   like a diamond in the sky.*
    *Twinkle, twinkle, little star,   how I wonder what you are?*

*Music Moments To Teach Academics: Language Arts and Music*

2. Look at a simple musical score and follow each stave with your fingers from left to right.

3. Place colored squares and rectangles of various sizes on the board in a row. As you read the shapes from left to right, have the students practice making long and short sounds depending on the size of the square or rectangle. Relate this to the long and short sound rhythms in sentence structure.

▌ ▍ ▍▍ ▋ ▍ ▋ ▍▍▋ ▍ ▋▍▍ ▍ ▍ ▋▍ ▋▋ ▋ ▍ ▋

4. Practice breathing into the belly (diaphragm) and send the speaking voice across the room in an arch for good projection. Make a game of it with partners calling questions and answers.

5. Use a block chart (see Resources) to track and map sounds from left to right, and top to bottom. Place an X in each box for a one-pulse sound. Repeat the pattern.

6. Listen to a simple piece of music that has clear phrases and a regular rhythmic structure (see Bibliography). Have your students "draw" the phrases with colored markers or crayons, practicing their strokes left to right.

7. Make or buy musical song-books. Tape record your voice singing or speaking the words/rhymes rhythmically so the students can listen and follow along in the book.

8. Stand in a circle and play a name game. One person says their first name, and the class echoes it back to them. Continue around the circle in a clockwise direction, until all the names have been echoed. Students are to look at each face as they repeat the name.

9. Make a picture card for each instrument or found sound in the classroom, one per student. Students hold their instruments at their desks. As the teacher holds up the picture card of one instrument, that student plays it and everyone turns with their eyes to look at the player.

10. The teacher holds her arms out to her sides, palms up, in front of the class, a bell in one hand. The students focus their eyes on the empty hand. When the teacher rings the bell, all eyes switch the the other hand. This helps to develop vertical eye tracking. Vary the activity with high and low for horizontal tracking.

11. Students can practice vertical and horizontal eye tracking as the teacher plays a steady pulse, moving objects left to right or up and down.

## Spelling

1. Practice speaking or singing long and short vowels, exaggerating their characteristics.

    e (quick, sharp *ee* sound)     e (long, smooth *eh* sound)

2. To practice silent "e," chant the spelling of a word and rest on the "e." Students can hear the silent "e" in their heads during the rest.

    C-A-K-E (think silent "e")     P-A-S-T-E (think silent "e")

3. Chant the spelling of each word four times: singing, speaking, whispering and shouting for interesting repetition.

4. Chant the letters using a steady pulse; chant the letters using rhythmic patterns.

    F-R-I-E-N-D         FR-I-EN-D
    *steady pulse*      *rhythmic pattern*

5. Create a spelling rap using the rhythmic patterns of a word, its spelling and a definition of the word.

    C-A-R, the car goes far!

6. Chant the letters using groupings of two (strong-light) or three (strong-light-light). Accent the first pulse of each grouping.

    **P**-A-**T**-T-**E**-R-**N**-S     **H**-O-T

7. Use the natural rhythm that occurs when spelling some words.

    M-**I**-S-S-**I**-S-S-**I**-P-P-**I**

8. Clap the vowels and pat the consonants.

    G     R     A     C     E
    *pat  pat  clap  pat  clap*

9. Play different instrument sounds for vowels and consonants.

    Vowels = metal sounds
    Consonants = wood sounds

10. Chant or sing common letter patterns/combinations and their sounds.

    S-H *Shh!*     T-H *Th!*     E-S-T *est!*     P-H *F!*

11. Create spelling chant using rhythm; create simple so-mi (five-three) melodies for these same spelling chants.

        Spoken:     ST-A-RR-Y, starry, starry, starry sky!
        Sung:       ST-A-RR-Y, star-ry, sta-rry, star-ry sky!
                       5 5-3-5 5- 3   5 - 5   3 - 3   5 - 5  3

12. Play a circle game with spelling. All students sit in a circle and keep a body percussion pattern going (e.g., pat-pat clap rest). On the first rest, the teacher says the name of a spelling word. On the second pattern rest, the next student in the circle says the first letter of the spelling word. Continue around the circle until the word has been spelled completely, the last person saying the spelling word again. The next person in the circle says the next spelling word and the game continues.

        CAP             C              A             P           CAP
*pat-pat clap-rest  pat-pat-clap-rest  pat-pat-clap-rest  pat-pat-clap-rest  pat-pat-clap-rest*

13. Create a more complicated body percussion pattern for older students.

                                     THOUGHT
      *pat-pat  clap-clap  tap-tap (chest) snap!*          etc.

14. Sing-spell eight letter words in a scale going up; reverse the spelling on the way down the scale.

          B    U    I    L    D    I    N    G
        (*do  re  mi  fa  so  la  ti  do*)
        (*1    2    3    4    5    6    7    8*)

15. Sing-spell two-letter words using so-mi (five-three) melodies; sing-spell three-, four-, five-, six- and seven-letter words using the corresponding notes of the scale.

          D    O    G
          F    R    O    G
          J    U    M   P    Y
       (*do  re  mi  fa  so  la  ti  do*)
       (*1    2    3    4    5    6    7    8*)

16. Trace the shape of a word with your finger while making your voice go higher and lower to match the shape of the letters.

                              t   h   i   r   s   t   y

## Music Moments To Teach Academics: Language Arts and Music

17. Use the letters of the musical alphabet (A B C D E F G) to create as many words as possible. Chant the spellings or sing the pitches.

    ACE   DEAF FEED BEG   BAGGAGE   FACE

18. Spell a word with your partner; alternate chanting each letter or spell half of the word and let your partner spell the other half; teacher calls out the first letter and the class calls out the second letter, etc. Vary these spelling games using question/answer and call/response forms.

19. Use the following rhyme to create a rondo form for a spelling song or rap. The students can get into groups and create a rap for each spelling word.

    A   *Spelling is <u>neat</u>, spelling is <u>fun</u>; how happy we'll <u>be</u> when it's <u>over</u> and <u>done</u>!*

    B   *Group One raps about the first spelling word.*

    A   *Spelling is neat, spelling is fun; how happy we'll be when it's over and done!*

    C   *Group Two raps about the second spelling word.*

    A   *Spelling is neat, spelling is fun; how happy we'll be when it's over and done!*

20. Spell the word as a class three times: slow, medium and fast.

    P   E   A   C   E;   P E A C E;   PEACE!

21. Spell the word as a class three times: soft, medium and loud.

    *peace*         peace         **peace**

22. Spell the word as a class or individually, starting soft and getting louder (crescendo); starting loud and getting softer (decrescendo).

23. Spell the word as a class or individually, starting slow and getting faster (accelerando); starting fast and getting slower (decelerando).

24. Spell the word out loud accenting consonants and saying vowels lightly; repeat, accenting the vowels and saying the consonants lightly.

25. Spell the word out loud using staccato (short and sharp) articulation; spell the word out loud using legato (long and smooth) articulation.

26. Spell the word using different styles of music: rap, opera, country, etc.

27. Play a different body percussion sound (clap, pat, stomp or snap) for each letter of the spelling word.

28. Play a steady pulse with body percussion or instruments while chanting spelling words.

29. Practice spelling the words using different combinations of voices: solo, duet, trio, etc.

30. Play with the spelling words by spelling them in a round in class. One group starts and another group follows behind.

31. Use this game and chant with your class for a fun practice of silent "e" spelling words. How can you adapt the rhyme to work with other spelling words? Other content areas?

    *Chant*  For <u>each</u> and every <u>letter</u>, we <u>do</u> the same 'ole <u>thing</u>,
    But <u>when</u> we get to <u>silent</u> "e," <u>we</u> must <u>sing</u>! <u>Tra-la</u>, la-la, <u>la!</u>

    *Game*  Pat own legs   clap own hands   clap partner's hands   clap own hands

    *Directions*  While chanting the poem, kids walk around the room to the beat to find their partner by "...*we must sing!*" After they say "*Tra-la, la-la, la*", the clapping/partner game begins. Each letter is only called out on the pat of the legs, in unison by the class together. When they get to silent "e", the kids reach their arms out to the sides and "sing" the "e". The teacher or the students then select or draw out of a hat the next spelling word. You can have even more fun by designating a style of singing, like opera, country or yodeling.

    *Tips*  It helps to have a steady pulse going throughout the game, both for the chant and the pat-clap section to keep everyone together. Practice the game while sitting at the desks first before adding the movement and partners to guarantee student success.

    *Examples*  ||:pat-clap-partner-clap    pat-clap-partner-clap:||

    (love)
    L
    V

    O
    E *(sung)*

    (taste)
    T
    S
    E *(sung)*

    A
    T

    (hue)
    H
    E *(sung)*

    U

*Music Moments To Teach Academics: Language Arts and Music*

**Words**

1. Chant two-syllable words on a steady pulse, accenting the appropriate syllable; chant three-syllable words in a similar fashion.

    | **flow**-*er* | **flow**-*er* | **flow**-*er* | **flow**-*er* |
    |---|---|---|---|
    | **flow**-*er*-*y* | **flow**-*er*-*y* | **flow**-*er*-*y* | **flow**-*er*-*y* |
    | *Va*-**nes**-*sa* | *Va*-**nes**-*sa* | *Va*-**nes**-*sa* | *Va*-**nes**-*sa* |

2. Chant the syllables of any given word in a rhythmic pattern. Try to use the natural speech pattern inherent in the word.

    *me-ta-**mor**-pha-sis*     *me-ta-**mor**-pha-sis*

3. Sing an accented syllable on a high pitch, unaccented on low pitches.

4. Use a speaking voice for accented syllables and a whispering voice for unaccented syllables.

5. Use a loud voice for an accented syllable and a soft voice for unaccented syllables.

6. While speaking a word, clap on the accented syllables.

7. One partner speaks the unaccented syllables; both partners speak the accented syllables.

8. Sing a different pitch for each syllable in a given word.

9. As students say each word, the teacher plays a drum on each accented syllable.

10. One instrument plays the prefix, the other plays the root word.

    UN  -  HAP-PY
    (*bell      woodblock*)

11. One instrument plays the root word (verb), the other plays the suffix.

    WALK - ING
    TALK - ING
    (*wood    metal*)

12. Write one or both words on the board. Use voices, body percussion or instruments to show the following:

    Antonyms - two opposite sounds, like loud/soft, fast/slow, high/low, staccato/legato, smooth/jerky

Homonyms - sounds the same/spelled differently, play two different wood sounds

13. Write a word on the board and the group performs the opposite.

    On the board:  LOUD     Class plays:  softly

14. Make a chart of sounds for each kind of word.

    *verb = metal, noun = wood, pronoun = drum, adverb = shaker, adjective = voice*, etc.

15. Choose three, short rhyming words to play this game (idea from *The Electric Company*, a children's television show in the 70's). You say the sound of the first letter, followed by the rest of the word. Repeat for the next two words, then say all three words, one after the other.

        C  -  UT   CUT  (dun duh dun duh duh)
        R  -  UT   RUT  (dun duh dun duh duh)
        N  -  UT   NUT  (dun duh dun duh duh)
        CUT  RUT  NUT  (dun duh dun duh duh)

16. Write a sentence on the board but leave out an important word. Read the sentence and have the class clap the number of syllables in the missing word. They can guess the word or another word that has the same number of syllables and would make sense in the sentence.

        The _____ jumped into the pond (clap once for blank).
        Possible answers: frog, boy, girl, etc.

17. Do the same game as above using a familiar song, but leave an important word/note out of the melody. Students can guess what word/note is missing and sing it back.

18. Practice dividing compound words by making a sound between the two joined words.

        over (X) board    flap (X) jack    moon (X) light

19. Use two different voices to say each compound word.

        **house***boat*    **sea***shell*    **car***port*

20. Music: *Music for Dancers, #19 Mango Walk.* Write several compound words on cards and cut them in half (one word on each half). Give each student a card. As the music plays, students travel around the room, looking for someone to create a compound word with. Pause the music and students have to find a partner to make a compound word with (even the nonsense ones are fun). The class looks around and reads the new compound words. When the music resumes, they travel to find a new partner or change cards.

*Music Moments To Teach Academics: Language Arts and Music*

21. When spelling contractions, play one sound for the first word, another for the second word, and a third sound for the apostrophe.

22. Sounds For Nouns: Write nouns that can be expressed with vocal or instrumental sounds on cards. Hold up a card and the class can make the sound or show one student the card privately and he/she gives the class a "sound clue" to guess the word.

    Suggestions: *lawn mower, cat, ocean, car, etc.*

**Punctuation**

1. Punctuation Play

    | Symbol | | Instrument | Explore different ways to: |
    |---|---|---|---|
    | Period | . | Hand Drum | a. use your voice to "draw symbols" |
    | Excl. Point | ! | Slide Whistle/WB | b. use energy to express symbols |
    | Comma | , | Cabasa | c. read text, insert sounds |
    | Quot. Marks | " " | Maracas | d. show flash card/make sound |
    | Colon | : | Tic Toc Block | e. use claps, snaps, pats, stomps |
    | Semi-colon | ; | Agogo Bell | f. sing a sentence, punctuate |
    | Quest. Mark | ? | Triangle | g. punctuate same sentence diff. |
    | | | | h. silent read, play only punctuation |

2. Draw the different symbols for punctuation and vocalize the movement with your voice.

3. Write the separate words of a sentence that uses several punctuation symbols on large cards. Mix up the order or the words and let the class figure out the correct punctuation to use (with sounds) for the sentence.

4. View the video *Victor Borge* (see Videography) to get additional ideas for musical fun with punctuation.

5. Practice reading sentences using instrument sounds for punctuation.

6. Try using different punctuation for the same sentence. How do you need to change your voice when you read it?

# Music Moments To Teach Academics: Language Arts and Music

7. Make up a song or rap about punctuation. It might go something like this, with instrument or vocal sounds to represent each symbol.

   *Punctuation, it's a sound celebration,*
   *It's a comma, quotation, and a point of exclamation,*
   *And a suggestion if you want to mark your question,*
   *Place a period at the end, then you know we'll comprehend!*

8. Experiment with vocal techniques for oral reading including pitch (high/low), volume (loud/soft), intensity, intonation (the quality of the voice) and expression (accents, emphasized words, broken, smooth) as they relate to punctuation.

## Rhymes

1. Choose a simple, nursery rhyme and chant it while patting the pulse on your lap. Accentuate/exaggerate the speech rhythm (patterns).

Did-dle did-dle dump-ling, my son John, went to bed with his stock-ings on,

One shoe off and one shoe on, did-dle did-dle dump-ling, my son John!

2. Half of the class claps the rhythm patterns of a simple nursery rhyme while the other half walks around the room with pulse. Switch parts.

3. Take two rhyming words from the same nursery rhyme and chant them on a pulse to create an accompaniment for the poem. Half of the class performs the repeated pulse-chant and the other half chants the poem.

   Pulse Chant:   *John,   on,   John,   on,   etc.*

4. Create a rhythmic pattern using rhyming words in phrases related to the poem. Half of the class performs the rhythmic pattern and the other half chants the poem.

   Rhythmic Pattern:   *La-zy   head,   out of bed!*

5. Play the musical name games (see Resources), finding rhymes for the names in class. Which names have many rhymes? Which names have no rhymes?

6. Play the word game #15, on page 50 using various rhyming words.

7. Eight counts: One partner says a simple word on pulse one of an eight-pulse count, while patting the pulse on his/her lap. The other partner says a rhyming word on pulse one of the second eight-pulse count:

   | Partner One: | 1 | 2 | 3 | 4 | 5 | 6 | 7 | 8 |
   |---|---|---|---|---|---|---|---|---|
   | | "Toy" | (pat) | (pat) | (pat) | (pat) | (pat) | (pat) | (pat) |

   | Partner Two: | 1 | 2 | 3 | 4 | 5 | 6 | 7 | 8 |
   |---|---|---|---|---|---|---|---|---|
   | | "Soy" | (pat) | (pat) | (pat) | (pat) | (pat) | (pat) | (pat) |

8. Chant or sing one-syllable rhyming words using a one pulse (*strong*) grouping. Chant or sing two-syllable rhyming words using a two-pulse (*strong light*) grouping. Chant or sing three-syllable rhyming words using a three-pulse (*strong light light*) grouping. Chant four-syllable rhyming words using a four-pulse (*strong light strong light*) grouping.

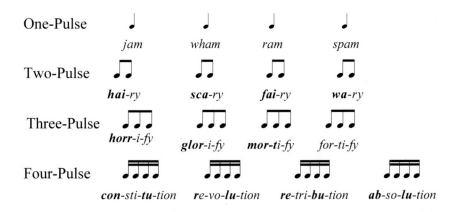

9. Play the Brainstorm Rhyming Game. One person says the name of a simple word followed by "which rhymes with. . ." in a rhythmic chant and the rest of the group comes up with a rhyming word. Continue the chant until all ideas are exhausted for that word. Take turns being the leader.

   **FINE** which rhymes with *line* which rhymes with *mine* which rhymes with *pine* which rhymes with *sine* which rhymes with *vine* which rhymes with *wine* which rhymes with *spine* which rhymes with *thine* which rhymes with *dine* which rhymes with *nine* which rhymes with *shine* which rhymes with *shrine* which rhymes with *stein* which rhymes with *sign* which rhymes with *twine* which rhymes with *swine!*

10. One partner chants a word on a low voice pitch. The other partner chants a rhyming word on a high voice pitch. The words can be chanted at the same time or one after another in a repeated pattern.

11. Half the class sings a word on the scale going up and the other half sings a rhyming word on the scale going down:

|  | 1 | 2 | 3 | 4 | 5 | 6 | 7 | 8 |
|---|---|---|---|---|---|---|---|---|
|  | do | re | mi | fa | so | la | ti | do |
| Group #1: | sun | sun | sun | sun | sun | sun | sun | sun |
|  | 8 | 7 | 6 | 5 | 4 | 3 | 2 | 1 |
|  | do | ti | la | so | fa | mi | re | do |
| Group #2: | fun | fun | fun | fun | fun | fun | fun | fun |

12. Sit in a circle. Repeat the following rhythmic pattern in unison as a group. The first person says a word on the first clap; the second person says a rhyming word on the next clap; the third person says a new word; the fourth person says a rhyming word. Continue around the circle. Select words to be used ahead of time and write them on a chart.

   Ostinato (repeated pattern):   ♩   ♩   ♩   𝄽

   *pat    pat    clap    (rest)*

13. Write so-la-so-mi melodies (or more complicated ones) to favorite nursery rhymes to sing in class.

14. Change the rhythm pattern of a well-known nursery rhyme to make it more challenging for older students:

   *Hump-ty Dump-ty sat on a wall! Hump-ty Dump-ty had a really great fall!*

15. Create a Rondo using the following A section. The class chants or sings the A section together, then each small group makes up another musical section based on a well-known or original rhyme. Between each small group, perform the A section again. Add instruments and body percussion to create a memorable and exciting experience.

   A Section: *Give me a riddle, give me a rhyme; give me a poem to pass the time! (repeat)*

16. One partner asks or sings a question with a noun at the end of the phrase and the other partner answers the question with a rhyming word at the end of their phrase.

   Partner One:  *Will you wash your socks today?*
   Partner Two:  *If I will, I cannot say!*

17. Make up sentences that contain two, three or four rhyming words and still make sense. Speak musically or sing the sentences as a class, placing accents on the rhyming words. Pat a pulse while you perform each sentence or add an instrument on each rhyming word.

   *The **frog** slipped off of the **log** and into the **bog** because of the **fog**.*

18. Practice speaking or singing a set of rhyming words three times: slow, medium and fast.

    SLOW:    *kiss*    *miss*    *hiss*    *bliss*

    MEDIUM:    *kiss  miss  hiss  bliss*

    FAST:    *kiss miss hiss bliss*

19. Practice speaking or singing a set of rhyming words three times: soft, medium and loud.

    SOFT:    *sea*    *free*    *knee*    *glee*

    MEDIUM:    sea    free    knee    glee

    LOUD:    **sea**    **free**    **knee**    **glee**

20. Practice speaking or singing sets of rhyming words twice: staccato (short, broken) and legato (smooth, connected).

21. Use different voices to make music out of rhymes and rhyming words: *sing, speak, whisper* and *shout*.

22. Substitute body percussion (*claps, pats, snaps* and *stomps*) for rhyming words within a given poem. Choose four rhyming words and create your own substitution poem.

**Example: "The Zeet" by Kerri Lynn Nichols**

*<u>Way</u> down <u>there</u> in the <u>land</u> of <u>Zeet</u>, I saw a <u>Zeet</u> with <u>very</u> sore <u>feet</u>, but*

*<u>That</u> poor <u>Zeet</u> was <u>learnin'</u> the <u>beat</u>; <u>learnin'</u> the <u>beat</u> with <u>sore</u> Zeet <u>feet</u>, so*

*<u>If</u> you want a <u>rhythm</u> with a <u>really</u> neat <u>beat</u>, <u>listen</u> to the <u>beat</u> in the <u>neat</u>, Zeet, <u>feet</u>!*

    KEY:  Zeet = clap = woods    feet = snap = metals

            beat = stomp = low drums    neat = pat = high drums

## Poetry

1. Examine the lyrics of poetic songwriters (Bob Dylan, Joan Baez, etc.). Listen to a piece and talk about the musical setting in relationship to the lyrics.

2. In small groups or individually, select or write a short poem and create a tune for it.

3. Take a familiar tune and write poetry (lyrics) to the melody.

4. Select a poem to read aloud. Add/create markings to indicate expression. You might add accents, dynamics (soft and loud), variations in vocal pitch, repetition of lines, solo or choral speaking or instrumental emphasis. Write a score for your poem on a large poster and perform with the class.

5. Develop a soundscape for a selected poem. Play creatively with words and sounds present or inferred in the poem. Employ the concepts of music to "disguise" the poem and then allow the class to figure out which poem you used.

6. As you read a poem, play with changing the rhythm of the words. First, speak it in a natural rhythm. Then, add pauses and changes in speed to add interest. Clap the rhythm of the words or play it on an instrument.

7. Create an ostinati (repeated pattern) for your poem. Select a few key words from the poem and chant or sing them in a repeated, short pattern as an accompaniment while others read the poem. Transfer words to body percussion, then to instruments to add interest.

8. Pat a steady pulse as you read a poem. Try pulses of different speeds. Is the poem *metered* (fits well to a steady pulse) or *free rhythm*?

9. As you speak the poem, mark the natural accents you feel in the text. Is the poem in groupings of two or three? An easy test is to play a two- or three-pulse accompaniment while saying the poem to see if it fits.

   Accompaniments:   Two:  *pat clap, pat clap*    Three:  *pat snap snap, pat snap snap*

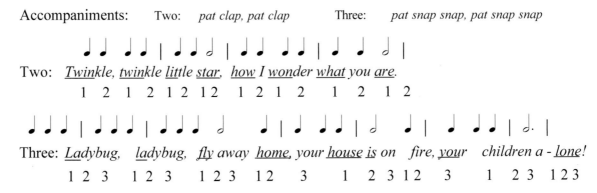

10. Explore poems for two or more voices (suggestion: *Joyful Noise* by Paul Fleischman) or write your own. Some parts are spoken alone and others together in different combinations of voices.

11. Present a poem through four different voices: sing, speak, whisper and shout.

12. Look at several poems and analyze them in terms of repetition and contrast (suggestion: *The Dreamkeeper And Other Poems* by Langston Hughes). Notice how these two concepts create a form for the poem.

13. Practice choral (together) reading as a class. Discuss tempo, pauses and voice inflection.

14. Read a poem to your class and allow the students to improvise a rhythmic accompaniment with body percussion or quiet instruments using pulses and patterns.

15. Write a poem that uses a variety of sound words and images. Create a soundscape for your poem.

16. Write sound words or words that imply sound on strips of paper and place in a jar. Each group draws five words out of the jar and writes a poem using those words and related ones.

17. Use well-known or original tongue twisters to learn about alliteration. These are fun to chant rhythmically or sing. Add a body percussion accompaniment to your tongue twister as you speak it.
    *Ninety-nine nuns interned in an Indiana nunnery!*

18. Notate the rhythm (patterns) of simple poems (see Resources).

    Baa, baa black sheep, have you any wool? Yes sir, yes sir, three bags full.

19. Tape record a poem in speech or song. Have your partner add an ostinati or sounds in the background.

20. Create a rap-poem to the rhythm of a familiar tune.

21. Make up a repeated chant about onomatopoeia (A section). Each group in class can create a section using these kinds of words.

    Ono-mato-poe-ia, bang, crash, boom!   Ono-mato-poe-ia, bang, crash, boom!

22. Check out the book and/or video, *Free To Be...You And Me* by Marlo Thomas and share the poetry and songs with your students. Create a musical drama inspired by the book.

*Music Moments To Teach Academics: Language Arts and Music*

23. Write a Sound Symphony. Sit in a quiet place for 15 minutes and write down every sound you hear. Listen at a deeper level each time you stop writing. Format the words and phrases into a metered poem or a free rhythm and share with the class. For examples of sound symphonies, see *The Listening Book* by Walter Mathieu.

24. Limericks are poems that are generated from a specific rhythm and meter and are usually humorous. Students can write their own limericks and create a pulse accompaniment with instruments, voices or body percussion to go with them. Here is an example from my sister, Kelli Jayn Nichols.

    *There once was a weirdo from France, who kissed all the girls while he danced,*
    *He was so fruity, they kicked his patootie, which ripped out the seat of his pants!*

25. Write a series of similes and metaphors on the board. As you point to each one, the students will respond with an instrument sound to indicate their response.

    Simile - *respond with wood sounds*    Metaphor - *respond with metal sounds*

26. The Saran Rap: Brainstorm the favorite foods of each person in the class and write them on the board. As a class, write a rap using the different foods. Create a beat-box accompaniment for your rap. Discuss the place of rap in our culture in terms of poetry.

27. Divide a poem into phrases. Speak the phrases as you draw a rainbow in the air with your hand. Can you find or write a poem that has phrases in AB form? ABA form? Rondo form?

28. Write the phrases of a poem on the board in a mixed-up order. Speak, sing and clap the phrases. Allow students to figure out the true order of the phrases in the poem. Perform each phrase of the poem differently using a musical concept.

29. Select a haiku poem. As a class or in small groups, add sounds to your haiku that reflect the essence of the poem. You can use different voices expressively, instrument or found sounds and silences.

30. Haiku poems are usually created in a three line form: five syllables, seven syllables, five syllables (ABA form). Use body percussion to internalize this syllabic structure and form. Transfer to voices, instruments or other sounds.

    1 2 3 4 5,   1 2 3 4 5 6 7,   1 2 3 4 5
    *pat pat pat pat pat ,  clap clap clap clap clap clap clap,  pat pat pat pat pat*

31. Here is a chant that follows the above syllabic pattern. You can speak the syllables in a variety of rhythmic patterns, similar to reading the words of a haiku.

    H - A -   I - K - U    (5)

    That is how you spell haiku,    (7)

    H - A -   I - K - U    (5)

32. Cinquaine (or cinquain) is also a syllabic form. The previous activities for haiku can also be applied to cinquaines. Make sure students are counting *syllables* and not *words*. Cinquain is a five-line poem with the following syllabic structure: 2, 4, 6, 8, 2.

    Baby    (2)
    stretching, grasping,    (4)
    reaches for the rattle,    (6)
    each day, a new kitchen journey,    (8)
    Giggle.    (2)

33. Add sounds to your cinquane. Here are some ideas for the poem above.

    *Line 1*    *goo goo gah gah sounds, cooing, etc.*
    *Line 2*    *ratchet sounds, rubber bands, pats on desk*
    *Line 3*    *shakers and rattle sounds*
    *Line 4*    *kitchen sounds (vocal) or kitchen sounds (spoons, glasses, etc.)*
    *Line 5*    *giggling musically (high and low, overlapping)*

34. Diamante poems are often shaped like a kite or diamond. It is a seven-line form. Create a chant about the diamante to help memorize the format.

    *Line 1*    *one noun*
    *Line 2*    *two adjectives modifying the Line 1 noun*
    *Line 3*    *three verbs describing the Line 1 noun*
    *Line 4*    *four noun - images (two refer to iLne 1 noun; two refer to Line 7*
    *Line 5*    *noun) three verbs modifying the Line 7 noun*
    *Line 6*    *two adjectives describing the Line 7 noun*
    *Line 7*    *the opposite of the Line 1 noun*

35. Transfer the shape pattern into pulses through body percussion:

*snap*

*clap    clap*

*pat    pat    pat*

*stomp stomp stomp stomp*

*pat    pat    pat*

*clap    clap*

*snap*

36. Transfer the body percussion of your diamante to instruments or voice sounds.

   *snap = metals, whisper*    *clap = woods, speak*
   *pat = shakers, sing*    *stomp = drums, shout*

37. Clap the rhythm of the words of your diamante. Pat a pulse while you say the poem.

38. Say or sing your diamante in a round (one group starting before the other group). Perform the lines in a pattern using fast/slow, high pitch/low pitch, loud/soft. Use crescendo and decrescendo as you read the diamante starting soft on Line 1 and 7, with Line 4 being the loudest.

39. Perform your diamante using different combinations of voices and/or instruments.

   *Line 1: solo*      *Line 5: trio*
   *Line 2: duet*      *Line 6: duet*
   *Line 3: trio*      *Line 7: solo*
   *Line 4: quartet*

## Stories

1. Tape record a short story and add sounds, sound effects and music to it.

2. Create one-line chants to memorize definitions for the parts of a story (plot, character, setting, conflict, resolution, etc.).

3. Read a story. Write a rap, summarizing the story.

4. Develop a soundscape for a scene or setting in a story.

5. Choose a familiar tune and tell a story through new lyrics.

*Music Moments To Teach Academics: Language Arts and Music*

6. Listen to a particular piece of instrumental music (see Discography) and write a story to go with it.

7. Choose a simple story and transform it into a sound story by adding voice or instrument parts for each character or recurring theme, object or phrase.

8. Create musical themes or chants using books that have repeated phrases in them.

    *Examples*  *Why Mosquitos Buzz In People's Ears*
    *Chicka Chicka Boom Boom*
    *Chicken Soup With Rice*
    *Where The Wild Things Are*

9. Design a "musical score" using images, shapes, designs and colors to outline a story. Use sounds and repeated words/phrases to create an interesting piece. You might employ titles, headings, pictures, and key words or characters. Map the score visually on a poster or make a chart to share with the class.

10. Explore the concept of story by listening to, singing and analyzing ballads.

    (*Wreck of the Edmund Fitzgerald, Harriet Tubman, Pete Seeger songs*)

11. Use a zipper song to tell a fairytale or to summarize a basal reader story.

    *Example*  *Jack and the Beanstalk (tune: Mary Had a Little Lamb)*

    *Verse One*  Once upon a time ago, time ago, time ago,
    Once upon a time ago there was a boy named Jack.

    *Verse Two*  Once upon a time ago. . . .he sold his cow for beans.
    *Verse Three*  Once upon a time ago. . . .his mother was so mad!

12. Share world cultural story-songs with your class (*Let Your Voice Be Heard, The Singing Sack, Songs and Stories of Uganda*). See the Bibliography for other examples.

13. Share appropriate musicals and operas for your grade level (check your local library). The music tells part or all of the story. There are many excellent selections for children.

14. Play with the form of a story, from simple to complex. Create three sections of music to relate the beginning, middle and end of any given story (A B C). Where is the repetition in the story? Contrast?

*Music Moments To Teach Academics: Language Arts and Music*

15. Read a story. What sounds were in the story (literal or implied)?

16. Use the concepts of musical expression to learn about story elements:

    *Humor: use silly voices, unusual instruments, wacky rhythms*
    *Exaggeration: loud/soft, slow/fast, high/low, staccato/legato, etc.*
    *Figures of speech: chant, sing in different styles*

17. Make up a chant-phrase for each character. You can describe the character or chant dialogue that the character might say.

18. Choose a short story. Divide the class into small groups. Each group will create and present a section or paragraph of the story musically.

19. When reading folk tales, play indigenous music from the specific culture in the background softly to create atmosphere. Listen to the music before and after the story and discuss it with your students.

20. Play incidental music designed to enhance reading comprehension (see Discography).

## Writing And Communication

1. Discuss the form of the five paragraph essay in terms of repetition and contrast.

    *A B C D A form*

2. Write about a musical concert, piece of music or favorite composer.

3. Use rhythmic pattern, pulse and flow to explore sentence lengths and rhythmic interest.

    *Jill and Jane went out to play.*

    *Once upon a time, there was a big, bad wolf.*

4. Use rhythmic pattern, pulse and flow to explore paragraph structures and rhythmic interest (e.g., use long and short sentences, word choice, etc.)

5. Music: *I Am the Song, #6 Journey to the Moon, K. Nichols.* Use soft, legato music to practice mirroring (copying the teacher or a partner silently in movement) to develop focus and vertical/horizontal eye tracking.

*Music Moments To Teach Academics: Language Arts and Music*

6. Use a familiar tune or rhythm to create a short song or chant regarding the purposes of writing. Here are some ideas.

| | | |
|---|---|---|
| *to prompt* | *to tell about something* | *to name something* |
| *to describe* | *to direct* | *to learn* |
| *to imagine* | *to express* | *to inform* |
| *to create* | *to explain ideas/procedures* | *to persuade* |
| *to entertain* | *to debate* | *to question/challenge* |

7. Music: *I Am the Song, #2 Samba, K. Nichols.* Use music with clear phrases (see Bibliography for additional examples) to enhance listening skills. One partner creates a pattern of movement or body percussion for eight counts and the other partner echoes that pattern on the next eight counts of music.

8. Turn simple songs into substitution games to develop inner hearing skills. Sing a song, making up hand motions for each word or phrase. The next time through, substitute the first hand motion for the first sung word or phrase, and so on, until the entire song is sung silently while the actions are performed.

9. Use the echo or question/answer process with voice, body percussion and instruments to develop conversation and listening skills.

10. Looping is a great technique to develop listening and multi-tasking skills. The leader claps a four-count pattern and while the class echoes it back, the leader claps a new pattern. Looping can be done with voices, instruments or body percussion, integrating other academic concepts like spelling words into the format. As the class becomes more skilled with looping, you can increase the phrases to eight and even 16 counts for an advanced challenge.

11. Audio record your instructions musically in a rap, chant or song for a class activity to help students develop listening skills.

12. Using musical concepts to explore speech and communication skills including voice pitch, volume, articulation, projecting and enunciation. Use age-appropriate vocal warm-ups (see Resources) to help develop these skills.

13. Check out the songs on the *Schoolhouse Grammar Rock* compact disc or video. The songs stick with kids and teach various grammar concepts.

14. Connect the six traits of literature with the elements of music (idea developed by Stephanie Davis, Denver, CO, used with permission).

*Music Moments To Teach Academics: Language Arts and Music*

| | | |
|---|---|---|
| *Music:* | RHYTHM | *Patterns of movement in space and time.* <br> Concepts: pulse, grouping, pattern |
| *Literature:* | CONVENTIONS | *Rules/regulations for clear communication.* <br> Concepts: punctuation, capitalization, word usage, mechanics, grammar, spelling |
| *Music:* | MELODY | *A series of related pitches, usually the lead part.* <br> Concepts: pitch, scale, interval, motive |
| *Literature:* | IDEAS & CONTENT | *Main subject and communication purpose.* <br> Concepts: theme, thesis, concept, purpose |
| *Music:* | FORM | *The way music is put together; the order.* <br> Concepts: phrase, repeat, contrast, section |
| *Literature:* | ORGANIZATION | *The way literature is best put together.* <br> Concepts: introduction, story, plot line, sentence organization, paragraphing, phrasing, conclusion |
| *Music:* | EXPRESSION | *How the music is performed; techniques used to communicate the message, tone or feeling of the music.* <br> Concepts: pace, dynamics, articulate, interpret |
| *Literature:* | VOICE | *Style, manner, personality of literature, appropriate for purpose and audience.* <br> Concepts: understandable, memorable, engaging, informative |
| *Music:* | TIMBRE | *Various qualities of sound; the unique voices of singing, speech and instruments.* <br> Concepts: body, voice, percussion, instruments |
| *Literature:* | WORD CHOICE | *Selection and variety of vocabulary that make the piece unique and meaningful.* <br> Concepts: vocabulary, descriptive |

*Music Moments To Teach Academics: Language Arts and Music*

---

| | | |
|---|---|---|
| *Music:* | TEXTURE | *The layers of the music; simultaneous parts.* Concepts: combinations, harmony, accompaniment |
| *Literature:* | SENTENCE FLUENCY | *Combination of a variety of sentence lengths to create a natural flow of ideas.* Concepts: natural flow in logic and meaning, variety in sentences |

---

15. Use additive form to explore the concept of inductive and deductive paragraphs. Play a repeated eight-count pattern on a woodblock. Then, layer in a different eight-count pattern on a bell. Keep adding parts (four or five) and listen to the sound with all parts playing simultaneously. Slowly remove one part at a time until only the first pattern remains.

   part one                                      part one, part two, part three, part four
   part one, part two                            part one, part two, part three
   part one, part two, part three                part one, part two
   part one, part two, part three, part four    part one

## Creative Writing

1. Music: *Dance Music for Children, #5 Shoemaker Dance, Shenanigans.* This music is in A B C (three different kinds of music) form and tells a story about when shoes were made by hand.

   | | |
   |---|---|
   | A | Sing the song while sewing with long, smooth strokes |
   | B | Tap-tap-tap the rhythm of the hammer with your fist |
   | C | Skip around the room to the music in your new shoes |

2. Music: *I Am the Song, #17 Waltz of the Toys, K. Nichols.* This music is in additive form. One "toy" is layered in each time the music repeats (a different instrument represents each toy). Students can draw or write down the toys they hear and create a story about toys on a shelf that come to life. This music was written as an introduction to *The Velveteen Rabbit.*

3. Music: *Music for Dancers, Too! #10 Locomotion.* Contrasting sections of music represent different cultural music styles. Listen to the music and write a story about a journey or world travel. Select one "location" and write about the setting and the people.

*Music Moments To Teach Academics: Language Arts and Music*

4. Music: *Music for Dancers, #20 Paraphony & Polyphony, K. Nichols.* A B form music (two contrasting sections that repeat). Write a short story about stillness and movement with an object for a theme.

5. Music: *I Am the Song, #6 Journey to the Moon, K. Nichols.* This is a through-composed piece of instrumental music (one section, constantly changing). Use as inspiration for stories about the beginning of the earth and space travel.

6. Music: *Dance Music for Children, #2 Cross Dance, Shenanigans.* A B form music. Create a story about the giants (A section, slow music) and the pixies (B section, quick and light music) in a far off castle or develop two other contrasting characters or ideas.

7. Music: *Music & Movement for Munchkins, Disc Two, #7 Fast & Slow.* AB repeated music. Create a story about two different tribes who are opposite in character: Tribe A and Tribe B. Occasionally, the music combines the A and B sections. Tribes can interact during these sections.

8. Music: *I Am the Song, #8-12 Sticky Finger Suite, K. Nichols.* Five short, contrasting pieces of instrumental music. Listen to each and draw a picture of a person, place or thing that comes to mind. Create a story in a small group using one idea or several.

9. Music: *Music for Creative Dance, V.3, #13 Fairytale, Eric Chappelle.* This music is written in A B C D C B A form. As you listen to the different sections which are contrasted or repeated, develop a plot line for a story with your group. Listen to the piece several times to outline your story and write a synopsis to share with the class.

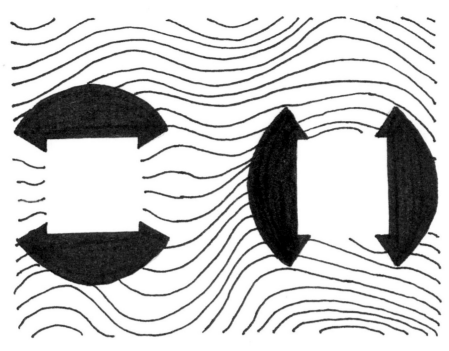

# Chapter Four:
# *Mathematics and Music*

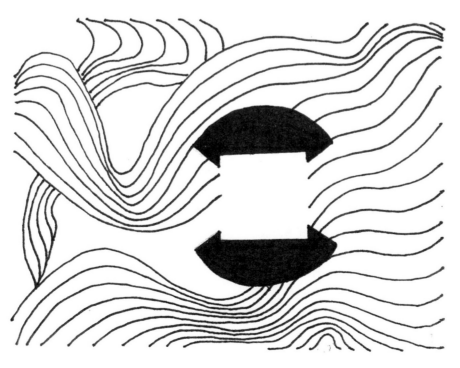

*Music Moments To Teach Academics: Mathematics and Music*

## MATHEMATICS CONCEPTS AND CONTENT

| | | |
|---|---|---|
| patterns | symbols (=, <, >, +, -, x) | equality/inequality |
| equations | function rules | inverse operations |
| addition | subtraction | multiplication |
| division | sum | difference |
| product | factors | numbers |
| rational numbers | whole numbers | counting |
| dimensions (two and three) | geometric shapes | triangle |
| square | circle | rectangle |
| parallelogram | rhombus | right triangles |
| oblique | oval | pentagon |
| cylinder | sphere | divergence |
| cube | parallel | perpendicular |
| theorems | skew | intersect |
| planes | abstract | notation |
| hexagon | angles | circumference |
| diameter | radius | area |
| width | length | perimeter |
| volume | ratios | prime numbers |
| trigonometry | transformations | tesselations |
| metric system | standard system | distance |
| weight | time | money |
| manipulatives | estimating | rounding |
| even numbers | odd numbers | fractions |
| decimals | percentages | relationships |
| mental math | negative numbers | integers |
| linear/nonlinear | quadratic functions | mean |
| median | mode | range |
| comparatives | digits | proportions |
| absolute value | exponents | square root |
| number theory | factorials | percents |
| story problems | pi | probability |
| statistics | factor trees | Fibonacci numbers |
| ordinal | mass | temperature |
| height | calibration | arch |
| symmetry/asymmetry | congruence | quadrilateral |
| ray | isosceles triangle | equilateral |
| rotation | cube | cone |
| inductive reasoning | true/false | reciprocal |
| historical math figures | applied math | pure math |
| place (1's, 10's) | grouping | graphing |
| random events | chance | frequencies |

*Music Moments To Teach Academics: Mathematics and Music*

**Numbers And Counting**

1. Speak/whisper/sing the numbers from 1-10 or 1-20 on a steady pulse. Play a pulse with clapping or instruments while you think the numbers silently in your head.

2. Sing *This Old Man (Knick Knack Paddy Whack)* with your elementary class.

3. Chant the numbers on a steady pulse, changing the pitch of your voice between high and low for each letter (one = high, two = low, three = high, etc.).

4. Chant the odd numbers loudly; chant the even numbers softly; reverse.

5. Chant the numbers using a fast-fast-slow pattern for groups of three numbers: 1 2 3, 4 5 6, 7 8 9, 10 11 12, etc. Experiment with other rhythmic patterns.

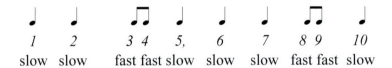

```
1     2     3 4   5,    6     7    8 9    10
slow  slow  fast fast slow  slow  slow fast fast slow
```

6. Sing the numbers using the pitches so and mi (high and middle).

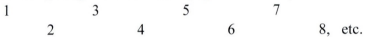

```
1        3        5        7
    2        4        6        8, etc.
```

7. As a class, count the numbers from 1-20 using a steady pulse. Each person secretly chooses two numbers that they will shout and play their instrument on (some numbers will not be chosen and there will be silences on those pulses). Students will need to follow the counting in their heads (*Idea adapted from Anne Green Gilbert*).

8. Chant the numbers with a steady pulse. Each person claps or plays their instrument on their birth date number (day, not year).

9. Walk around the room and chant the numbers on a pulse in groupings of two (loud/soft, strong/light, accented/unaccented).

**1**   2   **3**   4   **5**   6   **7**   8   **9**

10. Chant the numbers using different rhythmic patterns and rests (pauses).

11. Create chants to count by 2's, 3's, 4's, 5's and 10's.

12. Sing or speak the numbers starting on a low pitch and gradually raise the pitch of your voice; repeat, starting high and lowering your voice pitch.

13. Trace the shape of a number with your finger in the air as you change the pitch of your voice (one = short scoop up, then voice slides down).

14. Sing or speak the sound of the number as you trace it with your finger; repeat with other numbers and their sounds.

15. Create an interesting vocal piece based on numbers and their sounds. Each group can make up a repeated part for a specific number. Layer the separate parts into a full group piece.
    *One, wha wha nnnnnn, wha wha nnnnnn, one  (clap once)*

16. Select a group of seven or eight numbers and sing them on the notes of the scale (do-re-mi-fa-so-la-ti-do or 1-2-3-4-5-6-7-8). Try the singing game using even numbers only, odd numbers, prime numbers, etc.

17. Sing or chant the numbers in an alternating pattern. You can use different pitches to designate your placement in the sequence.

    | Numbers: | *1* | *3* | *2* | *4* | *3* | *5* | *4* | *6* |
    |---|---|---|---|---|---|---|---|---|
    | Pitch: | do | mi | re | fa | mi | so | fa | la |

18. How many letters can you sing/speak on a repeated pitch in one single breath?

19. Practice groups of numbers via call/response (QA) process.
    Teacher:  1 2 3          Class:  4 5 6

20. Practice groups of numbers via echo process.
    Teacher:  1 2 3          Class:  1 2 3

21. Practice chanting or singing the numbers in a round (canon). Divide the class in two groups. First group begins; second group begins when the first group finishes the first four numbers. Students keep a steady pulse to maintain synchronicity. For a variation, have the second group begin earlier or later and add more than two parts. Write the combinations on the board and discuss the relationships and patterns between numbers.

    Group #1:    1 2 3 4,  5 6 7 8,  9 10 11 12,  13 14 15 16
    Group #2:    (waits)   1 2 3 4,  5 6 7   8, 9   10 11 12

22. Can you chant the numbers slowly? Fast? Can you start slowly and get faster? Can you start fast and get slower?

23. Speak the first group of numbers using a legato (smooth, connected) voice and phrase; speak the second group of numbers using a staccato (broken, separate) voice and phrase.

24. Write a group of numbers on the board. Place a fermata over certain numbers and hold those sounds when you get to them; repeat the exercise using other music symbols such as accents (>).

25. Create a pattern with body percussion while chanting the numbers. Pat the odds and clap the evens. Develop more complex patterns involving stomps and snaps students.

26. Divide the class into two groups with instruments: woods and drums. As the class chants the numbers, those with woods play on the odd numbers while the drums play on the even numbers.

27. Use an additive form game to practice the numbers. Say the first number, then the first two, three and so on: 1, 12, 123, 1234, 12345, 123456, 1234567, 12345678, etc.

28. Music: *Music for Creative Dance, V.2, #5 Pizz-Ah! Eric Chappelle.* This music has 28 short sections. Practice writing a different number for each section of the music, or alternate between different numbers.

29. Music: *Music for Dancers, #1 Pulsation.* At the beginning of the music, one student makes a shape in the middle of the space and makes the sound of one number; the next student makes a shape attached to the first student while chanting the next number in the sequence. Continue until all of the students have joined in. Then, the leader runs to the end of the chain to starting the counting in reverse.

30. Sing a familiar tune with "number" lyrics. Sing a single number and practice writing it or combine numbers in a sequence using pitches.

    *Tune: Twinkle Twinkle*    One one, two two, three three, four
                                             Five five, six six, seven seven, more!
                                             Eight, eight, nine, nine, then there's ten....

    *Tune: Hot Cross Buns*    Three, two, one (rest), three, two, one (rest)
                                             One one one one, two two two two
                                             Three, two, one (rest)

*Music Moments To Teach Academics: Mathematics and Music*

31. Practice the vocal warm-ups (see Resources) using the numbers.

32. How many fingers do you have? Sing your response (1 2 3 4 5). How many legs does the spider have? Sing your response (1 2 3 4 5 6). Use the so-mi motive (five-three) to make up simple melodic responses.

33. Use groupings (meter) of strong and light pulses to practice the numbers.

    | Twos: | **1** | 2 | **3** | 4 | **5** | 6 | **7** | 8 |
    |---|---|---|---|---|---|---|---|---|
    | | **strong** | *light* | **strong** | *light* | **strong** | *light* | **strong** | *light* |

    | Threes: | **1** | 2 | 3 | **4** | 5 | 6 | **7** | 8 | 9 |
    |---|---|---|---|---|---|---|---|---|---|
    | | **strong** | *light* | *light* | **strong** | *light* | *light* | **strong** | *light* | *light* |

34. Write a rap about numbers and counting and develop an ostinato (repeated pattern) accompaniment for it.

    Ostinato:   *1 and a 2 and a 3   4   5*

35. Try singing simple, three note motives using the pitches of the scale. How many can you create?

    | 2 3 1 | 1 5 3 | 8 5 6 | 5 6 3 | 3 2 1 |
    |---|---|---|---|---|
    | *re mi do* | *do so mi* | *do so la* | *so la mi* | *mi re do* |

36. Practice chanting the numbers using different combinations of voices.

    Solo:  1 2 3 4 5                Duet: 6 7 8 9 10
    Trio:  11 12 13 14 15           Quartet: 16 17 18 19 20
    Tutti (everyone): 21 22 23 24 25

37. The class sits in a circle, patting a simple body percussion pattern on their laps. On the first clap, the first person says "one"; on the next clap, the second person says "two" and so on until everyone has participated. Create more difficult patterns for older students and have them count by 3's, 6's, 7's, etc.

    | *Voices* | "1" | "2" |
    |---|---|---|
    | *Pattern* | *pat pat clap* | *pat pat clap* |

38. Bounce tennis balls to the pulse as you chant the numbers. Try different variations.

39. Practice jump rope chants and songs with numbers at recess or recreational time.

40. Play rhythmic, hand games and clapping games to familiar chants (*One potato, two potato, three potato, four...*). Learn the hambone or make up your own (see *Step It Down* by Bessie Jones). Make up your own rhymes using numbers.

41. Music: *Dance Music for Children, #4 Seven Jumps, Shenanigans.* This folk music from Denmark has an additive AB form using fermatas (held notes). As the music begins, the class walks around to the pulse in a circle. On the first fermata (B section), everyone says "One!" and makes the shape of the number with their body. On the next fermata, "Two!" is added and so on until the music ends. There are seven "jumps."

42. Check out the *Schoolhouse Rock* video and compact disc, *Multiplication Rock* and other titles for fun, catchy tunes that help students remember facts.

43. Use a block chart to practice counting with a pulse. Place X's in the boxes to indicate sound, either vocal or instrumental. For older students, add other parts and create a more complex pattern. Block charts can be of any length (see Resources) and are repeated several times. For voices, say the number of each box there is an X under or write in a number word (one, two, three...) to be spoken.

| 1 | 2 | 3 | 4 | 5 | 6 | 7 | 8 |
|---|---|---|---|---|---|---|---|
| one |  |  | four |  |  | seven |  |
|  | two |  |  | five |  |  | eight |
|  |  | three |  |  | six |  |  |

44. Count the keys on a piano or keyboard. Can you sing them as you count? How many black keys are there? White keys? If you don't have a piano or keyboard, use the Melody Chart (see Resources).

45. Play 16 counts with a partner. One student keeps a steady pulse on a drum at a walking tempo. One person walks away from their partner and then returns while counting to 16. The other partner then walks away counting backward from 16 and returns. Simplify the game for younger students; add complexity for older students.

46. Make two sets of file cards. On one set, write single numbers, 1-10, and on the other, write a sound-action word (e.g., clap, snap, pat, stomp, sing, whistle, hum, etc.). Students draw one from each file and then perform the number via the indicated sound:

  *Card from pile one:*   4     *Card from pile two:*   clap
    *Solution:*   perform four claps

47. Can you show "five" musically in several different ways? Here are some suggestions.

   -five claps, five pats, five stomps, five snaps
   -whisper/sing/speak/shout "five", five times
   -play a rhythmic pattern of five on an instrument
   -play five pulses on an instrument
   -sing the first five notes of the scale (do-re-mi-fa-so)
   -make up a pattern and play it five times (pat clap clap)

48. Sing the song "I Know An Old Lady. . ." (additive form) making up new lyrics around numbers.

    *Example*

    | | |
    |---|---|
    | *Verse One* | I know an old lady who swallowed a one, <br> It wasn't much fun to swallow a one, <br> Perhaps she's done. |
    | *Verse Two* | I know an old lady who swallowed a two, <br> And what do you do when you swallow a two? |
    | *Verse Three* | I know an old lady who swallowed a three, <br> Fiddle-dee-dee, she swallowed a three... |
    | *Chorus* | She swallowed the three, to follow the two, <br> She swallowed the two, to follow the one, <br> I don't know why she swallowed the one, <br> I guess she's done! |

49. What other numbers do we use in our lives (telephone number, house/street number, date, social security number, etc.)? Assign different sounds to each digit and perform them in sequence.

    1-800-505-4237 (one clap, eight stomps, rests for zeros, etc.)

## Patterns

1. Look at the keys on a piano or keyboard. What patterns do you see? In the black keys? White keys?

2. Place a pattern of shapes on the board (triangle, circle, square, repeat). Assign a different sound to each shape (speak/sing/whisper, clap/pat/snap, or wood/metal/drum) to create a sound representation of the pattern.

3. Look at patterns found in the classroom. Where do you see repetition? Contrast? Play these patterns with body percussion or instruments.

   *Shirt:* stripe, polka dots, stripe, solid
   *Play:* wood, metal, wood, drum

4. Experiment with playing and singing the tones of a pentatonic (five-note) scale. You can use a xylophone or the black keys on the piano. In a pentatonic scale, there is a group of three notes, followed by a space and two more notes before the pattern is repeated. Many of our folk songs as well as melodies from the Far East and Africa were created using the five tones of the pentatonic scale. If you do not have access to an instrument, you can easily sing the pentatonic scale using solfege.

| **do** | **re** | **mi** | *(fa)* | **so** | **la** | *(ti)* | **do** |
|---|---|---|---|---|---|---|---|
| 1 | 2 | 3 | *(4)* | 5 | 6 | *(7)* | *(8/1)* |
| sing | sing | sing | think | sing | sing | think | sing |

5. Play "Copy Me." The class stands in a circle and the first person starts by making a repeated pattern of sound with voice, body or instrument. The class copies the leader until everyone is in unison. Then, the next person starts a different sound pattern and the group copies it. Continue until each person has created a pattern.

6. Play "Circle Of Sound" (idea from *Teaching The Three R's* by Anne Green Gilbert. used with permission). The class stands in a circle and the first person starts by making a repeated pattern of sound with voice, body or instrument while walking in a circle around the inside of the group. As the leader passes a person, that person joins in the pattern. When the leader returns to their spot in the circle, the others keep his/her pattern going until the second leader passes by them with a new one. You will hear two patterns simultaneously at any given time in the game. Advanced: send two people at once in opposite directions around the circle.

7. Create short ostinati (repeated patterns) and layer them together.

  *Rhythm:* ta ta ta-te ta ta-te ta-te ta-te ta
       ta te te ta ta ta-te ta-te ta- a

  *Melody:* middle low middle higher
      so mi so la
      5 3 5 6

  *Form:*  *binary (AB)*   *ternary (ABA)*
      *rondo (ABACADA)* *round (canon)*

*Music Moments To Teach Academics: Mathematics and Music*

*Expression:* *fast/slow/fast*      *loud/soft/loud/medium*
*staccato/legato/staccato*

*Timbre:* *wood/metal/wood/wood/drum*
*sing/speak/sing/speak/whisper*

*Texture:* *solo/tutti/solo/quartet*

8. Place long and short shapes on the board to create long and short sound patterns. Talk about Morse code which uses a combination of short and long sounds to relay messages.

9. Create your own code by assigning a number to each letter of the alphabet. Send your code to your friend via sound only and see if they can decipher the message. Use pauses (rests) between numbers to make sure your message is clearly received.

| 1 | 2 | 3 | 4 | 5 | 6 | 7 | 8 | 9 | 10 |
|---|---|---|---|---|---|---|---|---|---|
| a | b | c | d | e | f | g | h | i | j |
| 11 | 12 | 13 | 14 | 15 | 16 | 17 | 18 | 19 | 20 |
| k | l | m | n | o | p | q | r | s | t |
| 21 | 22 | 23 | 24 | 25 | 26 | | | | |
| u | | w | x | y | z | | | | |

*Hello: eight claps, five pats, 12 snaps, 12 snaps, 15 stomps*

10. Music: *I Am the Song, #1 Can You Feel The Happy Rhythm? K. Nichols.* Listen to this piece a few times and write down the pattern of form the sections create with repetition and contrast (Answer: A B C A B C A B).

11. Music: *I Am the Song, #2 Samba, K. Nichols.* On the first phrase of the music, the teacher makes up a pattern with claps or rhythm sticks. On the second phrase, the class repeats it. You can create four-pulse, eight-pulse or 16-pulse phrase patterns. This music is written in an overall A B repeated form.

12. Music: *I Am the Song, #14 Sansa Kroma, K. Nichols.* This music is written in A B A B A B A B form. For the A section, make a shape and clap your hands three times. Repeat this pattern four times total (A section). For the B section, walk around the room and clap the pulse or make up a new rhythmic pattern. Or, have the children sit in the circle and pat the pulse on their laps. They can count out loud as a group. Older students can chant multiples

together or individually around the circle. You could add boxes in a passing game for more of a challenge. How could you integrate addition and/or subtraction into the game?

13. Look in the Conceptual Discography (see Resources) for examples of music that reflect pattern through *form* or *rhythm*.

14. Play the Cup Rap game. Create interesting rhythmic patterns with a plastic cup (a variety of colors and sizes can be found in the picnic area of your local grocery store) and your desk. Organize the different sounds of the cup into patterns. Here are some suggestions.

    1. Pick the cup up and place it top side up on the desk.
    2. Grab the cup from the side.
    3. Pick the cup up and place it topside down on the desk.
    4. Tap a rhythm on the bottom of the cup.
    5. Pat a rhythm on the desk to the sides of the cup.
    6. Pick the cup up and touch the top to your other hand.
    7. Pick the cup up and touch the bottom to your other hand.
    8. Slide the bottom of the cup across the desk.
    9. Slide the top of the cup across the desk.
    10. Clap your hands above the cup.
    11. Pass or slide your cup to your partner.
    12. Scrape the ridges on the side of your cup with your nail.
    13. Pass the cup from one hand to the other.
    14. Speak or sing into the cup.
    15. Tap the sides of the cup.

15. Music: *Music for Dancers, #1 Pulsation, K. Nichols*   Form: A B repeated.
    A: *Create a rhythmic pattern of sound/movement with your partner. You may use voice, body percussion or small percussion instruments.*

    B: *Wave goodbye to your partner and move around the room by yourself with pulse to find a new partner.*

16. Music: *I Am the Song, #13 Walkin' Now in Beauty, K. Nichols.*
    Folk dances use patterns in rhythm (counting), in form (contrasting and repeated sections), and in formations (co-centric circles, stars, parallel lines, etc.). Here is a simple folk dance to teach pattern. Stand in a circle formation and number off by twos:

    A section:   *Walk clockwise in the circle for eight slow pulses*
                 *Turn and walk counterclockwise, eight slow pulses*

*Music Moments To Teach Academics: Mathematics and Music*

    *B section*     The "one's" walk to the center of the circle for four slow pulses, then backwards for four pulses to return to their spots; Then, the "two's" walk to the center of the circle for four slow pulses and then backwards for four pulses to their spots.

17. Look in the Discography and Bibliography for other suggestions of simple and complex folk dances that engage pattern (suggestions: *Rhythmically Moving* Series by Phyllis Weikart/Gemini, *Best of the Shenanigans* by the Shenanigans, and Sanna Longden's *Dances of Seven Continents* Series).

18. Experience a simple polyrhythm (meaning many rhythms) of two against three. As you practice, you will be able to hear and feel the rhythm in a grouping of two as well as three.

    Hands on lap: *together, R L R*     OR     *together, R L R*
    Counting:           *1   2 + 3*                   *1   + 2 +*

19. Block charting and circle drumming are two great activities you can use to explore the concept of pattern and build group synergy at the same time. Check out the bibliography for a list of good drumming titles.

    Block Charting: Mark X's in this pulse chart to create rhythmic patterns. Keep the drum part on the steady pulse (odd numbers); this keeps the rhythm steady. Example: Row 1 (across) would be played by maracas; Row 2 (across) by a bell; Row 3 (across) by the drum.

    | 1 | 2 | 3 | 4 | 5 | 6 | 7 | 8 |
    |---|---|---|---|---|---|---|---|
    | X | X |   |   | X | X |   |   |
    |   | X | X |   | X |   | X | X |
    | X |   | X |   | X |   | X |   |

    *Circle Drumming*     Sit in a circle with hand drums, congas or "found sounds." Warm up by playing a steady pulse.

    Number off by twos: Have the "one's" keep the pulse going and the "two's" make up a pattern against it.

    Switch parts.

    Play patterns using loud and soft (strong and light) strokes.
    Two = strong light         Three = strong light light

Music Moments To Teach Academics: Mathematics and Music

*Combine patterns of two and three.*
*Five = strong light, strong light light*

*The "1's" play the pattern of two while the "two's" play the pattern of three; switch parts. Notice changes.*

*One person starts a pattern and the next plays a new one that fits with it. Go around the circle.*

## Opposites

1. Show the difference between long and short through sound. Write long and short lines on the board or on file cards to create different combinations of sound. Use voices and/or instruments to make the sounds. Relate to the concepts of staccato and legato.

   ⎯⎯⎯    ⎯ ⎯ ⎯    ⎯⎯⎯    ⎯
   *triangle    wood wood wood    triangle    wood*

2. Show the difference between big and small through sound using the concepts of loud and small or different timbres.

   big           small
   *(loud drum)*   *(quiet bell)*

3. Experiment with drums that have different size drum skins (hand drums work well for this). Fill in the following blanks.

   *The bigger the drum skin, the _____ the pitch. (lower)*
   *The smaller the drum skin, the _____ the pitch. (higher)*

4. Show the difference between tall and short objects by using a high or low voice to describe them or play high and low pitches on an instrument.

5. Show the difference between many and few through sound. Divide the class into two groups: many with instruments and a small group with instruments. Take turns letting each group play. Which is louder? Which creates more sound? Take turns playing a solo, then all together, solo, all together.

6. Show the difference between near and far. One person plays a drum while standing in the middle of class. The person then walks outside of the class into the hallway and plays the drum. What differences do you hear? Take two plastic cups and tap them on your desk to copy the sound of footsteps that are getting closer to you. How would you change the sound to make the footsteps start close to you and get farther away?

*Music Moments To Teach Academics: Mathematics and Music*

7. Show positional and directional opposites through sound. You can use body percussion or instrument sounds.

      up/down          *clap your hands up high; clap them down low*
      over/under       *clap your hands over your desk; under your desk*
      right/left           *clap your hands to the right of your body; to the left*
      forward/backward  *clap your hands in front of your body; behind*

8. Show the difference between fast and slow. Sing a simple song fast; sing it slow; sing it at a medium speed. Repeat the exercise by playing the rhythm of the words fast, slow and medium.

9. Sing the scale on numbers, solfege or a vowel sound going up and going down.

| Up: | *do* | *re* | *mi* | *fa* | *so* | *la* | *ti* | *do* |
|---|---|---|---|---|---|---|---|---|
| | 1 | 2 | 3 | 4 | 5 | 6 | 7 | 8 |
| Down: | *do* | *ti* | *la* | *so* | *fa* | *mi* | *re* | *do* |
| | 8 | 7 | 6 | 5 | 4 | 3 | 2 | 1 |

## Time, Money And Measurement

1. Make a spinner fashioned like a clock with the numbers one through twelve around the edge. Spin the spinner and make the number of sounds (clap, play an instrument) indicated.

2. A metronome is a device used in music to count the pulses (beats) per minute. Set the metronome at various speeds and create activities to do to the pulse. If the metronome clicks 80 beats per minute, how long does each pulse take? What movements could we do in 60 beats? What pace is comfortable for walking? Stretching? Running?

   *Example:*    *60 beats per minute = 15 claps, 15 pats, 15 snaps, 15 stomps*

3. Compare the ticking of a wind up clock with a metronome keeping pulse. At what speed does the metronome need to beat to match the clock? How can we set it to be different from the clock?

4. Use a bell to ring for the different times of the clock. How many rings for 12 noon? 1:30? 8:00?

5. Let's create our own clock of sound with instruments or body percussion. Keep in mind the ratio between days, hours, minutes and seconds. Present the piece in "elapsed" time.

6. Chant the hours on the clock to memorize them. Turn the chant into a so-mi melody.

> *One o'clock, two o'clock, three o'clock, four,*
> so so so   mi mi mi   so so so   mi
>
> *Five o'clock, six o'clock, seven o'clock, more,*
> so so so   mi mi mi   so so so so   mi
>
> *Eight o'clock, nine o' clock, ten o'clock, eleven,*
> so so so   mi mi mi   so so so   so mi mi
>
> *Twelve o'clock is the very last one,*
> so so so so so mi mi mi mi
>
> *Now we go back and begin again!*
> so so so so   so so mi mi mi

7. Create a rhyme-chant using the hours on the clock.

> *When the clock strikes one, we'll have some fun!*
> *When the clock strikes two, I'll dance with you!*
> *When the clock strikes three, we'll sing with glee!*

8. Drop different coins on a desk and describe the difference in sound. Can you tell what coin is dropped if you close your eyes?

9. Create shaker instruments by placing coins in a plastic or metal container. Find how many sounds you can make with a dollar bill: crinkle it and straighten it at different speeds, rub two ends together, fold it tightly and tap on the desk, etc.

10. Create a code of sound for different amounts of money.

> *Pennies = woodblock   Dimes = cow bell or triangle   Dollars = drum*
>
> $2.45 = (two drum beats, four bell sounds and five taps on the woodblock), etc.
> Dime (one bell sound) = 10 pennies (10 sounds on the woodblock), etc.

11. Play the Hickory Dickory Dock game. Chant the poem or make up a melody for the words to sing. Children sit in a circle and chant/sing the poem; the "mouse" walks around the outside of the circle. At the end of the poem, the "mouse" tags the "cat" (anyone in

*Music Moments To Teach Academics: Mathematics and Music*

the circle) and the cat chases the mouse around the circle and back to their spot. The second time, the clock strikes two, so the mouse tags two cats, and so on:

*Hickory dickory dock (clap), the mouse ran up the clock (clap),*
*The clock struck one (bell), the mouse ran down, hickory dickory dock (clap)!*

The clock struck two (two bells), he lost his shoe. . .
The clock struck three (three bells), he bumped his knee. . .
The clock struck four (four bells), he shut the door. . .
The clock struck five (five bells), he's still alive. . .
The clock struck six (six bells), he did some tricks. . .
The clock struck seven (seven bells), he looked to heaven. . .
The clock struck eight (eight bells), he wasn't late. . .
The clock struck nine (nine bells), the mouse was fine. . .
The clock struck ten (10 bells), he found a pen. . .
The clock struck eleven (11 bells), he fell back to seven. . .
The clock struck twelve (12 bells), he jumped to the shelf. . .

12. Write lyrics about different coins or bills to a familiar tune. Here is an example from Kathi Naffah, Denver, CO, to the tune of B-I-N-G-O.

*There is a coin that's brown and round and penny is its name-O,*
*P-E-N-N-Y, P-E-N-N-Y, P-E-N-N-Y and penny is its name-O.*

It's worth one cent, no more, no less, and penny is its name-O,
P-E-N-N-Y, P-E-N-N-Y, P-E-N-N-Y and penny is its name-O.

Lincoln is the president, his face is on the penny,
P-E-N-N-Y, P-E-N-N-Y, P-E-N-N-Y and penny is its name-O.

There is a coin that's made of nickel, nickel is its name-O,
N-I-C-K-E-L, N-I-C-K-E-L, N-I-C-K-E-L and nickel is its name-O.

There is a coin that's silver thin and dime is its name-O,
D-I-M-E dime, D-I-M-E dime, D-I-M-E dime and dime is its name-O.

Even though it's very small, it's worth ten cents, count them all,
1-2-3-4-5, 6-7-8-9-10, the dime is silver thin and it is worth 10 cents-O

There is a coin that's big and round and quarter is its name-O,
Q-U-A-R-T-E-R, Q-U-A-R-T-E-R, Q-U-A-R-T-E-R and quarter is its name-O

Washington, the president, his face is on the quarter,
Q-U-A-R-T-E-R, Q-U-A-R-T-E-R, Q-U-A-R-T-E-R and quarter is its name-O

13. Create a soundscape for a grocery store or another setting where money is exchanged.

14. Sit in a circle. Take a penny, dime, quarter, fifty-cent piece or silver dollar and as you sing this so-la-mi tune, secretly pass the coin behind backs around the circle. One person is in the middle with their eyes closed. At the end of the song, they must go to a person and sing their question. The person in the middle gets three chances to find the coin before it is revealed. The person in the middle changes places with the person who had the coin and the game starts again. Repeat with different coins.

    *Penny, penny, who has the penny? Who has the penny hiding in their hands?*
    so mi  so mi  so  mi la  so mi     so mi la  so so mi la so so    mi
    *"Do you have the penny"? ("Yes, I have the penny" or "No, I do not")*
    so  so  mi   la  so  mi       so  so mi   la  so mi       so mi la so-mi

15. Older students can do a search and find all the songs they can that refer to money (e.g., *Cabaret*, Pink Floyd's *"Money,"* Shania Twain's *"Ka-Ching,"* etc.)

16. Write chants to memorize units of measurement for length, volume and weight. Use different voices to chant (sing/speak/whisper/shout). Play the rhythm of the words with body percussion or an instrument while you say or think them. Keep a steady pulse on a drum and chant in a call/response style.

    *millimeter, centimeter, decimeter, meter, decameter, hectometer, kilometer*
    *milligram, centigram, decigram, gram, decagram, hectogram, kilogram*
    *milliliter, centiliter, deciliter, liter, decaliter, hectoliter, kiloliter*
    *inch, foot, yard, mile*
    *ounce, pound, ton*
    *teaspoon, tablespoon, cup, pint, quart, gallon*

17. Place a ruler on the desk. With your finger, tap a pulse on each number consecutively as you begin on one end and travel to the other. Count out loud. Start with the standard side of the ruler and at the end, go to the metric side to compare. For more complexity, subdivide the units of measurement.

    | Inch | = | *walk (1)* | *walk (2)* | *walk (3)* | *walk (4)* |
    | 1/2 inch = | | *run-ning* | *run-ning* | *run-ning* | *run-ning* |
    | 1/4 inch = | | *wig-gle jig-gle* | *wig-gle jig-gle* | *wig-gle jig-gle* | *wig-gle jig-gle* |

18. Time and Space. How many beats/paces does it take to walk across the room? What if we moved twice as fast? Twice as slow? Can we pace out a square to the beat of the music?

*Music Moments To Teach Academics: Mathematics and Music*

**Fractions And Ratios**

1. Explore whole, half, quarter, eighth and sixteenth notes using rhythmic notation. Clap or play these note values or use the movement words described in the Resources chapter in this book. Create simple sound computations to further understand the relationships of these fractions. You can use the standard music notation for this activity or shapes:

   | whole note | half note | quarter note | eighth note | sixteenth note |
   | whole rest | half rest | quarter rest | eighth rest | sixteenth rest |

   *Whole note =  two half notes OR four quarter notes OR eight eighth notes OR 16 sixteenth notes*

2. What combinations of note values can you play in a four-pulse phrase? An eight-pulse phrase? A 16-pulse phrase?

   *four-pulse phrase:* one half note, one quarter note and two eighth notes
   *eight-pulse phrase:* one whole note, one half note, eight sixteenth notes
   *16-pulse phrase:* two whole notes, two half notes, two quarter notes, two eighth notes and four sixteenth notes

3. Use the space between notes (intervals) on the keyboard or piano to explore ratios (or use *The Melody Chart* in the Resource chapter). Play or sing them to hear the difference between the intervals. For advanced students, talk about the ratios of the string lengths (inside the piano) to the pitch that is produced at the keyboard. Here are the intervalic ratios.

   <u>Interval</u>
   Semitone/Half step (C to C#, E to F, B to high C, etc.)
   Second/Whole step (C to D, E to F#, Bb to high C, etc.)   Ratio: 1:2
   Third (C to E, D to F#, G to B, etc.)   Ratio: 1:3
   Fourth (C to F, D to G, F to Bb, etc.)   Ratio: 1:4
   Fifth (C to G, D to A, F to high C, etc.)   Ratio: 1:5
   Sixth (C to A, D to B, etc.)   Ratio: 1:6
   Seventh (C to B, F to high E, etc.)   Ratio: 1:7
   Octave (C1 to C2, D1 to D2, etc.)   Ratio: 1:8

4. Draw a pie on the board. "Slice" it into four, even pieces. Number each piece of the pie, one through four. Divide the class into four groups: shakers, metals, woods, drums. Point to a sector and the corresponding group can sound their instruments (1/4 of the class). Point to two sectors and half of the class plays. Point to three sectors and three-fourths of the class plays. Try other pies divided in thirds, fifths, sixths or eighths. Change the groups of instruments to body percussion or voices.

5. Give each student a pair of rhythm sticks, an instrument or use body percussion. Write a number on the board and ask the class to play one-quarter of that number with pulses. Try different numbers with different fractions.

        Number: *8*         Fraction: *1/4*         Play: *two pulses*
        Number: *15*        Fraction: *1/3*         Play: *five pulses*

6. Write fractions on the board. Assign one group to play metals instruments for the numerator, the other to play woods for the denominator.

7. Use block charts of different sizes to teach fractions. Color in or place X's in the box where you want sound. In the following chart, how many boxes do we need to color in (and play on) to be playing for half of the time? Create other combinations or change the size of the chart. If there are four parts, how can you make a part play twice as much as the one under it?

| 1 | 2 | 3 | 4 | 5 | 6 |
|---|---|---|---|---|---|
|   |   |   |   |   |   |
|   |   |   |   |   |   |

8. Sing the song *Twinkle, Twinkle* or other familiar song. How many phrases does it have (six four-pulse phrases)? How can we sing one-half of the song? How would we sing one-sixth of the song? How would we sing two-thirds of the song?

9. Write or select a four.line, rhyming poem. As you perform the poem, speak one quarter of it (one line) and whisper three quarters. Change the fractions and voices. Divide the class into groups, half speaking the poem and half clapping the rhythmic patterns of the words.

10. In small groups of four or five, create ratios as you speak a simple poem or sing a simple song.

    *Solo*         *I'm a little teapot, short and stout,*         Ratio 1:1
    *Duet*         *Here is my handle, here is my spout,*         Ratio 1:2
    *Trio*         *When I get all steamed up, then I shout,*         Ratio 1:3
    *Quartet*         *"Tip me over and pour me out!"*         Ratio 1:4

11. Use sound to work with equivalent fractions. Write two equivalent fractions on the board but omit one of the numerators or denominators. Students can clap or play their instrument to indicate the missing number.

        1/2 = 3/?         3/5 = ?/10         4/12 = 1/?

12. In a three-pulse measure (3/4 meter), a quarter note accounts for what fraction of the measure (1/3)? A half note (2/3)? An eighth note (1/6)?

13. Singing in harmony (notes below or above the melody that sound good with it) creates a variety of ratios. Try playing them on a keyboard or xylophone to hear the different relationships between pitches.

    | | | | | | | | |
    |---|---|---|---|---|---|---|---|
    | *Thirds* | Ratio 1:3 | Part 1: | do | re | mi | fa | mi |
    | | | Part 2: | mi | fa | so | la | so |
    | *Fourths* | Ratio 1:4 | Part 1: | do | re | mi | fa | so |
    | | | Part 2: | fa | so | la | ti | la |
    | *Fifths* | Ratio 1:5 | Part 1: | do | re | mi | re | do |
    | | | Part 2: | so | la | ti | la | so |
    | *Sixths* | Ratio 1:6 | Part 1: | do | re | mi | re | do |
    | | | Part 2: | la | ti | do | ti | la |

14. The harmonic intervals above can also be inverted (turned upside down) to create a different interval. Play these on an instrument or on The Melody Chart.

    | *Scale* | C | D | E | F | G | A | B | c |
    |---|---|---|---|---|---|---|---|---|
    | | 1 | 2 | 3 | 4 | 5 | 6 | 7 | 8 |
    | | do | re | mi | fa | so | la | ti | do |
    | | (low) | | | | | | | (high) |

    | Thirds (Ratio 1:3) | Inversion | Sixths (Ratio 1:6) |
    |---|---|---|
    | Low C and E | | E and high C |
    | Fourths (Ratio 1:4) | Inversion | Fifths (Ratio 1:5) |
    | Low C and F | | F and high C |
    | Seconds (Ratio 1:2) | Inversion | Sevenths (Ratio 1:7) |
    | Low C and D | | D and high C |

15. Make Straw Panpipes using plastic drinking straws of a standard size. By cutting the straws into different lengths and taping them side by side, from longest to shortest, students should try to create an eight-pitch scale. Sound is created by blowing *across* the

tops of the straws (like a flute). Students may need extra straws to "figure out" the ratios that create the correct pitch sequence. Keep track of the various methods they use to solve the problem and discuss them in class. Play your panpipes in class, do some measuring of straws and document your findings. Make another row (one octave lower) by placing tape over the bottoms of the straws.

16. Music Suggestion: *Music for Dancers, #20 Paraphony & Polyphony.*
Divide the class into two "tribes." the *rational* and *irrational* numbers. Students can write rational and irrational numbers on sheets of paper and tape them to their shirts. Place a tape line through the center of the room. On the A section music, the rational numbers dance on their side of the room and play light, metal and shaker (agreeable) instruments. On the B section music, the rational numbers freeze and the irrational numbers dance on their side of the room, playing drums and woods (disagreeable) instruments. Repeat this sequence until the last section of music, where the two tribes mingle and make peace. During the activity, numbers can be persuaded to "defect" and become a member of the opposing tribe. How would they need to change their numbers in order to do this?

*Rational Number*   Any number that can be written as a fraction
*Irrational Number* Any number that can NOT be written as a fraction
                    (e.g., pi, square roots of 2, 3, 5, etc.)

## Operations

1. Do the above activity using *whole* and *prime* numbers.

    *The Ready-for-PRIME-time Numbers*
    *2, 3, 4, 5, 7, 11, 13, 17, 19, 23, 29, etc.*

    *The NOT-so-ready-for-prime-time Numbers*
    *6, 8, 9, 10, 12, 14, 15, 16, 18, 20, 21, 22, etc.*

2. Assign sounds to each symbol used in equations. Read the equations out loud but substitute the instrument sounds for the symbols.

    + *(plus)*   claves      − *(minus)*     guiro

    × *(times)*  drum        / *(divide)*    triangle

    = *(equals)* cymbal      ≠ *(not equal)* vibraslap

*Music Moments To Teach Academics: Mathematics and Music*

3. Substitute body percussion for the numbers in an equation while exploring equalities and inequalities.

$$5 + 2 = 2 + 5$$

*(five claps  claves  two pats  cymbal  two pats  claves  five claps)*

4. Make up a chant about *inverse operations*.

> *Inverse operations, it's quite a cool sensation.*
> *Subtract and add, divide and multiply, inverse operations!*

> *seven + six is thirteen;   thirteen - six is seven*
> *two x four is eight;   eight / four is two*

5. Use rhythm instruments or body percussion to practice the four operations: *add, subtract, multiply* and *divide*. You can give verbal instructions or write an equation on the board.

$$3(8 - 4) + 2 = \underline{\qquad}$$

*Play eight pulses; subtract four pulses (play four pulses).*
*Multiply the remaining pulse by three (play 12 pulses).*
*Add two (play 14 pulses).*

6. Divide your class into four groups: addition, subtraction, multiplication and division. Each group creates a math rap for their operation. Use the chant below for an A section and create a rondo form.

> Chant         *Add, subtract, multiply, divide,*
> A section     *Each one full of operational pride!* (repeat)

7. Chant an addition equation and play the answer on your instrument. Repeat for other operations: *addends/sum; factors/product; divisor, dividend/quotient; minuend, subtrahend/difference*.

> Chant   *"Five plus three is"* (play your instrument eight times)
> *"Two times six is"* (play your instrument 12 times)
> *"Twelve divided by three is"* (play your instrument four times)
> *"Four minus three is"* (play your instrument once)

8. Create chants and repeat the previous exercises to learn the three properties: *commutative, associate, distributive*. Divide the class into three groups and let each write a rap or song to a familiar tune to tell about/explain their property.

*Music Moments To Teach Academics: Mathematics and Music*

<u>*Commutative*</u>     <u>*Associative*</u>     <u>*Distributive*</u>
$A + B = B + A$     $A + (B + C) = (A + B) + C$     $A(B + C) = (A \times B) + (A \times C)$
$A \times B = B \times A$

9. As a class, decide what sounds you will use for the operational symbols as well as the numbers in a given equation. Write these on the board or give each student a sheet with the codes on it. Play an equation musically and see if the students can write down the equation on their paper using the code.

10. Music: *Rhythmically Moving, V. 7, #10 D'Hammerschmiedsgesell'n.* This music is written in A B (binary) form. The A section is divided into groupings of three. Students can create body percussion patterns with a partner using three and multiples (sets) of three.

    A section: *Sixteen groups of three (48 pulses/counts)*
    *Suggestion: pat clap clap (16 times)* <u>OR</u> *pat clap clap R L both (eight times)*

    B section: *Skip around the room to find a new partner*

11. Create equations using grouped pulses in twos and threes and other combinations of twos and threes. Remember to accent Pulse 1 in each group.

    <u>Four groups (sets) of three</u>
    **strong** *light light,* **strong** *light light,* **strong** *light light,* **strong** *light light*
      **1**    2    3    **1**    2    3    **1**    2    3    **1**    2    3

    <u>3 + 2 + 2 + 3</u>
    **strong** *light light,* **strong** *light,* **strong** *light,* **strong** *light light*
      **1**    2    3    **1**    2    **1**    2    **1**    2    3

12. Use movement and body percussion to show addition and subtraction equations.

    $8 - 3 = 5$    *Walk and clap eight pulses forward (counting forward); walk and snap three pulses backward (counting backward); hold on five.*
    $4 + 2 = 6$    *Walk and clap four pulses forward; walk and snap two pulses forward; hold on six.*

13. Chant or add percussion instruments to factor trees to practice factoring. It is usually helpful to maintain a steady pulse while chanting as a class. The strong beats are underlined.

*Music Moments To Teach Academics: Mathematics and Music*

$$72$$
$$6 \times 12$$
$$2 \times 3 \ \ x \ \ 4 \times 3$$
$$2 \times 3 \times 2 \times 2 \times 3$$

Chant

*Seventy-<u>two</u> is <u>six</u> times <u>twelve</u>, two times <u>three</u> times <u>four</u> times <u>three</u>,*
*<u>Two</u> times <u>three</u> times <u>two</u> times <u>two</u> times <u>three</u> (drum drum drum)*

14. You can also chant the factor trees while keeping a rhythmic pattern with rhythm sticks (*floor, click, floor, click*) or hand clapping patterns with a partner.

15. Chant or sing the folk song, *Weavily Wheat*. Substitute other equations for the ones in the original song.

> *D'wan none your weavily wheat, d'wan none your barley,*
> *Take one down and pass it 'round and bake a cake for Charley!*
> *Five times five is twenty-five, five times six is thir-ty,*
> *Five times seven is thirty-five, five times eight is for-ty!*

16. Chant the times tables. You can write the factors and their products into a block chart (see Resources) and transfer it to instrument sounds as an interlude (Pulse 8 = rest).

| Pulses | 1 | 2 | 3 | 4 | 5 | 6 | 7 | 8 |
|---|---|---|---|---|---|---|---|---|
| | 8 | x | 4 | = | thir- | ty | two | |

## Geometry

1. Show *congruent* and *similar* by making or collecting instruments. Play the instruments and describe the differences or similarities you hear.

   | | |
   |---|---|
   | Congruent | *same shape and size (duplicate)* |
   | Example: | *two 10" hand drums* |
   | Similar | *same shape but a different size* |
   | Example: | *two rectangle-shaped woodblocks, different sizes* |

2. Music: *Music for Dancers, #6 The Space Between Your Ears.* Use the contrasting sections of this piece to practice drawing different lines, angles and shapes. Use large paper and markers for good flow and control. What shapes use curved lines? Straight lines? Zigzag lines? How would you use your voice to show curvy, straight and zigzag lines? What instruments could you use to reflect these different kinds of lines?

A Sections: curved or zigzag (follow the rhythm or grouping of three)

B Sections: straight or zigzag (follow the rhythm, pulse or grouping of two)

3. Use the same music to practice drawing circles, squares and triangles.

4. Trace a large circle on your desk or in the air while singing the scale up and down, beginning and ending at the same point on the circle and the same note (*do*). Repeat the activity with other shapes.

5. Trace the circle with your finger (starting at the top) while sliding the pitch of your voice around: *high to middle to low to middle to high*. Repeat the activity with other shapes.

6. Use grouping to trace triangles and squares. Conduct these on your desk, in the air or on the board. Say the number as you move your finger to it.

   3/4 time:    *3 (start here)*        4/4 time: *4 (start here)*

   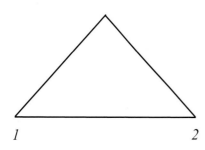
   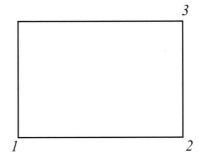

7. Create or borrow a catchy tune to help students remember *pi* to the fifth decimal point or other facts. Here is an example from Scott LaViollette, Olympia, WA.

   Borrowed tune      *"867-5309" by Tommy Two Tone (1980's)*
   *(lyrics talking about a girl's phone number)*

   New lyrics         *"3.14159" by Scott LaViollette*
   *(lyrics talking about this amazing number)*

8. Take your class Geometry Caroling. In small groups, older students can take familiar caroling tunes and write math lyrics to them. Share them in class and pick the best ones to go caroling in the hallways of the school.

*Music Moments To Teach Academics: Mathematics and Music*

Tune: *O Christmas Tree/O Tannenbaum*

New lyrics  *Geometry, geometry, you make such pretty shapes for me,*
*Geometry, geometry, you make such pretty shapes for me!*
*Acute or right, even obtuse,*
*Across from the hypoteneuse,*
*Geometry, geometry, you make such pretty shapes for me!*

*Rectangles, kites and even squares,*
*You find these shapes most anywhere, . . . . . . .*

*A pentagon, five sides hath thee,*
*I found a large one in D.C., . . . . . . .*

9. Find or make instruments that use some of the shapes you are learning in class. Discuss the differences in sound and how the sound waves travel within the shape.

| | | | |
|---|---|---|---|
| Circle | *Hand drum, tambourine* | Rectangle | *Wood block* |
| Sphere | *Maracas* | Cube | *Box shakers* |
| Cylinder | *Rainstick, quica* | Cone | *Conga drum* |
| Triangle | *Triangle* | | |

10. Create chants and tunes to memorize geometric formulas: *radius, diameter (2r) and circumference (2 pi r).*

    Tune  *Mary Had A Little Lamb* or *London Bridge*
    Example:  *Area is pi r squared, pi r squared, pi r squared,*
    *Area is pi r squared, that is the formula!*

11. Geometric definitions, formulas, and information for chanting or singing

    Radius  *The distance between the center of a circle and any point on that circle.*

    Diameter  *The distance between one point on the circle, through the middle, to another point on the circle. (2r)*

    Circumference  *The distance around the outside of a circle. (2 x pi x r)*

    Area  *The total space inside the circle. pi(r squared)*

    Volume  *Sphere: 4/3pi x r squared     Cube: length x width x height*

    Surface Area  *Sphere: 4pi x r squared     Cube: 6(side squared)*

12. Explore squares. Write lyrics about squares to a familiar tune (e.g., Sesame Street's *Hip To Be A Square* from Huey Lewis' hit song). Chant the definition and formulas of a square.
13. Create "square" rhythm patterns using a four-pulse phrase, four times.
14. Divide the class into four groups and stand in a large square around the room: one group is one side of the square. Assign different sounds to each group (four voices, four body sounders, four instruments, etc.). One side plays four pulses, then the next side, etc.
15. Get into a group of four (quartet). Chant and play the following or make up your own.

    *Squares have four equal sides, 1     2     3     4*

16. Other facts about squares

    Perimeter = *4 x the length of one side*
    Area = *the length of one side squared (side x side)*
    Angles = *all angles are equal in a square (90 degrees)*

17. Trace an equilateral triangle with your finger and voice. Repeat the exercise for an isosceles triangle and a scalene triangle. Where are the long sounds? Shorter sounds? Try this activity with squares and rectangles as well.

18. Divide the class into three groups: woods, metals, drums. Assign an instrument for each shape (square, circle, wood). Write shapes on the board or cut them out of colored construction paper. Place in patterns and point to them as the students play the correct sound.

19. Create a musical piece or story about The Triangles. There are three tribes: *Isosceles, Equilateral* and *Scalene*. You could even create a hero, *The Right Triangle*. Use the chants below (to the rhythm of *Ladybug, Ladybug, Fly Away Home*) or create your own. The students can develop a storyline together, then work in small groups to develop their own tribes, integrating information about their particular triangle into the story musically.

    Together    *Triangle, triangle, shape with three sides,*
                *Which one will you be? You'll have to decide!* (repeat)

    Answer 1    *Isosceles triangle, two sides the same,*
                *With one side that's different - it's part of the game!*

*Music Moments To Teach Academics: Mathematics and Music*

Answer 2    *The <u>sca</u>lene is <u>one</u> with no <u>two</u> sides a<u>like</u>,*
*The <u>shape</u> has been <u>squished</u> like the <u>frame</u> of a <u>bike</u>!*

Answer 3    *The <u>equi</u>lateral <u>triangle test</u>*
*is <u>three</u> sides the <u>same</u> so it's <u>clearly</u> the <u>best</u>!*

20. As the teacher touches the sides of the shape, the students play a pulse. Repeat the exercise for triangles, squares, rectangles, pentagons and hexagons.

21. Set theorems to rhythm or melody to aid in memorization. Use accents and percussion to give it a jazzy sound that is fun and memorable.

    *The sum of the angles of a triangle is 180 degrees.*

22. Use rhymes and instruments to learn about angles. Use a small instrument (triangle) to represent *acute angles*, a medium size instrument (woodblock) to represent *right angles*, and a big instrument (drum) to represent *obtuse* angles.

    *Acute angles look so small, they're difficult to see at all.*
    *Acute! There is no substitute!*

    *The right angle, it's plain to see, looks like an L at 90 degrees.*
    *Out of sight, with angle right!*

    *Obtuse angles, wide and big, are silly looking thingamajigs!*
    *Hanging loose, with obtuse!*

23. Draw angles on the board; students identify by playing the correct sound.

24. Match various kinds of lines with musical ideas.

    | | |
    |---|---|
    | parallel | *sing or play harmony that is parallel to the melody* |
    | perpendicular | *clap hands, criss-cross palms* |
    | intersecting | *use rhythm sticks, click together* |
    | horizontal | *piano or xylophone playing* |
    | vertical | *recorder or clarinet playing* |
    | diagonal | *cello or string bass playing* |

25. What kind of lines can you see on a musical score? Look at a variety of scores to find some of the following examples.

|  |  |
|---|---|
| staff lines | *horizontal* |
| bar lines | *vertical* |
| repeat signs | *vertical* |
| note stems | *vertical* |
| staff and bar lines | *perpendicular* |
| phrase and slur markings | *curved* |
| # and natural symbols | *diagonal, intersecting* |
| eight note flags (connected) | *diagonal* |
| ledger lines | *horizontal* |
| quarter rests | *zig zag* |

26. What kind of shapes can you see on a musical score?

27. Use musical elements to illustrate the concepts of symmetry and asymmetry.

   a. Play a rhythm; partner echoes exactly (symmetry)
   b. Play a rhythm; partner changes their answer (asymmetry)
   c. Create a body percussion pattern in two or four (symmetry)
   d. Create a body percussion pattern in three or five (asymmetry)
   e. Play eight steady pulses with the class (symmetry)
   f. Play eight sounds anytime you feel like it (asymmetry)
   g. Play a standard rhythm:   ta   ta   ta te   ta (symmetry)
   h. Play a syncopated rhythm:   te ta   te ta   ta (asymmetry)
   i. Sing the scale going up and down (symmetry)
   j. Sing a few notes of the scale going up and different ones going down (asymmetry)
   k. Speak a poem, sing a song or listen to music that is written in a symmetrical form (see Discography).
   l. Speak a poem, sing a song or listen to music that is written in an asymmetrical form (see Discography).
   m. Speak the words of a sentence with a symmetrical pattern of loud, soft, loud, soft, etc.
   n. Speak the words of a sentence with an asymmetrical pattern of loud, loud, soft, medium, loud, medium, soft, etc.
   o. Create a symmetrical rhythmic improvisation of 16 pulses (four phrases of four pulses)
   p. Create an asymmetrical rhythmic improvisation of 17 pulses (with no regular phrases)

28. Place different designs or shapes on the board. As you point to each, the students will respond in sound. How else might you show the relationship between shape and sound?

|  |  |
|---|---|
| Symmetrical | *steady pulse* |
| Asymmetrical | *erratic rhythm* |

29. Folk dances use many math concepts, particularly within the subject of geometry. Here are a few ideas for using folk dances to teach math in the classroom. See the Bibliography and Discography for suggestions on learning folk dances or making up your own to traditional music (fake folk dancing!).

| | |
|---|---|
| Spatial concepts | *folk dances teach spatial awareness through many formations: circles, co-centric circles, square sets, partners, parallel lines, etc.* |
| Patterns | *symmetrical and asymmetrical counting patterns, repetition and contrast, directional changes, "mixers," where at the end of the section, you are standing with a new partner.* |
| Sequencing | *chain of steps, soldering sections together, form of the music, watching-doing-listening, etc.* |
| *Basic Folk Dance | *The basic folk dance, which you can modify for a variety of concepts, is:* |

*Circle Formation:  eight counts walk clockwise*
*four counts walk into the circle*
*four counts walk out of the circle*

30. Use a simple round or canon to illustrate the concept of tesselations. In a four part canon, the tessellation looks like this.

| 1: | **Phrase One** | Phrase Two | Phrase Three | Phrase Four |
|---|---|---|---|---|
| 2: | Phrase Four | **Phrase One** | Phrase Two | Phrase Three |
| 3: | Phrase Three | Phrase Four | **Phrase One** | Phrase Two |
| 4: | Phrase Two | Phrase Three | Phrase Four | **Phrase One** |

| | |
|---|---|
| Phrase One | *Row, row, row your boat,* |
| Phrase Two | *Gently down the stream,* |
| Phrase Three | *Merrily, merrily, merrily, merrily,* |
| Phrase Four | *Life is but a dream!* |

31. Many compositional techniques in music are similar to the concepts of transformational geometry. Using a note cell (melodic motive or three notes), compare and contrast these forms.

*Original*      Here are three examples of a melodic motive (note cell).

*\*Sequence*      Play the same motive, one note higher or lower than it is originally written. Relates to the concept of translations (slides) in geometry.

*Inversion*      The inverted form of the motive presents the notes as a mirror image (upside down) of the original. Relates to the concept of reflection, using a horizontal midline.

*Retrograde*      The retrograde form of the motive presents the original motive backwards, from the end to the beginning. Relates to the concept of reflection, using a vertical midline.

*Retrograde-Inversion*      The retrograde inversion form of the motive presents the original motive upside down and backwards.

32. Chord inversions relate to transformational geometry as well. Chords are several notes played together at the same time. For our purposes, the lower octave of notes will be written using capital letters and the higher octave will be written using lower case letters. Follow along on The Melody Chart or play these inversions on a keyboard or xylophone.

C MAJOR CHORD (notes played simultaneously)
Root Position: C E G    First Inversion: E G c    Second Inversion: G c e

| *C* | *D* | *E* | *F* | *G* | *A* | *B* | *c* | *d* | *e* | *f* | *g* | *a* | *b*, etc. |
|---|---|---|---|---|---|---|---|---|---|---|---|---|---|
| *1* | *2* | *3* | *4* | *5* | *6* | *7* | *8(1)* | *2* | *3* | *4* | *5* | *6* | *7* |
| *do* | *re* | *mi* | *fa* | *so* | *la* | *ti* | *do* | *re* | *mi* | *fa* | *so* | *la* | *ti* |

F MAJOR CHORD (notes played simultaneously)
Root Position: F A c    First Inversion: A c f    Second Inversion: c f a

| *C* | *D* | *E* | *F* | *G* | *A* | *B* | *c* | *d* | *e* | *f* | *g* | *a* | *b*, etc. |
|---|---|---|---|---|---|---|---|---|---|---|---|---|---|
| *1* | *2* | *3* | *4* | *5* | *6* | *7* | *8(1)* | *2* | *3* | *4* | *5* | *6* | *7* |
| *do* | *re* | *mi* | *fa* | *so* | *la* | *ti* | *do* | *re* | *mi* | *fa* | *so* | *la* | *ti* |

G MAJOR CHORD (notes played simultaneously)
Root Position: G B d    First Inversion: B d g    Second Inversion: d g b

| *C* | *D* | *E* | *F* | *G* | *A* | *B* | *c* | *d* | *e* | *f* | *g* | *a* | *b*, etc. |
|---|---|---|---|---|---|---|---|---|---|---|---|---|---|
| *1* | *2* | *3* | *4* | *5* | *6* | *7* | *8(1)* | *2* | *3* | *4* | *5* | *6* | *7* |
| *do* | *re* | *mi* | *fa* | *so* | *la* | *ti* | *do* | *re* | *mi* | *fa* | *so* | *la* | *ti* |

## Other Categories

1. Explore the concept of chance and math using music. Check out the *John Cage* video (see Videography) and music suggestions in the Discography for other examples. Here are a few suggestions for creating chance music in the classroom.

    *Dice Rolls*  Assign different sounds or notes that correspond to the numbers on the dice. Roll the dice several times to create your piece: write down the order of your piece.

    Roll a three; the drum will sound three times.
    Roll a six; improvisation by all groups.
    Roll a two; the woods play fast.
    Roll a two and a three; the drum and woods play.

*Music Moments To Teach Academics: Mathematics and Music*

*Cut and Paste* — Write out the words to several familiar tunes and then cut the words or phrases apart. Mix them up, and draw out eight to create a new song.

*Aleatoric Music* — With your marker, divide a large poster board into several squares. Fill each square with either a color or pattern which is assigned to a particular sound or group of people. As the conductor draws his/her baton across the different squares, the sounds will change. The conductor can move the baton slowly or abruptly and the musicians must work hard to follow with sounds.

Example:
*Red square - vocal hisses and shakers*
*Polka dot square - everyone plays a pulse*
*White square - silence*

*Circles* — Similar to the idea above, place three different colored circles made of yarn, fabric or plastic tubing on the floor in close proximity. Each colored circle is assigned to a specific sound or group of sounds. Conducting is performed with the feet, but you may add hands or elbows to create combinations of sounds.

Groups: *voices, body percussion, found sounds*

*Equations* — Write out a series of equations, simple or complex and create a piece of music based on the numbers and symbols used.

Example: $5 + 2 - 6 \times 3$

Five people make sounds, then add two more. Six stop playing (solo), then three strong beats from everyone to end.

2. Create fun raps about complex mathematical concepts. Here is a speech piece written by Ken Lochner, Olympia, WA.

Part One
*Proba__bili__ty, sta__tis__tics, devi__a__tions and the like,*
*In my cerebral cortex bunched together, oh so tight!*
*If    I    could  just   get    some   rest.*
*I'd study even better for my comprehensive test!*

Part Two
*Bibli, bibli, __ bibliography the bibli, bibli, __bibliography the*
*Bibli, bibli, __ bibliography the bibli, bibli, ___oh well!*

100

Part Three  *Foot-notes, foot-notes, don't forget the foot-notes!*
*Foot-notes, foot-notes, don't forget the foot-notes!*

3. Create more complex rhythmical patterns using block charts. Use this code to make patterns that use quarter notes, eighth notes, sixteenth notes and triplets.

     One X in a box      =   *quarter note ("walk" pulse)*
     Two X's in a box    =   *eighth notes ("run-ning" pulse)*
     Three X's in a box  =   *triplets ("triplety" pulse)*
     Four X's in a box   =   *sixteenth notes ("wiggle jiggle" pulse)*

4. Use block charts for graphing information, points and equations. Play the information and compare the visual with the auditory. Use other graphs in class to create music, using voices sounds and pitches, rhythm patterns or instruments.

5. Wolfgang Amadeus Mozart wrote a piece of music called *Table Music, Duet For Two Violins*. This piece can be read right side up and upside down. Two violinists stand on opposite sides of a table with the music between them. Harmony is created as both views of the notes are played simultaneously.

6. Stretch a long piece of masking tape across the floor of the classroom to create a number line. Use shorter pieces of tape to indicate number placement, both positive and negative. Play with the number line through movement and sound. While a person moves on the number line, the others can play pre-assigned instruments to reflect the position on the line.

     *Positive numbers*  Play the number of pulses with wood instruments or claps.
     *Negative numbers*  Play the number of pulses with metal instruments or pats.
     *Zero*              Play a short, tremolo on the drum.

7. Add sounds to story problems in class. You can add sound effects for things in the story, play the numbers and symbols, or the answer.

8. Use instruments and sounds to teach the concept of sets.

     *-Create a set of ocean sounds*
     *-Create sets of wood, shaker, metal and drum sounds*
     *-Create a set of vocal sounds*
     *-Create a set of farm sounds*

*Music Moments To Teach Academics: Mathematics and Music*

9. For numbers 1 through five, younger students can do Touch Math. Each number has dots placed on it which students can touch with their pencil as they say the number or add numbers. Coordinate the rhythmic patterns with others in class or clap them together while the teacher points on the board

| | **1** | **2** | **3** | **4** | **5** |
|---|---|---|---|---|---|
| Say | *1* | *2, 3* | *4, 5, 6* | *7, 8, 9, 10* | *11, 12, 13, 14, 15* |

10. Stone passing games are great for learning spatial, rhythmic and other mathematical concepts. You can use familiar rhymes or songs or make up your own. River stones work great, but you can also use bean bags and a whole variety of objects. Start by passing one around the circle on the pulse, and gradually add another object as students are successful. To get kids started, decide which direction you will pass (generally to the right, although it is a good brain challenge to try it both ways), and practice chanting and doing the following without an object.

| Say | *pick* | *pass* | *pick* | *pass* |
|---|---|---|---|---|
| | (pick it up) | (pass it right) | (pick it up) | (pass it right) |

11. Search your library for examples of Baroque music, particularly the music of Johann Sebastian Bach. He was considered the "mathematician of music" and through listening and examining a score, students will find many relationships to math concepts they are studying. Check the Discography for other suggestions. Other great minds in our history that have long recognized music's strong relationship to mathematics, include Einstein, Mozart, Pythagorus, Yehudi Menuhin and Howard Gardner.

12. Twelve-tone composition was a technique that was born in the Twentieth Century as a rebellion to the emotional approach to writing music that took place in the Romantic Period (1820-1910). It is a mathematical approach to writing music with very strictly organized and often, to an untrained ear, sounds unpleasant and disorganized. Here is a basic introduction to this technique. It is best to play these on a keyboard if possible, but they can be worked out on paper with no regard to the "sound." Check out the Discography for listening examples.

    A. <u>Twelve Tones</u>

| C/B# | C#/Db | D | D#/Eb | E/Fb | F/E# | F#/Gb | G | G#/Ab | A | A#/Bb | B/Cb |
|---|---|---|---|---|---|---|---|---|---|---|---|
| 1 | 2 | 3 | 4 | 5 | 6 | 7 | 8 | 9 | 10 | 11 | 12 |

B. Create Your Tone Row - *Decide what order the tones will be played in. There are numerous possibilities. You can mix up the assigned tones/numbers above, or assign new numbers to the pitches.*

| D | E | F | C | C# | G | D# | A# | F# | G# | B | A |
|---|---|---|---|----|---|----|----|----|----|---|---|
| 3 | 5 | 6 | 1 | 2  | 8 | 4  | 11 | 7  | 9  | 12| 10|

C. *Rules - Tones MUST be used in this sequence (from left to right). You cannot use Pitch 6 (F) until Pitches 3(D) and 5(E) have been played. You MAY combine pitches (chords) to change the sequence, playing 3(D) and 5(E) together before playing 6(F). Repeat the sequence as needed.*

9. Compare and contrast different scales (major and minor) and modes as they relate to math. In scales, the variable placement of the half steps and whole steps changes the overall sound and emotional tone of the scale. See *Music for Dancers* (Bibliography) for clear descriptions and activities regarding the scales and modes.

10. The Circle Of Fifths/Circle of Fourths is another mathematical sequence using the pitches of the keyboard. These pitches repeat in a cycle and sequence. Use this information and the Melody Chart to help students find these patterns.

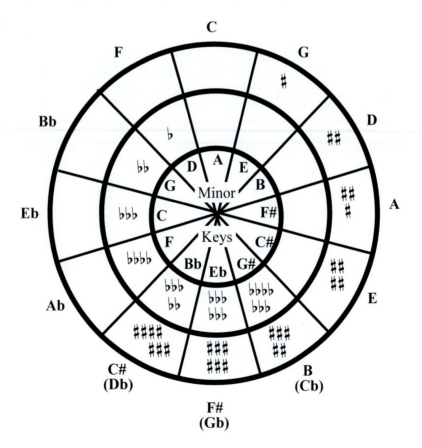

# Chapter Five:
# *Science* and *Music*

*Music Moments To Teach Academics: Science and Music*

## SCIENCE CONCEPTS AND CONTENT

| | | |
|---|---|---|
| properties | substances | materials |
| objects | living/non-living | components |
| structures | systems | matter |
| energy | change | inquiry |
| natural | synthetic | size |
| weight | shape | color |
| texture | density | motion |
| vibration | echo | pitch |
| sound | light | organisms |
| plants | animals | chemicals |
| boiling point | solubility | position |
| relative speed | sound waves | water waves |
| length | reflection | refraction |
| transmission | absorption | scattering |
| interference | increasing/decreasing | constant acceleration |
| frequency | amplitude | stored energy |
| heat | electrical | mechanical |
| nuclear | earth | universe |
| transference | rate and amount | conservation |
| particles | atoms | atomic bonding |
| evaporation | condensation | precipitation |
| freezing and thawing | natural forces | magnitudes |
| push and pull | balanced/unbalanced | weather and seasons |
| predict and observe | extinction and adaptation | fossils |
| environment | physical | natural disasters |
| rocks | soil | water |
| liquid | gas | vapor |
| atmosphere | spherical planets | solid interior |
| landforms | bodies of water | crust |
| hot convecting mantle | dense metallic core | hydrosphere |
| oceans and tides | seas | lakes |
| rivers | streams | plate tectonics |
| orbit | sun, moon, earth | asteroid |
| comet | solar system | galaxy |
| expanding universe | stars | celestial bodies |
| phylum | categorize | species diversity |
| external/internal | natural selection | biochemical |
| genetic | interact/influence | recycling |
| multicellular | tissues and organs | genes |
| DNA | molecules | continuity |
| human body and systems | digestion | respiration |
| reproduction | circulation | excretion |
| disease | movement | prevention |
| growth | vitamins and minerals | ecosystems |

*Music Moments To Teach Academics: Science and Music*

**Seasons**

1. Use Antonio Vivaldi's *The Four Seasons*, a set of pieces from the Baroque period. Compare and contrast the music in terms of the four seasons or for inspiration to write poetry or prose. For a contemporary musical setting of the seasons, see the piano-jazz version by George Winston.

2. Create a soundscape for each season, either as a class or in small groups, using the sounds of spring, summer, fall and winter.

3. Look for other songs about the seasons and sing them as a class.

4. Write a chant or tune about the seasons. Each small group can create a musical presentation for a different season. Perform the entire piece as a rondo.

        A    *Winter, summer, fall and spring,*
             *Challenges and changes bring (repeat).*

        B    *Winter group presentation*

        A    *All together*

        C    *Summer group presentation*

        A    *All together*

        D    *Fall group presentation*

        A    *All together*

        E    *Spring group presentation*

        A    *All together*

5. Ask a question in four pulses; your partner has four pulses to answer.

        Question    *What are the sounds of spring?*
        Answer      *Birds and bees and living things!*

6. In your group, write a rap about the opposite seasons (summer/winter, spring/fall) and perform it. Set your rap to a tune and perform again.

7. What activities do you see taking place in the fall? (Raking leaves, pumpkin carving, trick or treat, windy days.) What kind of rhythms are created as we do these activities? In a group of three, show three different fall actions that have rhythm.

8. Write a poem about a season and perform it musically. You may use voices, body percussion and instruments to express your poem.

9. Select a familiar tune (see Resources) and write seasonal lyrics to it.

10. Use the Winter Solstice as a theme for your class. There are many musical traditions that surround the Winter Solstice (see your local library or search on the net). Introduce your students to these traditions or create a presentation for parents. Do the same at the end of the year with the Summer Solstice.

11. Talk about the seasons as a cycle and a metaphor for life. Make up a special rhythm pattern for each season and put them together to create a piece of music.

12. Assign an instrument to each of four groups in your class. Show slides or pictures of things happening in a particular season. Students can indicate which season the picture belongs to via instrument sounds.

> *Spring*      *metals (bells, triangles, etc.)*
> *Summer*    *woods (woodblocks, claves, etc.)*
> *Fall*        *shakers (maracas, rattles, etc.)*
> *Winter*     *drums (hand drums, congas, etc.)*

13. Use your voice to create a collage of sounds for each season.

> Example:    *Fall    (whispers, screeches, hisses, howls)*

14. Use the following poem as the A section for a rondo. Groups can create a contrasting sections for each season.

> *Seasons come and seasons go,*
> *Out with the sun and in with the snow!*
> *And what to wear, you never really know,*
> *'Cuz seasons come and seasons go!*

*Music Moments To Teach Academics: Science and Music*

## Weather

1. Use a block chart to graph the weather each day in class. Your chart needs seven horizontal boxes (seven days of the week) and four vertical boxes (sunny, cloudy, rainy and windy). Mark an X or combination of X's for each day, then assign instruments and play the patterns on Friday.

2. In groups or as a class, compose weather soundscapes using voices, instruments and body percussion. Other students can guess the type of weather that is represented (windstorm, thunder and lightning, hailstorm, rain, etc.).

3. Select a short story that has weather as a theme (e.g., *The Snowy Day* by Ezra Jack Keats). Add sounds to the story for characters and themes to create a sound story.

4. Select or write a proverb about weather and create a musical setting for it with rhythm or melody. Other students can indicate whether the proverb is true or false through sounds (clap = true; snap = false). Here are a few examples (from *Teaching The Three R's* by Anne Green Gilbert).

    a. *When bees stay close to the hive, rain is close by.* (True)

    b. *A tough apple skin means a hard winter.* (Possible)

    c. *When ants travel in a straight line, expect rain; when they scatter, expect fair weather.* (False)

5. Write down words to describe the daily weather to see if there is a pattern which you can chant or play.

    | M | T | W | TH | F |
    |---|---|---|----|---|
    | rainy | cloudy | sunny | cloudy | windy |

6. Make up a multi-part speech piece using words about weather in various combinations. To add interest, speak or sing them in different voices.

    Part 1    *Hurricane, hurricane, lots of wind and rain! (rest)*

    Part 2    *Swirl and twirl in a big tornado!*

    Part 3    *Rain - drops,      rain - drops!*

7. Music: *Music for Dancers, #1 "Pulsation"*, by Kerri Lynn Nichols.
   This music has two, contrasting sections. Use chanting and movement to learn about the water cycle (idea from Anne Green Gilbert).

   | | |
   |---|---|
   | A section | *Water resting and rippling in a calm lake or pond. It slowly gets warmer and warmer and something begins to happen.* |
   | B section | Chant: *Evaporation! Evaporation!* (repeat) *Students begin to rise up out of the lake and evaporate.* |
   | A section | *Evaporated water is now floating softly and freely through the air. Slowly, it begins to collect into cloud groups.* |
   | B section | Chant: *Condensation! Condensation!* (repeat) *Clouds are bumping together and moving very closely.* |
   | A section | *Collected clouds begin feeling heavier and heavier, denser and denser, until something happens.* |
   | B section | Chant: *Precipitation! Precipitation!* (repeat) *The water droplets return to the lake and the cycle starts over.* |

8. Compare clouds and their weight to timbre:

   Heavy - *drums*     Medium - *woods*     Light - *metals*

9. Use fingers and hands in different ways to create the sound of rainfall and snowfall on the head of a hand drum or cardboard box. Compare and contrast.

10. Experiment with making a rainstick in class. You will need a long plastic or cardboard tube that can be sealed on both ends and some kind of seeds, kernels, rice or dried beans to go inside. You can either drive nails into the cylinder (closely in a coil from top to bottom) or put bunches of the plastic substance that holds pop cans together into the tube.

11. Play a Native American rain chant in class (see Discography) or create one with your group. Discuss the concept of the rain dance with the class.

12. Read *My Mama Had a Dancing Heart* by Libby Moore Gray to the class. Assign each group one of the seasons described to present musically.

13. Compare and contrast the differences in sound between woods, metals, shakers and drums. Repeat, using the four voices (speak, sing, shout, whisper) and the four types of body percussion (clap, snap, pat and stomp). By changing the shape of your hands or using different parts of the hand, how many clapping sounds can you create? Does a pat on the back sound the same as a pat on your lap? Why or why not?

14. Play a hand drum by dynamically bouncing your hand off the skin. Do you hear a ring? Now, slap the skin sharply with a flat hand (fingers "glued" together) and leave it attached to the drum (do not bounce it off). Do you hear a sharp crack? What causes the differences in these sounds?

15. Take a glass, plastic pop or water bottle and blow across the top. What sound results? How can you change the sound?

16. Find a place that has a rich, soundscape (downtown on a park bench, the nature preserve, etc.) and sit in a comfortable position. Write down every sound you hear for fifteen minutes. Be sure to listen at a deeper level each few minutes to hear sounds that may not readily be apparent. Share your findings with the class. How many different kinds of sounds did you hear? How would you categorize them?

17. Discuss the phenomenon of canine hearing. Bring a dog whistle and a referee whistle to class and compare. Why are dogs able to hear pitches that humans are not? Are these pitches high or low? What is their frequency?

18. Make a chart of sounds that are found in your classroom. Separate them into "alike and different" or other categories. Make a block chart and use sounds from the classroom to create a musical piece.

19. How many sounds can you produce from one instrument or object? Experiment and record your findings to share with the class.

20. Take a small cardboard box and stretch rubber bands around it and across the open side. Pluck the bands to produce pitches. What do you notice? What modifications can you make to change the sounds?

21. Cut plastic straws into various lengths and tape them together side by side with masking tape, from longest to shortest. Blow across the top to create a row of pitches, much like a panpipe. What happens if you change the lengths of the straws? Cover one end of the straws with masking tape. How do the pitches change?

13. Read *Water Dance* by Thomas Locker to the class. Assign each group one part of the water cycle to present musically. If your class is small, you can pick and choose which pages to present.

## Plants

1. Choose a familiar tune and write biology words to it (e.g., *Jingle Cells* to the tune *Jingle Bells*) to teach your curriculum.

2. Select a flower. How many petals does it have (clap the number)? How many leaves does it have (pat the number)? How many stems (stomp the number)? Now, play the answers in order.

3. Create Plant Chants using different groupings of plants. Layer parts, use different voices and speeds to make it interesting. After the speech is memorized, play the rhythmic patterns of the words on percussion or found sound instruments.

    Trees: *sycamore, Douglas fir, pine, maple, evergreen* (repeat)

    Flowers: *daisy, daffodil, marigold, rose* (repeat)

    Vegetables: *turnip, cabbage, potatoes and beets* (repeat)

4. Create a soundscape for the growth process of a given plant. Add movement to the music.

    *seed, germination, sprout, stem, flower*

5. Create a soundscape for the opening/closing of a blossom. Add movement to the music.

    Blossom   *daylight, open, expand (metals)*
    *night, close, contract (woods)*

6. Can you make the sound of a bee pollinating a flower? With your voice? What instruments could make that sound (*shakers, scrapers*)?

7. Play 16 Counts to show the growth process of a plant through movement:

    *eight pulses to grow, eight pulses to return to the earth*

8. Sing the pitches of the scale up and down to grow and return.

*Music Moments To Teach Academics: Science and Music*

9. Use the following chant to create a rondo, with small groups writing the contrasting sections.

*Air, water, soil and sun, all plants need them, every one.* (repeat)

## Animals

1. What kinds of animals make sounds? What kinds of sounds do they make? Can you make the same sound using your voice? An instrument?

2. Use the vocal warm-ups (see Resources) for young children. There are several animal sounds that can help to prepare the voice for singing.

3. What kinds of animal sounds would you hear under the ocean (whale song)? Play some recordings of these sounds for your class. You can create the same sound by moistening your middle finger and lightly gliding it across the skin of a hand drum.

4. Music: *Music for Creative Dance, V. 2, #1 Whales, Eric Chappelle.*
   Use the whale sounds in this piece of music to create an undersea scene with movement.

5. What kinds of animal sounds would you hear on a farm? In the jungle?

6. Create a rap about the different kind of snakes there are and their sounds.

*rattlesnakes, cobras, boa constrictors*

7. Which animals are big and which are small? What large instrument could we use for the elephant (bass drum)? What small instrument could we use for the sound of a bee (shaker)?

8. Which animals move fast? Slow? Clap your hands or play your instrument to show me the pace of a turtle. Can you do the same to show me the pace of a cheetah?

9. Play eight counts using the names of adult animals and their babies. One partner says the adult name and the other will answer with the baby name:

| Pulse | 1 | 2 | 3 | 4 | 5 | 6 | 7 | 8 |
|---|---|---|---|---|---|---|---|---|
| Partner 1 | Sheep | (clap) | (clap) | (clap) | (clap) | (clap) | (clap) | (clap) |
| Partner 2 | Lamb | (clap) | (clap) | (clap) | (clap) | (clap) | (clap) | (clap) |
| Partner 1 | Cow | (clap) | (clap) | (clap) | (clap) | (clap) | (clap) | (clap) |
| Partner 2 | Calf | (clap) | (clap) | (clap) | (clap) | (clap) | (clap) | (clap) |

10. Use the following Jungle Chant to explore jungle animal sounds. Chant the poem together, then play a drum for 16 pulses while the students move and improvise animals they might hear in the jungle.

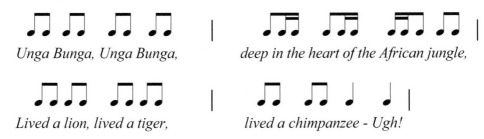

*Unga Bunga, Unga Bunga,*  *deep in the heart of the African jungle,*

*Lived a lion, lived a tiger,*  *lived a chimpanzee - Ugh!*

11. Play selections from *Carnival of Animals* by Camille Saint-Saens. As the students listen to each piece, they can write down animals the music suggests to them. Have the students move creatively to the music or allow them to draw pictures of the animals.

12. Sing the scale using different animal sounds. Hold up a picture of an animal and the students can sing that animal's sound. Change the picture as they sing down the scale on a different animal sound.

13. List eight animals you would find on the farm and sing the scale using their names. List other animal groups (ocean, jungle, desert, etc.).

| do | re | mi | fa | so | la | ti | do |
|----|----|----|----|----|----|----|----|
| *duck* | *goose* | *cow* | *horse* | *pig* | *dog* | *goat* | *cat* |

14. Music: *I Am the Song, #6 Journey to the Moon,* K. Nichols.
    Use this one section music to inspire an underwater improvisation, or a scene of three groups of animals (*ocean, land and sea*).

15. Music: *Music for Dancers, #4 The Hi-Lo Waltz,* K. Nichols
    This music has four contrasting sections: A B C D. Students can move around the room creatively in the following groupings.

    A section   *undersea animals and sounds*
    B section   *land animals and sounds*
    C section   *animals of the air and sounds*
    D section   *choose your favorite (combined)*

16. Sing *Old MacDonald* with your class to review the animals of a farm. Change the words to include different animal groups.

17. Sing *I Know an Old Lady,* but change the words to teach the food chain.

18. Create chants to learn animal groups and the manner in which they move or gather.

    *school of fish, flock of birds, litter of puppies, swarm of bees, brood of hens, string of ponies, pride of lions, colony of ants*

19. What kind of movements do animals make? What rhythm patterns are created by these movements? Can you clap or play them?

    Kangaroo - *hopping, bouncing*
    Horses - *galloping*
    Elephant - *sauntering*

20. Use this poem or write your own about any animal. Present the poem musically, paying special attention to the sounds of the poem. You may use voices, instruments and movement. Notice that there are rhythmic patterns inherent in the movement. Use these in your presentation.

    *Tadpole*
    *small, wiggly*
    *swimming, squirming, changing*
    *gills, fins, lungs, legs*
    *hopping, leaping, croaking*
    *large, muscular*
    *Frog*

21. Make up raps or use familiar tunes to review advanced concepts that relate to animals: *evolution, adaptation, extinction, speciation* and *natural selection*.

22. Make a list of endangered animals and the places they reside. Create a piece about these animals to sing for Earth Day.

23. Make up a chant of animals that are hatched from eggs: *fish, insects, birds, reptiles, amphibians.*

24. Play the music of Paul Winter (see Discography) which centers around endangered species, including the recorded sounds of whales, wolves and coyotes. Check out the *Living Things* website (see Websites) for additional music, concert dates and other ideas for classroom use.

25. Use the following chant to create a game for categorizing animals, plants and minerals. Students must identify items from pictures or list their answers in a chant.

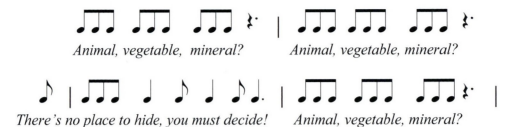

*Animal, vegetable, mineral?  Animal, vegetable, mineral?*

*There's no place to hide, you must decide!  Animal, vegetable, mineral?*

26. Use the rhythmic poetry of Ogden Nash to learn about animals. Then, write your own Ogden Nash style poem. Accompany your voices with a steady pulse on a drum or other instrument sounds. You can check out an Ogden Nash book from the library for examples.

27. Create a Four-Legged Chant using the names of animals that have four legs. Use a four-pulse beat on a drum between each phrase.

> *Horses, cows, dogs and cats* (pulse) (pulse) (pulse) (pulse)
> *Tigers, lions, deer and rats* (pulse) (pulse) (pulse) (pulse)

28. Repeat the above exercise using animals that have two legs or more than four legs.

29. Write a song about bugs called *Don't Bug Me*, using a familiar tune/rhythm.

30. Repeat the above exercises for various groups of animals: *dinosaurs, mammals, canines/felines, etc.*

31. Listen to some birdsong recordings. Take a field trip to a forest and try to identify the various birdsongs you hear. Return to the classroom and make up your own birdsong using the Melody Chart. What instruments can copy the sounds of birds? Write a piece with the class using different songs of birds you heard on your field trip and created with your groups. Add contrasting sections of speech using names and other facts about birds.

32. If you live nearby a wolf haven or zoo, take your class to a Howl In, where wolves communicate through "song."

## Earth

1. Create a nature soundscape for a given landscape: *ocean, jungle, desert, mountain, forest, etc.*

2. Talk about the earth with your class in terms of rhythms, pulses and cycles. How can we recreate these in class through sound?

    Examples:   *earth rotation, day and night, waves and tides, seasons*

3. Play selections from *Nature Music* for your class. Some of these blend sounds from nature with composed music (see Discography). Great for relaxation, reading, focus activities or group work as well as science experiences.

4. Make up chants for the different forms of water or landforms.

    *river, ocean, sea, stream, waterfall, lake, creek, pond*

    *mountain, valley, hill, plain, canyon, butte, range, cliff*

5. Divide the class into three groups. Each group creates a musical piece for one of the following themes.

    *atmosphere, hydrosphere, landforms*

6. Talk about recycling with your class. Recycling is finding a way to reuse something instead of throwing it away. Have the students gather items from home (garage, kitchen, etc.) that can produce sound in some way and bring them to class to create a group rhythmic improvisation.

7. Draw symbols on the board to represent different landforms. Use contrast and repetition to create form. Use the pitch of your voice to trace the contour of the landform.

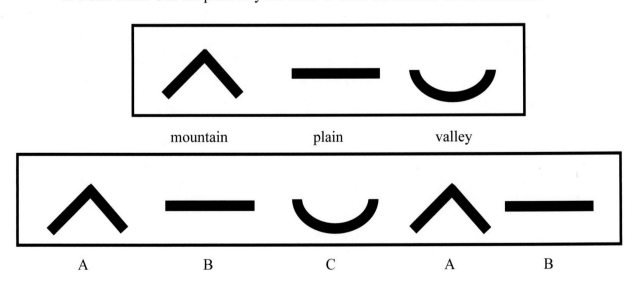

8. Use a familiar or original tune to write a song about ecology. Here is an example based on the tune *We Didn't Start The Fire* by Billy Joel:

WE DIDN'T START POLLUTING *(lyrics by Kerri Lynn Nichols)*

CHORUS:
*We didn't start polluting, but we know we might, and we can see the light.*
*We make a resolution, 'cause we want to right it, so we'll try to fight it.*

VERSE ONE:
Oil spills everywhere, not a minute left to spare,
Lysol, lots of junk, filling up our world with gunk.
When will people realize? Seas destroyed before our eyes,
Clean it up, get straight, do it now, we just can't wait.

(Repeat the Chorus between after verse)

VERSE TWO:
Politicians matching wits, ecosystem's on the fritz,
Freeway garbage piled high, as the speeding cars go by,
Aerosols fill the air, doesn't anybody care?
Dead birds on the shore, we can't take it anymore!

VERSE THREE:
Chemicals in our food, can't be up to something good,
Pepto Bismol, stomach pains, pumping poison in our veins.
We've been hypnotized by a toxic pesticide,
How long will it be 'til we take responsibility?

VERSE FOUR:
People won't you hear the call? Start with something very small,
Don't break burning bans, pick up and recycle cans.
Car pool, pump your spray, things you do most every day,
Build parks, save a tree, hey, it's up to you and me!

BRIDGE:
*So when we are gone, the world will still go on, and on, and on,*
*And on, and on, and on, and on...*

(Repeat the Chorus and fade out)

## Geology

1. Use a familiar Rock-n-Roll tune to write lyrics about plate tectonics moving and grooving.

2. Use the following chant as an A section for a piece about the earth.

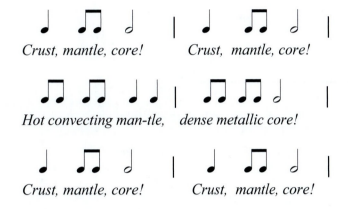

Crust, mantle, core!   Crust, mantle, core!

Hot convecting man-tle,   dense metallic core!

Crust, mantle, core!   Crust, mantle, core!

3. Talk about Yellowstone National Park with your students. What kinds of things would you see there (geysers, mud pots)? Use the following three sounds and movements to create a musical piece with your group. You may create an original rhythm/melody or use a familiar one. To notate your piece, cut out shapes of construction paper and glue to a poster board. To add complexity with larger, older groups, you can layer different parts in and add instrument sounds.

   Geyser (blue squares)      -   *exploding voice sound and body movement*
   Mud Pot (brown circles)    -   *slow, sustained glub sound and movement*
   Silence (white triangles)  -   *no sound and frozen body shape*

4. Use the geyser and mud pot sounds/symbols above to create groupings of twos and threes.
   
   4/4 time     geyser   mud pot   geyser   mud pot
   3/4 time     geyser   mud pot   mud pot

5. Discuss earthquakes and tremors in terms of vibrations. Use instruments to demonstrate. How would you play a 3.4 (Richter scale) earthquake differently from a 7.8 earthquake?

6. Look at pictures or drawings of the rock layers at the Grand Canyon. Where do you see contrast? Repetition? Recreate through music.

7. Write a Rock Rap about igneous, sedimentary and metamorphic rocks.

8. Chant geological facts, definitions and name identifications. Play the rhythmic patterns of the words on instruments. Find different kinds of rocks and tap them together to create rhythms.

9. Use pitch to learn the different rock layers of a given area. Use low, middle and high voices to chant or sing the names of the layers.

### Space

1. Play selections from Gustav Holst's *The Planets*. As the students listen to each piece, they can write down planets the music suggests to them. Have the students move creatively to the music or allow them to draw pictures of the planets.

2. Play other selections of music that relate to outer space such as *2001 Space Odyssey* and *Star Wars*. Relate to your curriculum.

3. Music: *I Am the Song, #6 Journey to the Moon, K. Nichols*. Create a movement drama about the first space flight to the moon, inspired by the music. Use the same piece of music to explore what gravity would be like on the moon.

4. Create raps or songs to familiar or original tunes about planet facts.

5. Sing *Twinkle, Twinkle*. Discuss the stars in the sky and other objects that appear to be stars.

6. Use slow, medium and fast selections of music to experience three different kinds of gravity through movement (suggestion: *Music for Dancers, Too! #11 Gravity*, or *Music for Dancers, #11 Three Paces, K. Nichols*).

7. Make a Gravity Block Chart. Create a box with eight horizontal boxes and three vertical boxes (three kinds of gravity). Each row of pulses sounds twice as fast as the one below it. Essentially, the bottom row plays whole notes (four long, sustained pulses), the middle row plays half notes (two pulses) and the top row plays quarter notes (steady one count pulse).

| 1 | 2 | 3 | 4 | 5 | 6 | 7 | 8 |
|---|---|---|---|---|---|---|---|
| X | X | X | X | X | X | X | X |
| X |   | X |   | X |   | X |   |
| X |   |   |   | X |   |   |   |

8. Practice orbiting an object or person in class using pulse counts. Travel around your desk, your neighbor or the room using four counts, eight counts or 16 counts. Which object or space takes longer to orbit? How many counts does it take to rotate 360 degrees on your own spot? Can you turn on your spot as you rotate around another object? How many counts does it take? Get in a group of three. One person orbits their desk, the second person orbits the first person and the third person orbits both of them around the edge of the room. Play a steady pulse on the drum to keep track of how many pulses each person takes to orbit.

9. How long does it take for the moon to orbit the earth? Play your answer in pulse on your drum. How long does it take the earth to rotate on its axis? Play your answer.

10. Chant the planets in order from the sun.

    Sun: *Mercury, Venus, Earth, Mars, Jupiter, Saturn, Uranus, Neptune, (Pluto)*

11. Divide your class into three groups. Each group writes a musical piece (song, rap, chant or expressive poem) about the sun, the moon or the earth. Perform the pieces in sequence in an A B C form.

12. Compare and contrast two planets with contrasting musical concepts.

13. Map out the planets in order from the sun with their respective distances on the classroom floor with masking tape. One person plays a steady beat on a drum while the others pace off the distances. How many pulses will be between each planet in order to approximate the ratio of distances?

14. Talk about the concept of the expanding universe. Divide your class into two groups: half movers and half instrument players. The movement group gathers into a tight bunch in the center of the space while the instruments play very quietly. As the movement group expands, the instruments grow louder. Continue the exercise, expanding and contracting the space and sound several times.

15. Create a rhythmic speech piece about comets and asteroids using this chant.

    *Comets and asteroids, comets and asteroids,*
    *Flying through the air like they just don't care!*

16. Explore gravity by creating sounds through a falling motion. Practice using weight differently.

*Music Moments To Teach Academics: Science and Music*

    a. Hand falling on to a drum head; bouncing off or sticking.
    b. Dropping sticks, balls and other objects on the floor or a desk.
    c. Mallets falling on xylophone bars (loose wrists), bouncing or sticking. Compare the sounds.
    d. Body percussion: hands fall to lap or chest, clap one hand on top.
    e. Use a squishy ball or hands/fingers to play a piano.

## Sound

1. Experiment with sound vibrations through a various means.

    a. Place two fingers on your throat as you vocalize. Try using different voices and compare your findings. Place your palm on your upper chest and repeat the exercise.

    b. Place a bowl of water on a table and wait until the surface is still. Release a drop of water onto the center of the water surface and observe the waves created. Compare these waves to sound vibrations.

    c. Practice striking a hand drum. What differences do you notice in the sound from striking it near the rim as opposed to striking it in the center? What creates these differences?

    d. Play a sound on a metal instrument (triangle, cow bell, church bell, gong). Why does the sound last so long?

    e. If your school has an orchestra, invite the teacher to class to give a demonstration about sound vibrations as they relate to stringed instruments. How are changes in pitch created on the strings? What are the mechanics of vibration inside the instrument?

    f. Play a conga drum or bass drum loudly. Can you feel the vibrations in your body? Have you ever heard the bass of a stereo in a car that is next to you on the road? Can you feel the vibrations of the music?

2. Write new lyrics to the Beach Boys' *Good Vibrations* to present your research and findings about sound vibrations.

3. Find sound examples of sound waves behaving in one of three ways.

    *bouncing off*      *traveling through*      *changing path*

4. Compare and contrast things that make sound with a game-song (suggestion, *One of These Things* from Sesame Street). Place three sound objects on the table, two alike and one different. Whistle a tune again or play 16 counts on a woodblock while the "contestants" think about their answer.

   Example: *triangle*     *metal pan*     **hand drum** (this one is different)

5. If you have a choir at your school, invite the teacher to class to give a demonstration about the sound producing mechanism of the voice and what techniques choir members use to improve their sound.

6. Examine the choir room to see if there are special sound panels built into the ceiling or walls. Go to a choir concert and observe the function of choir shells (large panels placed behind the risers to improve sound).

7. Talk about sound and vibration in terms of spoken consonants and vowels, singing and speech. What causes these differences?

8. Take eight glasses that are exactly the same size and place them in a straight row on a table. Fill each glass with a different amount of water, then tap each with a chopstick to hear the pitch. Compare and contrast your findings. What happens to the pitch if more water is added to the glass? What happens to the pitch if water is removed? If all the glasses are empty, do they have the exact same pitch? Why or why not?

9. Experiment with whirligigs and Boomwhackers™ or make your own. If you swing the whirligig at different speeds over your head, how many pitches can you hear? Does a short Boomwhacker™ have the same sound as a long one when struck on the ground? You can use soft, bendable plastic tubing for whirligigs and hard cylinders to make resounding tubes. What happens if you cap one end of the tube?

10. Find or make a drum that is fairly tall, with one end covered (skin) and one end open. Play the drum while it is sitting flat on the floor (skin up). Play the drum while it is tipped at an angle off the floor. What differences do you hear and why?

11. Play a xylophone from the big end to the little end. What makes each bar sound at a different pitch? What are the dynamics of the sound box? Does it make a difference if you strike a different place on the bar? What changes occur if you use a hard mallet (wood or plastic) instead of a soft one (yarn)? Why?

12. Bring a guitar to class and talk about how the strings are tuned.

22. Find three hand drums that are alike in shape and construction but are different sizes. Play each and compare the sounds you hear. Why does the larger drum sound with a lower pitch? Why does the smallest drum sound with the highest pitch?

23. Demonstrate the concept of frequency by playing pulses on an instrument or with body percussion at different paces. Watch the clock for 20 seconds. How many pulses can we play at a slow pace? Fast pace? Medium pace?

24. Demonstrate high and low pitches by singing up and down the scale

    | *do* | *re* | *mi* | *fa* | *so* | *la* | *ti* | *do* |
    |------|------|------|------|------|------|------|------|
    | 1    | 2    | 3    | 4    | 5    | 6    | 7    | 8    |

25. How do you make a loud sound? How do you make a soft sound? What must you do to change the volume of the sound?

26. In eastern countries, people practice making vocal sounds (called *toning*) in which more than one pitch can be heard at a time. These small, high tones that are produced are called overtones. To experiment with this concept, sing a middle to high pitch on the closed vowel *oo* (*u* sounds like *you*). Make your lips into a tightly formed circle as you sing the vowel and slowly change the sound to an *rrr* (*er*) sound and then to an *ee* (like *tree*) sound. Your lips will go from the tight circle shape to a smile (on *ee*) and back. If you listen carefully, you will hear overtones resonating above the note that you are singing.

27. Experiment with instrument making, either traditional (garden hose recorder, clay ocarina) or creating something original.

28. Discuss the speed of sound with your class. Compare to the speed of light. Apply information about the speed of sound to every day incidents: hearing a siren, yelling into a canyon, bathroom singing, etc.

29. Explore the phenomenon of high pitches (at certain frequencies) shattering glass.

30. Take a crystal glass, wet your index or middle finger, and lightly draw circles around the top edge to produce a pitch. Discuss the mechanics of this in class.

31. Compare and contrast the sounds of wind instruments and string instruments. How are they played? How is the sound different? How many variations of sound are there within each instrument family?

*Music Moments To Teach Academics: Science and Music*

32. Compare and contrast the concepts of dissonance (notes played together that seem to "clash" or sound unpleasant) and consonance (notes played together that create a pleasant harmony). Look in the Discography for listening examples. Discuss this in class. On your keyboard or other instrument, play these combinations.

    Dissonant    C and C# (semitone); C and F# (tritone)
    Consonant    C and E (third); C and G (fifth); C and c (octave)

    Listening Suggestion: *Music for Dancers, Too! #19, Consonance & Dissonance, Nichols.*

## Physics

1. Make up a chant about slow and fast moving molecules. Use whole notes, half notes and quarter notes to represent *solid, liquid* and *vapor (gas)* states of matter. Divide your class into three groups to create a short musical section about each state, using voices, instruments and dance.

2. Create chemistry chants of information and definitions.

3. Fill a plastic cup half full of water and cap with a lid. Shake the cup and describe the sounds you hear. Empty the cup and replace the water with ice. Shake the cup and compare the new sounds to the water sounds.

4. Create a rhythm/sound piece by looking at the diagram of atoms or molecules. Assign different sounds for each element.

    *hydrogen atom = one electron, one proton*
    *helium atom = two neutrons, two protons, two electrons*
    *lithium atom = four neutrons, three protons, three*
    *electrons water molecule = two hydrogen, one oxygen*

5. Chant chemical reactions or create rhythm pieces from them.

    *Sulfuric acid*    H20 + SO3 = H2SO4!

6. Chant and play the following words as a large group. Students can make lists of examples for *reflection* and *refraction* and chant them rhythmically.

*Re - flection, refraction, re - flection, refraction; a  mirror, an  echo, a  bend or a break!*

7. Assign instrument groups to opposing magnetic poles. Play a steady pulse on a drum to keep the beat. Students play their instruments as they walk around the room to the pulse. When the pulse stops, they make a shape with someone who has the opposite sound.

   *Positive = + = metals*   *Negative = - = woods*

8. Describe the motion of several objects and copy the rhythmic pattern of the movement in your body. Transfer the movement pattern to body percussion or instruments.

   Suggestions:   *swing, bicycle, grandfather clock*

9. Listen to and learn *Electricity* from the School House Rock series.

10. Experiment with the metal instruments (bells, chimes, triangles, gongs, etc.) and magnets.

## Machines

1. Divide the class into groups. Each group must form a machine with their bodies and use pulse, pattern and grouping to create the appropriate sounds. They may use voices, instruments and body percussion. The machine must be able to start or turn on, complete a work function and stop or break down. Share these pieces with the other groups and guess what the machines are. You can use traditional machines or create unusual ones.

2. Use voices, body percussion or instruments to recreate the sounds of a teeter-totter, swing, merry-go-round or other simple machines.

3. Brainstorm tools/machines that would be used to build a treehouse (e.g., hammer, saw, sander). Recreate the sounds in a musical composition. Repeat the exercise with a different theme and different tools.

4. Record different machine sounds from the office, classroom, home or other environments. Play the sounds in class and let students identify them.

5. Compare and contrast machines you would use in the home. Which ones are loud? Which ones create a pitch? High? Low? Combine sounds to create interesting music.

   *washing machine vs. washboard*   *dishwasher vs. microwave*
   *mixer vs. refrigerator*   *refrigerator vs. blender*
   *electric can opener vs. fan*   *timer vs. leaf blower*

6. Chant the six simple machines. Each small group creates a musical section about one of the six machines. Add an accompaniment with percussion instruments playing a pulse against the speech.

*Lever, wheel, pulley, screw,  wedge, inclined plane!*

    Group 1: (Levers)    Group 2: (Wheels)    Group 3: (Pulleys),  etc.
    Examples: *Crowbar, scissors, ice tongs, wheelbarrow, teeter-totter*

7. Create instruments using tools and parts of machines.

    Chime Tree   *Use fish line and nails or wrenches of different sizes, copper piping, drill, file, saw, etc.*

8. Turn on your computer and printer. Take notes about the sequence of sounds you hear. Notice any rhythms, pitches or unusual sounds that repeat. What kind of sounds does your computer make when you are connecting to the internet?

9. Find an old typewriter (electric or standard) from a thrift shop. Practice playing rhythmic patterns on the keys. What words can you type that create interesting rhythms?

10. What kind of tunes can you play using the pitches of a touch tone phone? Write a letter-code to communicate your sequence to a partner. Students can stand in the formation of the keys and sing the pitches for a fun group activity. What other sounds does the phone make?

# Chapter Six:
# Social Studies and Music

## SOCIAL STUDIES CONCEPTS AND CONTENT

| | | |
|---|---|---|
| cause and effect | years/decades/centuries | time line |
| historical events and people | calendar | BC and AD |
| millennia | continuity and succession | exploration |
| discovery | revolution | war and peace |
| civil war | issues/conflicts | industrialization |
| civil rights movement | information age | civilizations |
| turning points | continents | ideas/patterns of life |
| places | cities and counties | states and countries |
| region | community | native peoples |
| colonists | pioneers | immigrants |
| literature and music | customs and traditions | occupations |
| government | philosophy | religion |
| social issues | race and racism | language |
| identify past problems | photographs | drawings |
| artifacts | oral accounts | documents |
| graphs and charts | maps and tables | diagrams and texts |
| interviews | human resources | library and technology |
| fact/judgment/opinion | stereotype | conjecture and bias |
| relevant and irrelevant | commercials/advertising | perspective |
| argue for/argue against | land rights | free speech |
| church and state | Purists | abolitionists |
| equal rights | democracy vs. communism | individual rights |
| common good | Catholic vs. Protestant | property rights |
| religious freedom | equality and welfare | spirituality |
| progress | values and beliefs | conservation |
| printing press | atomic energy | genetic discoveries |
| television | radio | internet |
| land | family life | natural resources |
| telescopes | agriculture | railroads |
| power looms | steam engines | penicillin |
| irrigation | title, legend, grid, key | globe |
| satellite imagery | GIS data | transportation |
| literacy | population density | economics |
| vegetation | rainfall | urban vs. rural |
| climate | migration | power generation |
| pollution | housing and homelessness | forest fires |
| wildlife | natural hazards | erosion |
| farming | trade and commerce | waterways |
| buildings | trade | political alliances |
| recycling | product choice | recreation |
| consequences | alternatives | parks |
| society | survival | innovation |
| shelter, food, clothing | ethnic | subcultures |

*Music Moments To Teach Academics: Social Studies and Music*

| | | |
|---|---|---|
| books and movies | art and architecture | bridges |
| transmission | diffusion | interaction |
| foundational documents | U.S. Constitution | Bill Of Rights |
| rights and responsibilities | change and interpretation | equal representation |
| liberty | justice | pledge of allegiance |
| human dignity | rule of law | ideals and realities |
| citizenship | public policy | representatives |
| community service | voting | collective action |
| lobbying | republic | make and apply rules |
| law enforcement | consent | federal/state/local |
| legislative branch | executive branch | judicial branch |
| political parties | Democrats vs. Republicans | law interpretation |
| amendments | bills | initiatives |
| referendums | schools | health services |
| balance of power | monarchy | oligarchy |
| protest | pacifism | nations and world |
| international relations | territory | nuclear weapons |
| president | peace corps | volunteer |
| agreements and treaties | foreign policy | conflict/cooperation |
| classroom rules | family obligations | traffic safety |
| freedom of expression | freedom of the press | playground rules |
| common courtesy | sharing | consensus |
| dictator | socialist | curfew |
| food drives | school officers | making a difference |
| public service | scarcity | supply and demand |
| goods and services | produce and distribute | needs vs. wants |
| prices | incentives | profit |
| competitive market | economy | shortage vs. surplus |
| black market | durables | luxuries vs. necessities |
| work force | families | labor unions |
| agencies | small business | large corporations |
| traditional/command/market | capitalism | communism |
| new products | proprietorship | partnership |
| jobs | self-employment | non-profit status |
| money | earn, save and spend | investment |
| stocks and bonds | mutual funds/bank accounts | sales tax |
| minimum wage | inflation | slavery |
| underground railroad | emancipation | affirmative action |
| women's liberation | peace rallies | segregation |
| holidays | friends and friendship | foes |
| politeness and manners | empathy | cooperative learning |

*Music Moments To Teach Academics: Social Studies and Music*

**Calendar and Holidays**

1. Chant the months of the year rhythmically. Add a steady pulse instrument accompaniment or use body percussion. Play the rhythm of the words while you think the names of the months.

    *Ja<u>nu</u>ary,    Feb<u>ru</u>ary,    <u>March</u>,    <u>A</u>pril,*
    *<u>May</u>,    <u>June</u>,    <u>July</u>,    <u>Au</u>gust,*
    *Sep<u>tem</u>ber,    Oc<u>to</u>ber,    No<u>vem</u>ber,    De<u>cem</u>ber.*

2. Stand in a circle. Sing or chant the following song and play the game. When the group sings *January*, those born in January dance and play their instruments to the beat in the middle of the circle, then return to their spots. Repeat the song for each month.

    *Everybody born in January, dance around,*
    *Everybody born in January, dance around.*
    *Tra la la la (clap clap clap), Tra la la la (clap clap clap)*
    *Everybody born in January, dance around.*

3. Write a series of events on the board from the past, present and future. Divide the class into three groups: woods, metals and drums. Read the first event on the board and the appropriate group plays their instrument to indicate the correct answer. You can also use a chant for the entire group to say and play between each event.

    *Past, present, future (clap)    past, present, future (clap)*
    *Place the time  on the line,    past, present, future! (clap)*

    *woods - past    metals - present    drums - future*

4. Look on the calendar and select various holidays to research. Include holidays celebrated outside of the United States. Small groups can create a rap or song to a familiar tune about their assigned holiday. Information can include customs, traditions, origins and date.

5. Here is an old chant to learn the number of days in each month.

    *<u>Thirty days has</u> September, <u>A</u>pril, <u>June and</u> No<u>vem</u>ber,*
    *<u>All</u> the <u>rest</u> have <u>thirty</u>-<u>one</u>, ex<u>cept</u> for <u>February, just</u> for <u>fun</u>,*
    *It has <u>only twenty</u>-<u>eight</u> and <u>twenty</u>-<u>nine</u> on a <u>leap</u> year <u>date</u>!*

6. Chant the days of the week. Make up or borrow a tune for the words. Add a pulse with body percussion or drum. Play all instruments once together on the exclamation point of this chant.

    *Monday, Tuesday, Wednesday, Thursday, Friday, Saturday, Sunday!*

7. Sing children's songs about the days of the week or make up your own. Students can list the things they do on each day of the week and then create a musical setting of the information.

8. Find or write poetry or short stories about the days of the week or the months of the year. Add sounds and perform these expressively for class.

9. Create several raps based on different time elements of the calendar. Divide into groups and brainstorm ideas for each topic (days, weeks, months, years, decades, centuries, etc.).

10. Focus on the decades of the 20th century. What music examples can you find for each decade? What themes and styles are common in the musical selections?

11. Make a time line of eight calendar events and sing them using the pitches of the scale.

12. Write riddles or rhymes about different holidays using rhythmic speech. Add a melody or instruments.

13. What songs do you know from the familiar holidays? Can you hum the tune? Tap the rhythm of the words and the class can guess the song. Take a familiar tune and write words about a social studies concept.

14. Look at the Menorah, a candelabrum with nine candles used for Hanukkah. Can you see a pattern (four short candles, one tall, four short candles). Can you play this rhythm on your instruments? What other symbols are used for holidays? What patterns can we see and play?

15. What sounds do you associate with Halloween or harvest time? Make these sounds with your voice or instruments. What kinds of techniques make the music sound spooky or scary? (*minor scales, dissonance*)

16. What sounds do you associate with Christmas, Winter Solstice or Kwanzaa time? Make these sounds with your voice or instruments.

17. Write additional lyrics for the song *Over the River And Through the Woods* about traditions you experience with your family at Thanksgiving time.

18. Use the principles, themes and symbols of Kwanzaa (an African-American tradition) to inspire rhythmic poetry and musical compositions. Find songs to sing from the African-American tradition for each principle and create a program.

*Music Moments To Teach Academics: Social Studies and Music*

### History

1. Compare and contrast the events of any given time with the music of that same time. Our history is recorded in the music.

2. Explore the historical background of different songs (e.g., *Amazing Grace*, *The Star Spangled Banner*). Sing the songs in class and discuss the stories and traditions behind them.

3. Create history chants to memorize dates and events.
   *In fourteen hundred and ninety-two, Columbus sailed the ocean blue.*

4. Make up chants to remember facts (or fibs) about historical figures. Play an accompaniment on a drum or play the word rhythms on another instrument while thinking the information. Chant it using different voices (speak, sing, shout, whisper). Make up a body percussion rhythm to go with it.

   *George Washington, chopped down a cherry tree, crossed o'er the Delaware, had wooden teeth!*

5. Examine the flag of the United States Of America. Use your instrument to answer these questions: How many white stripes are there? How many red stripes are there? How many stars were on the original flag?

6. Sing songs from times of conflict and war to experience what the people thought and felt at the time:
   - Civil War/Slavery - *Dixieland, Follow The Drinking Gourd*
   - Underground Railroad - *Harriet Tubman*
   - Vietnam War/Protest - *Where Have All The Flowers Gone?*
   - Civil Rights Era - *We Shall Overcome*

7. Assign a war, period of time, conflict or other historical event to each small group. They can create raps about their themes or use the melody of a song from that time to write new lyrics.

### Geography

1. Create a city/urban or country/rural soundscape and share with the class.

*Music Moments To Teach Academics: Social Studies and Music*

2. Create chants for the states and their capital cities by region.

    *Olympia, Washington; Boise, Idaho; Salem, Oregon; Sacramento, California*

3. Learn your state song and sing it in class. Learn the state songs of other states you are studying and sing them in class.

4. Make up a chant for a capital, state and major products in that state.

    *Olympia, Washington; apples, evergreens, clean air, Washington!*

5. Play the names of the seven continents as you chant them. Assign one to each small group and create a musical rondo.

    *Africa, Asia, North America, South America, Europe, Australia, Antarctica*

6. Write the name of each continent on a piece of construction paper and spread them out on the floor of your classroom or gym. Play examples of music from the different continents. Students move to stand by the continent they believe the music comes from (*idea from Anne Green Gilbert*).

7. Use your voice, kazoo or slide whistle to trace the contour of the horizon, matching pitches for high and low points in the terrain. Create one sound for valleys, one for mountains and another for rivers.

8. Learn a folk dance from another country or make one up to traditional music, focusing on elements of that culture in your movements. See the Bibliography and Discography for suggestions. There are several good DVDs on the market that may be available through your local library. Invite someone from the culture into your classroom to share the dance firsthand whenever possible.

9. Sing simple folk songs from around the world. Use an authentic recording or teach by rote (suggestion: *Rise Up Singing!*). Talk about the oral tradition of a folk song and why it changes when passed from one person to the next.

10. Talk about the origin of the Orff instruments and play and listen to other instruments from different lands (suggestion: *Voices of Forgotten Worlds* by Larry Blumenfeld).

    Asia - *metallophones (metal alloy bars) - gongs, bells, chimes*
    Africa - *xylophones (wooden bars) - shekere, djembe, mbira*
    Europe - *glockenspiels (steel bars) - triangles, timpani*

11. Listen to varied examples of vocal aesthetic from different lands and reflect as a group.

*Music Moments To Teach Academics: Social Studies and Music*

12. Music: *Music for Dancers, Too! #10 Locomotion.* The contrasting sections of this piece were influenced by a variety of cultural influences: West Africa, China, North America, Australia, Europe and South America. Listen to the music and move to the pulse or rhythmic patterns. Students can draw the place they think the music is referring to or write down their impressions. Compare and contrast the musical style and interpretation of these pieces.

13. Divide your class into groups and assign each group a poem from a world culture. Each group will present their piece through sound and movement, using body signatures, characteristics and common instruments of that culture (they will need to do some research on this). Groups should emphasize the rhythms, style and imagery apparent in their poem. You can find many cultural poems on the web or at your local library.

### HAIKU

*Moon, sun's reflection. . .*
*lights the night, pulling at waves,*
*Sleeps in the morning.*

*Soft and still the pond. . .*
*A drop rippling gently,*
*Echoing the sky.*

*Storm, dark and brooding. . .*
*looms over the tall forest,*
*Angry and silent.*

*Rain, dancing lightly*
*washes green, slender grasses*
*In the fresh meadow.*

*Arching rainbow sky. . .*
*brings a day of sweet promise,*
*As loud as the drum.*

*Leaping waterfall. . .*
*splash and fall, singing your song,*
*To distant canyons.*

*The eagle and hawk. . .*
*circle the earth with full wings*
*And a beating heart.*

### NAVAJO PRAYER

*With Beauty before me, I walk*
*With Beauty behind me, I walk*
*With Beauty above me, I walk*
*With Beauty all around me, I walk*
*With Beauty within me, I walk*
*In Beauty, it is finished.*

*Music Moments To Teach Academics: Social Studies and Music*

ECCLESIASTES 3:1-8, THE BIBLE

*To everything there is a season,
a time for every purpose under the sun:
A time to be born and a time to die;
a time to plant and a time to pluck up that which is planted;
a time to kill and a time to heal. . .
a time to weep and a time to laugh;
a time to mourn and a time to dance. . .
a time to embrace and a time to refrain from embracing;
a time to lose and a time to seek. . .
a time to rend and a time to sew;
a time to keep silent and a time to speak;
a time to love and a time to hate;
a time for war and a time for peace.*

SUGGESTED CULTURAL POETRY RESOURCES

The Dream Keeper and Other Poems by Langston Hughes

Native American Songs and Poems, edited by Brain Swann

The Classic Tradition of Haiku: An Anthology, edited by Faubion Bowers

Laughing Tomatoes and Other Spring Poems by Francisco X. Alarcon

Russian Poetry for Children by Elena Sokol

E.E. Cummings: Complete Poems 1904-1962 by e.e. cummings, et al.

The Collected Poems of William Carlos Williams, edited by A. Walton Litz, et al.

This Same Sky: A Collection of Poems from Around the World by Naomi Nye

The Random House Book of Poetry for Children, edited by Jack Prelutsky

The 20th Century Children's Poetry Treasury, edited by Jack Prelutsky

The Book of Little Folk, by Lauren A. Mills

Earth Prayers from Around the World, edited by Elizabeth Roberts

14. Expose your students to quality music and dance performances, documentaries and authentic recordings from a variety of cultures. See the Bibliography and Discography for suggestions. Invite local artists or parents of students in to your class to share their cultural traditions first hand.

15. Try to bring in a handmade instrument from a non-industrial nation. Allow students time to examine the instrument and write down their observations. What can we learn about the land and the peoples based on the construction of this instrument? What is its function? How is it played?

    Example     *Talking Drum (handmade in West Africa)*
    Materials   *Animal skin, carved log, mud for glue, animal tooth inside, curved wooden mallet*

    *Previous knowledge: These drums were used as a kind of telephone, often played near a waterway to communicate with another village. The rattle (tooth) inside is considered the spirit of the drum.*

16. Create a rap about landforms, assigning each group a landform to explain through music.
    *valleys, mountains, plains and desert. . .*

17. Use the tune of *Frere Jacques* to create a song about vegetation and wildlife.
    *Vegetation, vegetation, wildlife, wildlife,*
    *Flowers, trees and green things, animals and birds that sing,*
    *How they grow, how they grow.*

18. Create soundscapes, raps or songs about various climate zones and conditions.
    *rainy tropical, semi-arid, warm rainy, cold moist, polar ice caps, etc.*

19. Use pulses to travel from one state to another. It would take three pulses to travel from Washington to California: *Washington (x), Oregon (x), California (x)*.

20. Music: *I Am the Song, #14 Sansa Kroma, K. Nichols.* This A B form song is a new arrangement of a traditional tune from West Africa. Sing the song and add the dance-game and instruments in your class. This is a great piece for initiating a new student into the group. *Sansa* is a hawk rumored to bring orphaned children to live with a new family in the village community.

    |   |   |   |
    |---|---|---|
    |   | A | *Swing arms down (clap clap clap)* |
    |   |   | *Swing arms up (clap clap clap) (repeat)* |
    | Words: | B | *Sansa kroma, nee nay woo, ah chay chay ko ko mah,* |
    |   |   | *Sansa kroma, nee nay woo, ah chay chay ko ko mah.* |
    |   |   | *(Repeat)* |

21. Music: *I Am the Song, #13 Walkin' Now in Beauty, K. Nichols.* This piece was written collaboratively with students as a response to learning about Native American culture

and their appreciation of that experience. Sheet music for voices, instruments and the circle dance can be found in the book *Inspirations* by Kerri Lynn Nichols.

22. Music: *I Am the Song, #18 Leaves That Fall*, K. Nichols. Listen to the piece with your students and sing along once you know it. Bring some fall leaves into class and ask students to describe them using various senses (touch, sight, smell). Generate a discussion about how leaves are a metaphor for the peoples of the world.

23. Music: *Peace Is the World Smiling, Music for Little People.* Play selections from this CD and let students sing along. Write your own song about peace in the world and perform it for parents and community.

## Community Groups

1. Play musical name games with your students each day. Use the ones in the Resources section of this book or make up your own.

2. Sing welcome songs each morning and closing songs each afternoon to bring your group together. Create other musical traditions or customs with your class.

3. Play stone (or other) passing games in a circle with your class that require cooperation. Use chants, rhymes or short songs to facilitate the pulse (*pick, pass, pick, pass*):

    *In the quiet, when you're all alone, wish upon the magic wishing stone,*
    *Hide the stone and may your wish come true, pass the magic on to someone new!*

4. Read the story *Stone Soup* and add sounds for each ingredient placed in the pot. Make up a song about sharing and cooperation to go with the story.

5. Recognize different personalities in the group as they relate to musical concepts (Music Suggestion: *Music and Movement for Munchkins, Disc Two, #7 Fast and Slow, #27 Walk and Rock or Music for Dancers, #17 Ching, Clop Boom!*).

    | *Pace* | fast (busy person), medium (balanced), slow (laid back) |
    | *Grouping* | twos (direct, goal oriented), threes (meandering) |
    | *Timbre* | woods, metals, drums, shakers (relate to emotions) |

6. Discuss what kind of moods we go through on different days (sadness, joy, anger, etc.) and play music that "sounds" like each feeling (see Discography). Listen to other examples and allow students to identify an emotion or feeling the music seems to imply.

7. Experiment with listening and cooperation by creating a rhythm or drum circle with your students (using traditional instruments or found sounds). One person plays an eight-count

rhythm and the group echoes it back. Continue around the circle until everyone has had a turn, then improvise together. One or two people should keep the steady pulse strongly on a low drum in the center of the circle. Focus on listening to others in the group, leaving some space in the sound for others to play, while adding your own rhythm to the group sound.

8. Play 16 Counts with the class. One person keeps a steady, walking pulse on a drum or other instrument. The class walks around to the pulse in free space until count 16, at which point they must get into a group designated by the leader. Here are some suggestions for the calls.

> *Group size: pair, trio, quartet, quintet, etc.*
> *Similarities: wearing same color, same height, birthday months,*
> *etc. Differences: opposites or similarities*

9. Chant the names of the people in your family and their "roles."

> *mother, father, sister, brother, aunt, uncle, grandma, grandpa,*
>
> O R
>
> *Joyce, Richard, Kelli, Dave, Ruth, Brian, Edna, Horace*

10. List other community groups that exist locally: unions, churches, dance companies, organizations, etc. Make up a song, chant or rap about these groups and their functions in society.

## Civics and Government

1. Chant the branches of the government and their functions.

> *executive, legislative, judicial*

2. Make a hierarchal list of eight government officials and sing them on the scale from low to high (e.g., council person, mayor, governor, senator, etc.).

3. Write a speech and rhythm piece about segregation and emancipation, using definitions and examples of each in your lyrics.

4. Create a freedom piece about the different freedoms we have in our country (e.g., freedom of speech, freedom of the press, etc.).

5. Make up a rap about all of the things that sales tax pays for.

6. Chant the traffic safety rules, both for pedestrians and drivers. The more rhythmic, the more memorable the information will be:

    Examples   *Don't end up in a heap! Look before you leap!*

                     *Red light stop, yellow light slow, green light go!*

7. To illustrate the concept of conflict resolution, lead your students through the following activity with a partner. Then, lead a discussion about how the students were able to negotiate to resolve the problem.

    *Partner 1*   Plays an eight-count rhythmic pattern on an instrument.
    *Partner 2*   Plays a different eight-count pattern on their instrument.
    *Third Time*  Together, create a new eight-count pattern that uses something from the previous two patterns. Then, share all three with the class.

8. Discuss a current issue that has two or more opposing views. Assign each small group a view and have them write a rap or song to state and support that point of view.

## Economics

1. Use the following chant to inspire a piece about supply and demand. Make a list of the students' needs and wants to create contrasting sections to the chant:

    A   *Needs and wants, supply and demand, (repeat)*
         *How can I purchase the very best brand?*
         *Needs and wants, supply and demand!*

2. Sing *I've Been Workin' On The Railroad* and talk about the occupation and time this song refers to. What other work songs do you know from this occupation? Other ones? What groups used (or use) singing to motivate the work force? (chain gangs, slaves, etc.)

3. List all of the different places you hear music. What kind of music is playing at the grocery store? Describe it. What is the purpose of this music?

4. Make a list of various occupations. What sounds do you hear in these occupations? Create a soundscape for each. Are there any rhythmic movements created by these occupations? Recreate one of these rhythmic movements and we will try to guess what occupation you are referring to.

5. Chant occupations that take place in or around water. Chant occupations that take place outdoors. Make other lists of occupations and chant them rhythmically. Chant the occupations and we will try to guess the category or theme that connects them.

*Music Moments To Teach Academics: Social Studies and Music*

6. Sing Sesame Street's *Who Are The People In Your Neighborhood* (see *The Sesame Street Songbook*). Add your own occupations and lyrics using this tune or another one.

7. What kinds of transportation do you see in the city? Country? What modes of transportation do children use? Can you make the sounds of some of these transportation objects? What kinds of rhythms or tones do you hear?

    Examples    *planes, trains, cars, trucks, garbage truck, fire engines, bicycles, scooters, mopeds, boats, helicopters, etc.*

8. Think of a product your company wishes to sell and write a commercial jingle for it. Perform for the class.

# Chapter Seven:
# *Visual Arts and Music*

*Music Moments To Teach Academics: Visual Arts and Music*

## VISUAL ARTS CONCEPTS AND CONTENT

| | | |
|---|---|---|
| art elements | line | texture |
| shape | space | color |
| principles of design | balance | dominance |
| contrast | repetition | rhythm |
| theme and variation | unity | types of lines |
| thin and thick | diagonal | zig zag |
| curvy | straight | scribbled |
| dotted | oval | curlicue |
| jagged | wavy | checkered |
| patterned | organic vs. inorganic | circles |
| squares | rectangles | pentagons |
| cylinders | pyramids | cones |
| positive and negative space | tessellations | color wheel |
| primary colors | secondary colors | tertiary colors |
| warm and cool colors | neutrals | lights and darks |
| harmonious colors | contrasting colors | tints (add white) |
| shades (add black) | bleeding | fading |
| radial balance | informal balance | symmetry/asymmetry |
| regular/irregular pattern | dominance | perspective |
| draw and sketch | paint | watercolors |
| oil paints | acrylics | medium |
| depth/dimension | overlap | fore/background |
| middle ground | shading | hatching/crosshatching |
| distance and horizon | vanishing point | two-dimensional |
| three dimensional | contour | elaboration |
| opaque vs. transparent | clay | sculpture |
| originality | natural expression | creativity |
| artistic or aesthetic view | strokes | composition |
| technique | collages | form |
| evaluating | revising | focus |
| density | linear | tone (values) |
| function or purpose | style | realism |
| abstract | famous artists | cubism |
| vertical vs. horizontal | emotional response | interpret |
| symbols | textiles | image |
| art history | culture | commercial art |
| folk art | decorative | architecture |
| fluency | flexibility | rough vs. smooth |

*Music Moments To Teach Academics: Visual Arts and Music*

1. Music: *Music for Dancers, #3 Twos & Threes.* Use the three contrasting sections of music to practice making curved, straight and zigzag lines or triangles, squares and circles.

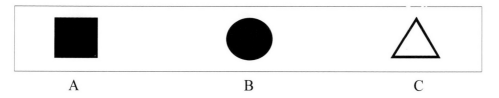

    A                      B                      C

2. Music: *Music for Dancers, #13 Staccato Legato.* Use this piece to draw jagged and smooth lines. Follow the rhythm of the piece with your hand as you create lines and shapes on the paper. When the music changes, change colors or mediums.

3. Music: *Music for Dancers, Too! #2 Strong & Light, K. Nichols.* This song is written in an A B repeated form. The A section is in a meter (grouping) of three pulses (strong-light-light), great for practicing curvy lines and loops, vertically, horizontally and diagonally. The B section music is grouped in twos (strong-light) and works well for practicing straight lines. Use the same music to practice making shapes or letters with straight lines and curved lines.

4. Explore the lines of Southwest art while using music for inspiration (Music Suggestion: *Music for Dancers, Too! #11 Gravity).* This selection has contrasting sections or music to inspire straight, curvy, and zigzag lines.

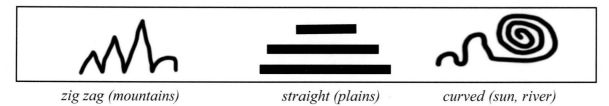

*zig zag (mountains)*          *straight (plains)*          *curved (sun, river)*

5. See Chapter Four (*Mathematics And Music*) for additional ideas about lines and shapes.

6. See the Discography for selections to support relaxation for artwork and to practice brush strokes in the air.

7. Show several musical scores to the students. Allow them to take any shape, line or symbol they see in a musical score and use them to create an original picture.

8. Compare and contrast pointillism and staccato symbols in music. Use this technique to create a picture.

9. Create an original painting. With a group, improvise music to go with the painting.

10. Music: *I Am the Song, #8-12, Sticky Finger Suite, K. Nichols.* Listen to each of these short selections of music and create a picture in response to various music concepts:

    a. *Listen and visually create the rhythms of the piece.*
    b. *Listen and visually create the melodies of the piece.*
    c. *Choose different color schemes related to the emotional quality of the music.*
    d. *Draw a character or setting for each piece.*

11. Examine famous works of art and create musical pieces that represent them. What art concepts are prominent in the art work? What music concepts relate to these?

12. Show the DVD *I See a Song* by Eric Carle or look at the book. Discuss how the artist has visually represented the music.

13. Cover a bulletin board with butcher paper. Choose a theme/setting such as a marsh. The class improvises marsh sounds with voices, body percussion and instruments while one or two students paint their marsh interpretation on the board. Repeat the exercise with different themes and combinations of painters and musicians. Both the music and the painting are improvised.

14. Compare and contrast visual art and music contemporaries of any given period.

15. Select a block chart from the Resources chapter in this book. Color the boxes in with a pattern, then translate that pattern into music.

16. Create Touch Musical Concepts: Visual Art For The Blind. Cut out several cardboard lines or shapes and glue them down to a flat piece of cardboard to create a texture to be "read." Choose a musical concept.

    *Pulse - Glue long, even strips vertically across the page. To "view," close your eyes and run your fingers across the page to "feel" pulse.*

17. Experiment with different ways of creating a musical score, where symbols, shapes, lines, designs, patterns, colors, pictures and blocks relate to different sounds. Create these on large poster boards and share with the class.

18. Map different pieces of music you hear. Maps can include pulses and phrases as well as contrast and repetition.

*Pulse Map*  *Phrase Map*  *Pulse/Phrase Map*

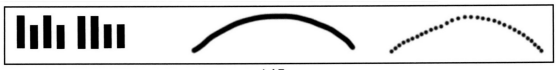

19. Play different timbres in voice, body percussion and instruments. Allow the students to find different ways to visually represent the "tone color" of each timbre.

    *drums*   *metals*   *woods*   *shakers*
    *shout*   *sing*     *speak*   *whisper*
    *stomp*   *pat*      *clap*    *snap*

20. Choose a piece of music that is written in additive form (see Discography) and draw or paint a different layer for each part added. You can relate this to foreground/middle ground/background, vertical/horizontal space or layer one design over another.

21. Create symmetrical and asymmetrical drawings or shapes in relation to musical concepts.

    *Grouping* Twos (symmetrical)      Threes (asymmetrical)
    *Pattern* Regular (symmetrical)    Irregular (asymmetrical)
    *Form* Balanced (symmetrical)      Abstract (asymmetrical)
    *Pace* Metronome (symmetrical)     Rubato (asymmetrical)

22. Music: *I Am the Song, #21 Follow Me, Moon, K. Nichols.* Sit across the table from your partner with a large piece of paper between you. Choose the "leader." On the first section of music, with your markers, you will mirror your partner's movements on the paper. When the music changes, you will shadow your partner's movements. When the music repeats, change leaders. Share your drawings with the group. You may use any musical selection that has two contrasting sections (see the Discography).

23. Use permanent markers to make designs on hand drums (the Remo drums with synthetic, replaceable heads). Glue designs or braided materials on the sides.

24. Make instruments in class as an art project. Use different containers or paper mache to create maracas and hand drums. Create non-traditional instruments and decorate them in an unusual way.

25. Find examples of musical notation, both past and present, and practice making the symbols with calligraphy. Create a picture using only musical symbols.

26. Match up musical and visual art styles and periods. Play music to inspire artwork.

    Example   *Play Debussy (see Discography)*
              *Impressionism: practice techniques (watercolor, etc.)*

*Music Moments To Teach Academics: Visual Arts and Music*

27. Compare Mussorgsky's *Pictures At An Exhibition* (Ravel's orchestration) with the artwork that inspired it. Create your own exhibition of artwork inspired by musical selections.

28. Listen to music that has a strong, lyrical, melodic quality (see Discography for examples). Draw or paint the contour (shape) of the melody, as it rises and falls, on your paper or canvas.

29. Divide the class into three groups: woods, metals and drums. Each instrument family will correspond to a primary color in the following Color Wheel Game. When the teacher points to a color, the corresponding instrument group plays. For secondary colors, two groups will play. Divide the class into additional groups to review tertiary colors:

    Primary  *Red - drums*    *Yellow - metals*    *Blue - woods*

    Secondary  *Purple - drums and woods play together*
    *Green - metals and woods play together*
    *Orange - metals and drums play together*

30. Assign one instrument sound for cool colors and another for warm colors. Point to a color on the color wheel and the students respond with sound.

    Warm Colors  *shakers*    Cool Colors  *metals*

31. Show examples from Disney's *Fantasia*, which is contains animation that has been inspired by and created to express classical music selections.

32. Show Dr. Seuss's *My Many Colored Days*, which uses color and music to examine and express different emotional states.

33. Create musical game boards or aleatoric charts (for chance music) on large paper with paints, markers and construction paper.

34. Choose a musical concepte(g., *pattern*) and create a visual expression of it. See the artwork in *Music for Dancers (artwork by Robin Adalina Landsong)* for examples.

35. Compare positive and negative space (visual art) to the concepts of sounds and rests (music). Create a representation of a rhythm or song that has sound (positive space) and silences (negative space).

36. Create artwork for a CD cover and disc around a theme concept.

37. Listen to an example of *theme and variations* music (see Discography). Create a piece of artwork based on a visual theme and its variations.

38. Match the concepts of music with the concepts and techniques of art. Ask the students to find these connections and create art experiences around them.

| <u>Music</u> | <u>Visual Art</u> |
|---|---|
| Pulse | Lines, Rhythm |
| Pattern | Pattern, Rhythm |
| Grouping | Symmetry, Asymmetry |
| Pitch | Depth, Dimension |
| Scale | Color Wheel |
| Interval | Space |
| Motive | Focus |
| Phrase | Strokes |
| Repetition | Repetition |
| Contrast | Contrast |
| Pace | Fluency |
| Dynamics | Light and Dark |
| Articulate | Critique |
| Interpret | Interpret |
| Timbre | Density, Color |
| Texture | Overlap, Layering |
| Harmony | Balance |

39. Music: *Music for Dancers, #13 Staccato Legato, K. Nichols.* This music consists of two contrasting sections of music. The A section is staccato (jumpy, accented, broken) while the B section is legato (smooth, connected). Practice contrasting strokes to the music with paints, markers or colored pencils.

40. Color in every other box in a block chart to create a checkered pattern. Assign sounds and play the pattern in class while looking at the chart.

41. Music: *I Am the Song, #17 Waltz of the Toys, K. Nichols.* This music starts with a single part and then layers in a new part upon each repetition of the music (additive form). Start by drawing thin lines and as each part is added, increase the thickness of the lines.

42. Practice making curvy, dotted and jagged lines in silence. What rhythmic patterns can you create as you draw these lines or combine them? Can the class draw these rhythms in sync?

*Music Moments To Teach Academics: Visual Arts and Music*

43. Create a percussion piece using materials from the art classroom: paper, scissors, brushes, tables, paint cans, etc.

44. Examine or create abstract art while listening to music of the same nature. See the Discography for suggestions.

45. Music: *Music for Dancers, #16 Voices, K. Nichols.* Listen to this piece of music. Can you hear the melody (a horizontal line of sequential sound)? Can you hear the harmony (vertical lines of simultaneous sound)? Draw a horizontal representation of the melody. Draw a vertical representation of the harmony.

46. Listen to and compare composed music (e.g., Baroque style) and free improvisation (e.g., jazz style). Relate to the inorganic vs. organic (realism vs. abstract) approaches to visual art. Create a piece of artwork for each listening example.

47. Sing a simple round like *Row, Row, Row Your Boat*. Write the words on the board to show the form of the round. Relate this musical technique to the art technique of tessellations. Can you create a drawing of these tessellations using boats, oars and waves?

48. Assemble collages as a representation of aleatoric or chance music. Use the collages as "notation" for an improvised musical performance.

49. Music: *Music for Dancers, #10 Rondo ala Copland.* Listen to this piece of music. Have the students stand in a circle, each with a different color scarf (seven colors in all). For the A sections, copy the teacher's movements. For each contrasting section, the teacher can call out a color and those students move to the center to improvise movement with their scarf. Listen to the music a second time, while recreating the form of the piece with paper and colored markers.

# Chapter Eight:
# *Wellness and Music*

## WELLNESS CONCEPTS AND CONTENT

| | | |
|---|---|---|
| body systems | functions and structures | emotional health |
| heart and lungs | limbic and motor systems | nervous system |
| physical health | puberty (changes) | adolescence |
| adulthood | sexual activity (risks) | pregnancy |
| disease | prevention and treatment | emergency crisis |
| stress | nicotine, alcohol, other drugs | addiction |
| dependence | first-aid skills | environmental factors |
| exercise | safe, respectful behavior | cardiovascular |
| advertising | social skills | relationships |
| emotional responses | decision-making | risk taking (healthy) |
| health occupations | mind-body connection | creativity |
| intergenerational | relaxation | five senses |
| aroma therapy | ambiance | Feng Shui |
| goal setting | journaling | toning and chanting |
| extra-sensory perception | energy work | massage |
| chiropractic | naturopathology | brain health |
| memory and recall | drum circles | bonding |
| Braindance | patterning | sensory integration |
| breathing/respiratory | spine | extremities |
| movement | vestibular stimulation | dance |
| aging | healing | anxiety/depression |
| growth hormones | seratonin | active vs. passive |
| music-making | possession stage | catered lifestyle stage |
| being state stage | continuum | living vs. retirement |
| listening | loneliness | space and time |
| self space/general | directions | pathway |
| focus | size | level |
| rhythm | pace | energy |
| weight | flow | force |
| body parts | body shapes | balance |
| opposites | fitness | body in motion |
| skills for life and activity | rules and procedures | safety |
| sportsmanship | cooperation | teamwork |
| games | play | strength-endurance |
| flexibility | leisure | nutrition |
| food groups | dietary guidelines | meats |
| dairy | fruits and vegetables | legumes |
| sugars, caffeine, chemicals | water | coordination patterns |
| fundamental movement | limbic system | integration |

*Music Moments To Teach Academics: Wellness and Music*

**The Human Body**

1. Place your palm over your heart and tap the pulse-rhythm with your other hand on your lap, desk or drum. Is the pattern even or uneven?

2. Run around the space and repeat the above exercise. Has the pulse of your heartbeat changed? How? Take several deep, slow breaths. How does this effect your heartbeat? Play these differences on your desk or instrument.

3. Hold your breath comfortably for several seconds. This is like a fermata in music. How does this effect your heart-pulse? Now, let your breath out in a big burst (sforzando).

4. Inhale deeply while placing your hands around your ribcage. What do you notice? Exhale fully.

5. Is your breathing slow or fast? Loud or soft? Create a steady pulse of upbeats (inhale) and downbeats (exhale).

6. Inhale deeply and exhale with a sigh on a vowel sound. Repeat for all of the vowels.

7. Inhale deeply and exhale on a high pitch sliding to a low pitch. Repeat, starting on a low pitch and ending high. Can you repeat the exercise using loud to soft and soft to loud? Try it using a hum. How can you hum if your mouth is open?

8. Inhale fast and exhale slowly; Inhale slowly and exhale fast. Inhale slowly and exhale slowly. Inhale fast and exhale fast.

9. Inhale a full breath and release on a pulse of hisses: S S S S S S S. Try double hisses (SS SS SS SS) and triple hisses (SSS SSS SSS SSS) using a steady pulse.

10. Combine the rhythmic patterns of the heart and lungs by playing them together on two different instruments.

11. How would your heartbeat pattern or breath pulse change if you had one of the following conditions? Play these changes on instruments. Start with regular patterns and then change them.

*Irregular Heartbeat*        *Heart Attack*        *Smoking*
*Asthma Attack*        *Exercising Vigorously*        *Emphysema*
*Sleeping*        *Drug Ingestion*        *Stressful Situation*

12. Can you rattle the bones in your body? Half of the class will play shakers while the other half moves their bodies to rattle their bones. What other instruments can make bone-rattling sound (*woods*)? Let's add these to our composition.

13. Sing the song *Dem Bones* (*Dry Bones*) as you move the various bones described in the music. Play rhythm sticks on the rests (pauses) in the melody.

    *Dem bones, dem bones, dem (X) dry bones,*
    *Dem bones, dem bones, dem (X) dry bones,*
    *Dem bones, dem bones, dem (X) dry bones,*
    *Now hear the word of the Lord! (X X)*

    The toe bone's connected to the (X) foot bone,
    The foot bone's connected to the (X) ankle bone,
    The ankle bone's connected to the (X) leg bone,
    Now hear the word of the Lord! (X X)

    The leg bone's connected to the (X) knee bone,
    The knee bone's connected to the (X) thigh bone,
    The thigh bone's connected to the (X) hip bone,
    Now hear the word of the Lord! (X X)

    The hip bone's connected to the (X) back bone,
    The back bone's connected to the (X) shoulder bone,
    The shoulder bone's connected to the (X) neck bone,
    The neck bone's connected to the (X) head bone,
    Now hear the word of the Lord! (X X)

    *Dem bones, dem bones gonna (X) walk around,*
    *Dem bones, dem bones gonna (X) walk around,*
    *Dem bones, dem bones gonna (X) walk around,*
    *Now hear the word of the Lord! (X X)*

14. Compare muscles to rubber bands. Stretch large rubber bands across a shoebox or other small box. Experiment with stretching and releasing the bands as your partner stretches and releases his/her muscles.

    *Tension/Relaxation*        *Contract/Expand*

15. How do our muscles and bones work together in the body? Let's play a duet of these movement/actions with our instruments.

    Woods and Shakers - rattle the bones in the body
    Rubber Band Box and Drums - pluck for the muscles in the body

16. Create chants about other body systems using pulse and pattern. Add instruments or sounds that reflect the system patterns.

17. What different body parts are used to sing? Where are they in the body and how do they work together?

    *lungs, diaphragm, mouth, lips, tongue, vocal chords, etc.*

18. As I play an instrument, you will move the corresponding body part. Use the chart below as a key:

    | | | |
    |---|---|---|
    | Head = *woodblock* | Fingers = *triangle* | Spine = *ratchet* |
    | Hips = *hand drum* | Elbows/Knees = *guiro* | Toes = *shakers* |

19. As I play each block on the temple blocks (there are five different pitches), move your body at one joint. Change the speed, pulse and pattern of the pitches.

20. Walk with a pulse in your feet around the room while clapping a different pattern with your hands. Move your feet in a rhythmic pattern while clapping the pulse with your hands.

21. How many different musical sounds can we create with our bodies? What body parts make these sounds?

    | | | |
    |---|---|---|
    | *voice, throat, lungs* | *chest, lap (patting)* | *claps, snaps, stomps* |
    | *tongue clucks* | *teeth clicks* | *feet walking* |

22. Sing *The Hokey Pokey* and move your body parts to the words.

23. Chant or sing the following song. Point to or touch the body part as you sing. Start out slowly and each time you repeat, get faster. Make up new words for different parts of the body.

    *Head and shoulders, knees and toes, knees and toes!*
    *Head and shoulders, knees and toes, knees and toes!*
    *Eyes and ears and mouth and nose,*
    *Head and shoulders, knees and toes, knees and toes!*

24. Sing other songs that teach the parts of the body or make up your own:

    *Eye Winker Chin Chopper, Looby Loo, Father Abraham*

25. For young children, sing many songs that have hand motions or actions to work on small-motor/upper body skills. It is fun to act out the hand motions with your feet and legs (lower body) the second time.

    | *Itsy Bitsy Spider* | *This Old Man* | *The Bus Song* |
    | *He's Got the Whole World* | *I'm a Little Teapot* | *Patty Cake, Patty Cake* |
    | *Where Is Thumbkin?* | *Pick a Bale of Cotton* | |

26. What body parts are used to play the following instruments? How are they used? Think of other ways the instruments could be played. What other instruments can you think of? What body parts are used to play them?

    Hand Drum - *hands, knuckles, fingers, palms, back of hand, knee, elbow, head, hip, fingernails, forehead.*

    Xylophone - *fingers, hands, knuckles*

    Recorder - *mouth, lips, lungs, fingers, hands, firms, spine*

## Five Senses

1. Music: *I Am the Song, #2 Samba, K. Nichols.* Use the song as a copy-me game with the teacher. Place an object or two-handed percussion instrument (cow bell, hand drum, etc.) in your hands. Students face the teacher. Make up a four-pulse phrase with your instrument while moving it right to left, up to down or diagonally. Freeze while the students copy with their instruments. Continue this game throughout the song. It assists in developing eye tracking.

2. Play the game *Say Say Oh Playmate*, doing the actions with your partner. Repeat the exercise with eyes closed.

3. Practice reading a music score: left to right, top to bottom. For younger students, practice following the words to a well-known song or create picture symbols for the song.

4. Use the Orff symbols for percussion instruments to designate what sounds to play. You can use these symbols or create your own.

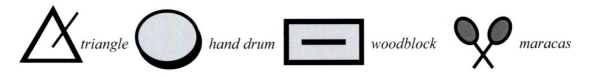

5.  Use short vertical lines to indicate pulses or patterns. Students look at the lines and play the rhythm on their instrument.

6.  Use colors or shapes to indicate different sounds:

    Yellow = *voices*    Red = *body percussion*    Blue = *instruments*

7.  Create partner clapping games to familiar rhymes to work on hand-eye coordination.

    Pattern:  P   C   R   C   L   C   B

    Key:  P : pat both hands on your lap         C : clap your hands together
          R : clap your partner's right hand     L : clap your partner's left hand
          B : clap both hands with your partner

8.  Play *Button, Button, Who's Got The Button?* and other circle "hiding" games. Sing the song as the object is passed behind backs. The person in the middle of the circle must guess where the object is at the end of the song. Fake passes are part of the game.

9.  Sing *Me Stone Miss Mary, Obwisana* and play other stone passing circle games with your students. Start with one stone and add more as needed.

10. Music: *I Am the Song, #14 Sansa Kroma, K. Nichols*. Use this music to do rhythm stick activities. Practice playing pulses and patterns with the sticks, echoing a partner or in unison with the class. Combine the techniques below to create interesting patterns.

    a.  Click your sticks together, right stick on top; click your sticks together, left stick on top; alternate. Click them on a pulse; click them on a pattern.

    b.  Tap both sticks on the floor together; alternate tapping the right stick and the left stick. Tap them in a pulse; tap them in a pattern.

    c.  Tap the sticks on different body parts: lap and shoulders. Alternate or cross your sticks as you tap them on your body. Tap one stick on the floor and one stick on your lap; switch.

    d.  Toss the right stick (half toss) into the right hand; repeat with the left stick. Alternate right and left tosses. Toss both sticks at the same time. Switch-toss the sticks laterally into the opposite hand (takes practice). Toss the one in your strongest hand over the other stick.

e. Once you become adept at the above techniques, try them with your eyes closed. Keep this activity safe by never tossing your stick above your neck or out of your space.

11. Play different instrument sounds from behind a desk. Students can respond through movement, drawing or giving verbal answers.

12. Listen to these three instruments: *triangle, drum, woodblock*. Describe the sound of each instrument. Compare and contrast.

13. Hang up a large towel or sheet to make a hidden screen. Play three different sounds from behind the screen. What sounds did you hear? How many times? Find new ways to play this game.

14. Play the Echo Game with your partner using body percussion or small percussion instruments. One partner claps an eight-pulse phrase and the other echoes it back. The first partner claps their phrase again, but this time, the second partner changes one thing about it. The third time, partner one claps their phrase and the second partner completely changes it.

15. List sounds you might hear during the day. What sounds might you hear during the night? Create these sounds.

    *fire engine, whispering/gossiping, scream, laugh,
    shout, cheer, cry, talk, sing, sneeze, cough, whistle*

16. Find different textures that you can touch: skin, carpet, hairbrush, desk, fabric, wall, ceiling, etc. What kind of sound would you make to describe each texture? What instruments "sound" like each texture?

17. Name some different textures/touches: smooth, slippery, bumpy, sharp, scratchy, rough, etc. How can we recreate these textures in sound?

18. Feel the vibrations as you play the drum or blow on a bottle. Where do you feel the vibrations? Play a recorder or vibraslap. How are the vibrations the same or different? Where do you feel vibrations in your body when you sing? Speak? Shout? Whisper?

19. Close your eyes and I will hand you an instrument. Can you identify the instrument using your sense of touch?

20. Touch two different instruments: a triangle and woodblock. Are they the same temperature? Why or why not?

21. What vocal or instrumental sounds could you make to express the following tastes?
    *sweet, salty, sour, bitter, bland, spicy*

22. Use different touches to produce a variety of sounds on your hand drum.

    a. *gently flutter your fingertips on the skin*
    b. *circle your palm across the surface of the skin, back and forth, fast and slow*
    c. *sharply flick your fingernail off the skin of the drum*
    d. *bounce your knuckles on the skin, on the rim*
    e. *strike the skin with a flat, sharp, stiff hand*
    f. *bounce your hand off the skin loosely*

23. Bring some spices for your class to smell. Disguise the bottle so they will need to use their sense of smell to identify the spices. Chant the spices rhythmically.

    *Cloves and spice,   oh how nice!   Cinnamon, garlic,   peppermint and thyme!*

24. Describe different smells rhythmically through rhymes. Add actions and keep a steady pulse on a drum. Play the rhythm of the words on a wood block to accompany the voices.

    *Pepper, mustard,   cinnamon stick,   eat too much and you'll   really get sick!*

25. Bring a tasty treat into class for the students to share. Afterwards, have them write a rhythmic poem or song about the treat.

26. What songs do we know that refer to food? What tastes are the songs referring to? How do we feel about those tastes? Let's sing the songs in class.

    *I Think I'll Eat Some Worms*     *On Top of Spaghetti Hot*
    *Patty Cake*                      *Cross Buns*
    *Bananas.Coconuts & Grapes*       *One Potato, Two Potato*
    *Soup, Soup*                      *Toot Sweet*

27. Make up a chant or tune about the five senses. Ask each small group to create a musical piece about one of the senses. Perform all of the parts together into a Sensory Rondo.

## Music Moments To Teach Academics: Wellness and Music

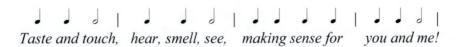

Taste and touch, hear, smell, see, making sense for you and me!

28. List all the things you might see in a day. Make up a rap or song about them. Repeat the exercise for the other senses. Share your pieces with the class.

**Nutrition**

1. Chant the different food groups: *fruits and vegetables; nuts, seeds and legumes; meats; dairy; fish and poultry, breads and cereals.*

2. List all the foods you can think of for the dairy group. Make up a rap or song about them. Repeat the exercise for the other food groups. Share your pieces with the class.

3. Assign an instrument sound to each food group. Hold up a picture of some kind of food. Students indicate which food group it belongs to by playing the correct instrument.

4. Choose eight foods that belong to a food group and sing them on the notes of the scale. Repeat the exercise for other food groups.

| eggs | milk | cheese | cream | butter | ice cream | yogurt | curds |
|------|------|--------|-------|--------|-----------|--------|-------|
| do   | re   | mi     | fa    | so     | la        | ti     | do    |

5. Use the tune of *The More We Get Together* to make up a song about the importance of drinking water. Eight glasses of water per day are needed for optimum brain function and to wash toxins from the environment and foods out of the body. Make up a pulse accompaniment by striking glasses with different amounts of water in them.

   Sung    *The more we drink our water, our water, our water,*
           *The more we drink our water, the healthier we'll be!*
           *To wash out the toxins and keep our brains rockin'!*
           *The more we drink our water, the healthier we'll be!*

   Spoken  *One glass, two glasses, three glasses, four,*
           *Five glasses, six glasses, seven, eight and more!*

6. Make up a chant or song about vitamins and minerals. Make a list of different vitamins and minerals, the foods they are found in and what they do. Use this information to create lyrics for your rap or song.

7. Talk about sugar, caffeine and other chemicals. Make up a chant about them and the foods they are found in.

8. Make a list of foods that are good for us, ones that we should limit, and ones to avoid for health's sake. Create three different musical settings for each: good, moderate and bad. What instruments and voices should we use to express each list?

9. What ingredients are needed to bake a cake? Can you chant them in a rhythmic pattern?

    Divide into groups and let each group make up a chant and movement sequence for one of the ingredients. Layer the parts in as you "mix up the batter."

10. Make up a nonsense recipe for a fictional food. Turn this into a rap or song and share with the class. Add instruments or other sounds.

## Movement

1. Use a variety of props in a rhythmic activity to increase coordination and overall fitness. Use pulse and pattern games, grouping and partner games to motivate the activities. Add clear, pulse music at the correct tempo to support the work.

    a. Bounce a ball to the pulse of the music; bounce it in a rhythmic pattern; bounce it in a grouping of two (bounce-catch) or three (bounce-catch-hold). Bounce it to a partner or around a group of four.

    b. Follow the rhythm stick activities described earlier.

    c. Toss bean bags and catch them to a pulse or rhythm.

    d. Play hopscotch using a variety of pulses and patterns. Try it sideways, backwards or with a partner. Make up rhymes or chants that match the pattern of your feet.

    e. There are numerous jump rope chants and songs to practice jump roping. Use a pulse and counting or patterns to increase the difficulty (suggestions: *Let's Slice the Ice, Circle Round the Zero* and *Step It Down*). Search for these chants on the internet.

    f. What other props can you use rhythmically?

2. Play rhythmic or motivational music to practice exercises or calisthenics.

3. Use folk dances and square dances to teach other movement skills as well as formation, rhythm and cooperation.

4. Find and play the old *Chicken Fat* record for kids to do warm-ups and exercises.

5. Start a stomp or step group at your school. Resources can be found in the list of links on page 247. These groups focus on rhythmic movement, discipline and cooperation with others.

6. Incorporate creative dance into lessons to foster creativity, problem solving, learning, cooperation and increase brain function.

7. Use pulse, pattern and rhythm to practice skills for sports: basketball, soccer, tennis, etc.

8. Use soft, relaxing music (see Discography) for cool-downs, stretching and breath work before and after a period of activity.

9. Use appropriate music to practice the concepts of movement. For more ideas, see *Music For Dancers* by Kerri Lynn Nichols or *Teaching Creative Dance* by Anne Green Gilbert:

*Place* (self and general) - *Music for Dancers, #20 Paraphony & Polyphony.*
   A section: non-locomotor movements; B section: locomotor.
   *Music for Dancers, Too! #3 Jammin' in De Jungle.*
   A section: locomotor movements; B section: non-locomotor movements

*Size* (big, medium, small) - *Music for Dancers, #16 Voices.*
   Start by moving with the pinky finger. As the music repeats, add bigger body parts until you are dancing with full body. Reverse.
   *Music for Dancers, Too! #7 Shape, Wiggle & Go!*
   A section: make big shapes; B section: small wiggles; C section: travel medium

*Level* (high, middle, low) - *Music for Dancers, #4 The Hi-Lo Waltz; Music for Dancers, Too! #4 Ups & Downs.*
   On the high notes, move at a high level. On the middle notes, move at a middle level. On the low notes, move at a low level.

*Direction* (right, left, up, down, forward, backward) - *Music for Dancers, #5, Ladders; Music for Dancers, Too! #8 Questions and Answers.*
   Move in a direction. When the music changes, move in a different direction.

*Pathway* (curved, straight, zig zag) - *Music for Dancers, #17 Ching, Clop, Boom!*.
   A section: move in a straight pathway; B section: move in a curvy pathway; C section: move in a zig zag pathway.
   *Music for Dancers, Too! #13 Circles & Squares.*
   Listen to the music and experiment with movement in curvy, straight and zigzag pathways both on the floor and in the air.

*Focus* (single, multi) - *Music for Dancers, #10 Rondo ala Copland.*
   When one instrument is playing, focus on one body part, person or spot while you move. When there is more than one instrument playing, move while changing your focus to different things.
   *Music for Dancers, Too! #10 Locomotion.*
   A section: dance using single focus (look at one object, person or thing)
   B sections: dance using multi-focus (keep changing your focus)

*Pace* (fast, medium, slow) - *Music for Dancers, #11 Three Paces; Music for Dancers, Too! #11 Gravity.*
   When the music is fast, move fast. When the music is slow, move slowly.

*Rhythm* (pulse, pattern) - *Music for Dancers, #1 Pulsation; Music for Dancers, Too! #1 One Bent Tulip.*
   When the music starts, move to create a rhythmic pattern. When the music changes, travel around the space with a pulse.

*Energy* (sharp and smooth) - *Music for Dancers, #13 Staccato Legato; Music for Dancers, #19 Consonance & Dissonance.*
   Move sharply and smoothly to match the energy of the changing music.

*Weight* (strong and light) - *Music for Dancers, #12 Quiet in the Library; Music for Dancers, Too! #12 Fee Fie Fo Fum.*
   Move lightly during the quiet music, strongly during the loud music.

*Flow* (free and bound) - *Music for Dancers, #13 Staccato Legato; Music for Dancers, #20 Paraphony & Polyphony.*
   When the music is flowing, move freely with your body. When the music is rhythmic, move stiffly or make shapes with your body.

*Body Shapes - I Am the Song, #2 Samba; Music for Dancers, #19 Mango Walk.*
   Half of the class freezes into shapes while the other half moves around those shapes. Movers copy a shape and then that person gets to move around. Take turns until the music is finished.

*Body Parts - Music for Dancers, #6 The Space Between Your Ears; Music for Dancers, Too! #6 Jigalig.*
   During the first section of music, move one body part. When the music changes, move a different body part.

*Relationships - I Am the Song, #21 Follow Me, Moon; Music for Dancers, Too! #The Return.*
   During the A section, mirror your partner in self space. When the music changes, shadow your partner through the room. Change leaders as the music repeats. Also, good for moving with props.

*Balance (on and off) - I Am the Song, #6 Journey to the Moon; Music for Dancers, Too! #9 Purcell Canon.*
   Slow, sustained music good for practicing yoga or balancing shapes. Practice going between on balance and off balance.

## Brain

1. Sing songs in class. Singing tones resonate the cells of the brain and body and promote health and healing. Particularly beneficial if you can add harmony to the singing.

2. Play musical-memory games and name games. Add hand motions and cross-lateral movements whenever possible to integrate both sides of the brain.

3. Play and listen to a variety of styles of music in class for different activities. Research has shown that a musical aural environment is an essential part of healthy brain development.

4. Use mallet instruments and rhythm sticks for various activities in class to stimulate the brain. Use hands simultaneously, alternating and crossing over each other.

5. Create body percussion pieces where the students are patting different parts of their bodies in different ways (sharp, smooth, strong, light) to provide sensory integration experiences.

*Music Moments To Teach Academics: Wellness and Music*

6. Check out the *Sound Health Series* of CDs. You can google these classical music CD's for thinking, reading, creating, concentrating and a wide variety of classroom activities which are available on several websites for purchase.

7. Play echo games in class, with one person clapping, saying, singing or playing a musical phrase and others echoing or changing it (QA). Try the skill of *looping*. The teacher plays a four-pulse phrase and, while the class is echoing, plays the next four-pulse phrase. This is a great brain game that challenges students to listen to a new pattern while playing the preceding one. This skill is often called *multi-tasking*, yet in actuality the brain is switching back and forth quickly between two skills.

8. Play *Chop Chop* with a partner. Place a chopstick, end to end, between your palm and your partner's palm. Move your hands without letting the chopstick fall to the floor. Once you feel confident, move your bodies around the room while balancing the chopstick. Take turns leading and following, changing directions and the position of the chopstick. Vary the brain integration by both using right hands, opposite hands or left hands. Try the activity with your feet, foreheads, shoulders and in other ways that challenge you (Music Suggestion: *I Am the Song, #6 or 12; Music for Dancers, Too! #9 or 21)*. (Idea adapted from Anne Green Gilbert).

9. Find ways in your daily classroom activities and experiences to practice the eight brain connection patterns discussed earlier in this book: *breath, tactile, core-distal, head-tail, upper-lower, body sides, cross-lateral and vestibular*. Use selections from *I Am the Song, Music for Dancers* and *Music for Dancers, Too!* that are four-five minutes in length.

10. For a great tactile activity, gather up balls of different sizes: tennis, playground, large exercise, etc. Divide the class into partners and give each pair a ball. One person lies on their stomach, while the other partner traces by rolling the ball along the edge of the body. Roll the ball over the length of the spine, adding gentle pressure and release. Find different ways of using the ball to massage your partner. Switch roles. Play relaxing music for this activity and keep the lighting soft (suggestion: *Will Ackerman: A Windham Hill Retrospective, #6)*.

11. Practice the movement patterns that conductors use when they lead an orchestra. Students may draw these on paper first to get a feel for the shape of each pattern. For a brain challenge, use both hands in a mirror image.

*Music Moments To Teach Academics: Wellness and Music*

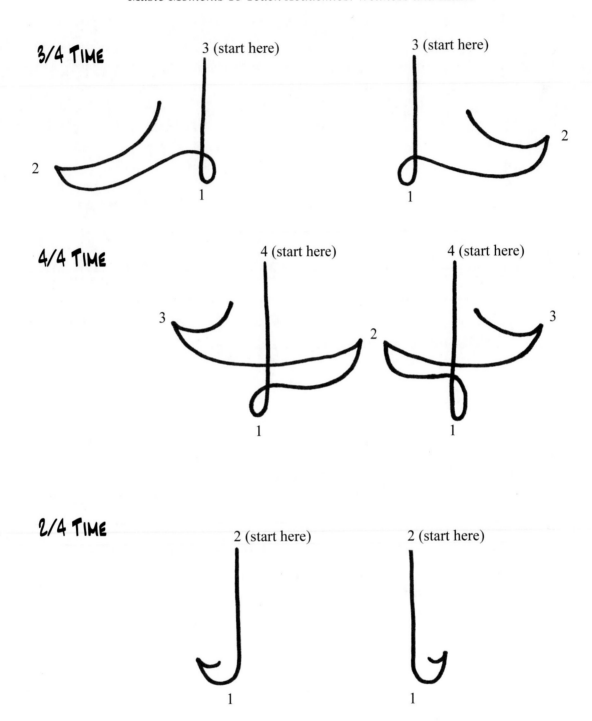

9. Integrate drumming or rhythm circles often to provide brain stimulus for your students. These can be done with body percussion, found sounds or traditional instruments. Two or three students should maintain a steady pulse in the center and the other students can improvise using some of the techniques described earlier and in the Resource section of this book.

## Wellness

1. How can you use your voice to express different emotions? Anger? Joy? Love? Sadness? Describe the changes in your voice. How do we interpret other people's voices and what they may be feeling?

    *pitch, volume, accents, staccato or legato, fast or slow, etc.*

2. Music: *I Am the Song, #8-12 Sticky Finger Suite, K. Nichols.* Listen to the various examples of music. What emotion or feeling do you associate with each? Write down your thoughts. What colors do you associate with these feelings? Can you cut out pictures, faces or scenes that seem to reflect each piece of music?

3. Music: *Journeys (all selections recommended), Carlos Nakai.* Lie down in a comfortable position or rest your head on your desk. Turn the lights down and listen to the music. Allow your creative mind to journey to a special place. Visualize every detail of the place and allow yourself to "be there" emotionally. Breathe in through your nose and out through your mouth as you are listening, relaxing your muscles. At the end of the listening period, allow yourself to "awaken" slowly. Without talking, draw a picture of the place or journal your thoughts and reflections.

4. Stand in a circle. One person walks along the inside of the circle, past the others, moving in his/her own rhythm. The group copies the movement and rhythm to affirm this person until he/she returns to his/her place in the circle. Repeat the exercise with the rest of the class.

5. Music: *I Am the Song, #14 Sansa Kroma or #8-12 Sticky Finger Suite. K. Nichols.* Sit with a partner, one behind the other. When the music starts, the back person lightly taps the pulse of the music on the front person's shoulders. The front person pats the pulse on their own lap. When the music changes, the partners turn around and repeat the process. Remember that there is more than one possible pulse (slow, medium, fast).

6. Provide healthy snacks for yourself and your students. Encourage students to choose protein snacks (which give your body/brain energy) over carbohydrates (which produce a tired, heavy feeling).

7. Encourage your students to actively make music over passive involvement whenever possible. Research has shown active music-making to be substantially more beneficial in terms of brain stimulus, skills development, motivation and overall wellness.

*Music Moments To Teach Academics: Wellness and Music*

8. Play recorders to develop strength against asthma (a growing epidemic for children in our country). This instrument is inexpensive, easy to learn and fun to play in a group.

9. Use active music-making in your class to help students combat anxiety, depression, loneliness and to develop bonds and community.

10. Incorporate environmental sounds (waves, waterfalls, rain) into the fabric of your class setting. These can be less "distracting" than some musical compositions and can enhance a relaxed learning atmosphere.

# Chapter Nine: Pedagogy: Tips for Success

*Pedagogy: Tips For Success*

1. Be positive. Sometimes kids portray a negative attitude toward music activities because it is "cool." If you are positive and energetic, and confident with your attitude towards music, your class will follow you. Provide older students with information about music, the brain and learning so they know that your motivation is to help them be successful.

2. Integrating music into your curriculum is not an easier method of teaching, but a better one that will enhance your students' learning and energize you as a teacher.

3. Use a "trial and error" approach as you get started with these music experiences. Trust that you know your students and that, together, you will figure out the best way to apply the suggestions in this book and create your own.

4. Take time in class to do team building activities using music and by other means. This helps to create a group synergy where students "buy in" to what is happening in the classroom. Spending time building the community of the group will save time and energy later and can prevent conflicts and competition from happening in class. Foster a cooperative learning model where I win when you win.

5. Structure provides a framework for creativity in any field. Give students the skills, structure and safety net they need to step out and take risks. At the same time, the less *you* do, the more *they* do, so allow space for them to try out new ideas, make mistakes and create successes for the group to build upon.

6. Spend some time gathering materials (CD's, songs, books, instruments and other music props) and building a quality, support system for your music endeavors. See the Resources section of this book for suggestions of excellent materials. Your support system can include online resources, local music specialists and musicians, and community music organizations.

7. As you integrate quality music experiences into your curriculum, be open to the students' suggestions and provide opportunities for them to listen to "their" music. A good rule of thumb is that music used in the classroom must not offend any person or any group of people. Kids understand the idea of community and generally want to do things that benefit the group. <u>Always</u> preview anything you plan on sharing with the students and if you have a question, ask your supervisor or a supportive colleague.

8. Create a pleasant learning environment that takes into account the lighting, sound, color scheme and space in the classroom. Here are some general suggestions to get started. You and your students can discuss others as the school year goes along. You will spend quite a bit of time together in the space and it is important that it supports learning.

*Lighting*  Fluorescent lighting is not learner-friendly. Bring in additional lighting (floor lamps or other small lights) to enhance or replace the track lighting or install adjustable lighting.

*Sound*  Take note of unusual noises that create a constant web of sound above and beyond the voices and movement in the classroom (fans, heating/cooling systems, freeway noise). Add nature sounds or very soft classical music to the setting.

*Colors*  Too many warm colors (reds, oranges, yellows) can breed a hyperactive classroom state while too many cool colors (blues, purples) can subdue or tire students. The best scheme is a blend of the two, or greens, which contain both elements of energy (yellow) and relaxation (blue).

*Space*  Arrange the furniture, equipment and your materials to provide the largest space for movement and group activities possible. Sort through things you do not need and do a "spring cleaning." A cluttered space is a stressful space for students and can tax the time of the teacher who can not find materials readily. Use large, clear (so you can see what is inside of them) storage boxes that you can stack for easy access to props and instruments. Create an organization system that the students can be in charge. This will save you time while also building ownership for the students and pride in the space.

9. Post the elements and concepts of music where the students can *access* and *use* them. This allows both you and the students to refer to the chart when you are integrating music into the classroom. Students gain new vocabulary and concepts which they can apply to other academic areas.

10. Use a conceptual focus when you teach a lesson. There should be one concept (academic, music or other) that runs through the various parts of the lesson. Provide opportunities for the students to work with the concept through introductory activities, exploration, skill development, creating and reflection/assessment (from teacher-directed to student-generated learning).

11. *Hear, see, say* and *do* the concept at the beginning of every lesson. This clarifies the focus of the lesson. By presenting the concept through four modes, you are working towards a 90% retention rate.

12. Present classroom activities through one mode at a time so that students can grasp the information. Take into account different learning styles, multiple intelligences and special needs within each setting.

## Pedagogy: Tips For Success

13. Use the *Three-Times-Is-A-Charm* rule: present your conceptual information at least three times over the course of a grading period. The first time, the students are being presented with new information. The second time, they are processing challenges and additional information. The third time, they are affirming what they know and restating it.

14. Music Moments should be designed using the following principles:

    1. *Socially enjoyable and stress free.*
    2. *Educationally fun.*
    3. *Everyone participates through listening, singing, playing instruments and incorporating rhythm activities.*

15. Foster an environment where every student knows each person's name and contribution to the group. Teach your students to value opinions and feelings and work hard to show respect for each other. Create goals as a team that are challenging but within reach.

16. Develop many modes of assessment that take into account multiple ways of knowing, individuality and self-evaluation. These might include writing and presenting songs or raps, playing instruments, group projects, video or audio taping, portfolios, artwork, dramatic presentations, tests, reports, interviews or observations. Create an assessment plan for your own teaching so that you can continue to improve. Ask your supervisor or a trusted colleague to help you and do some kind of journaling to keep track of your progress and reflections.

17. When you are clapping with young children (K-two), they will be more successful if you have them clap with one hand above the other (vertically). Meeting hands together at the midpoint of the body is a more advanced concept that is established after children progress through a variety of movement patterning stages. Patting is a better choice than clapping, with both hands on the body, either on the lap or the shoulders, where kids can "feel" the pulse.

18. Use circles as a ritual in your classroom for singing, rhythm or drum activities, sharing thoughts and ideas and for class discussions. In a circle, everyone can be seen and has an equal place and voice.

19. Whether you consider yourself a "singer" or not, sing with your students. The benefits far outweigh the challenges and you do not have to be a trained vocalist to lead songs. Once the kids know them, you will start the first two words and off they will go. If you make it a tradition, the students will really look forward to this time together. Find colleagues,

local artists, and CD's to support your efforts. Don't give up! Start with songs you are comfortable with and build upon your successes. Keep a notebook of your songs and lyrics that the students can access and copy. Eventually, you may have students who would like to act as the "song leader" for the day. Sing songs at any time of the day: welcome/good morning songs, songs for special occasions, transitions, music moments, clean-up time and saying goodbye.

20. Sing songs in an appropriate range for *children's voices*. This is generally between middle C (do) and high c (do). The younger the voice, the smaller the range (space between highest and lowest note in the song) should be. *So-mi, so-la-mi* and *pentatonic* songs are great for K-3rd grade, but other songs are acceptable. Use your best judgment and common sense when screening "children's music." As students become older, they can sing increasingly difficult songs. If you start a song too low, students will opt to "talk" through the pitches of the song instead of tune to the actual pitches and this is unhealthy, especially for the young voice. Many pop artists sing in a range that is not appropriate for children. When working with kids, use as little "weight" and vibrato in the voice as possible and try to keep the simple, pure quality of a child's voice. Men can use their falsetto, if they know how to, to match the range of the children.

21. Treat instruments with care. Learn appropriate technique from available sources and share that with the students. For the younger children, make instruments that can take the "wear and tear" of that age level. Purchase *high quality* instruments: choose a few key items instead of buying many at a cheaper cost and quality.

22. Incorporate as many movement activities as possible into the day for the students and yourself. Movement is the key to learning and is essential for brain function. Many of the music activities in this book are linked to academic concepts through movement. For more ideas about linking movement to your curricula, see *Teaching The Three R's Through Movement Experiences* by Anne Green Gilbert.

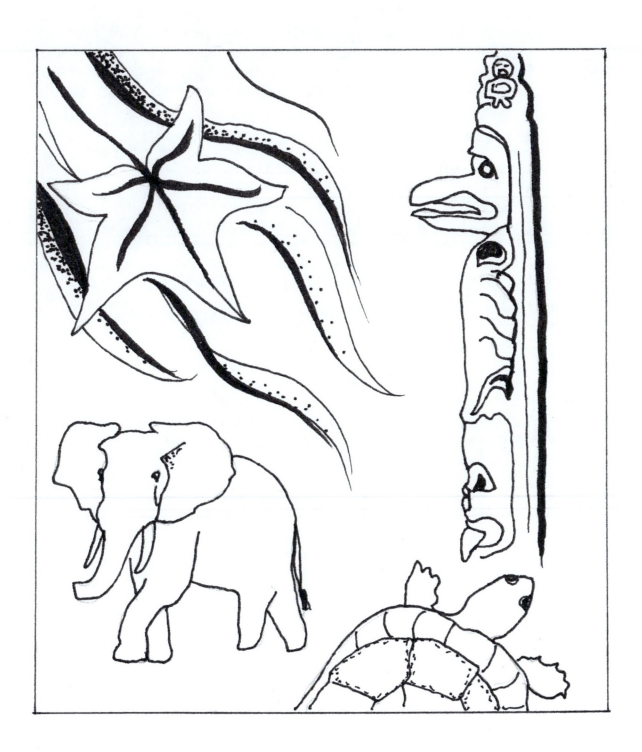

# Chapter Ten:
## *Resources*

## MATERIALS

1. **STREAMERS**

You can make these out of plastic table cloths that can be purchased at the arts and crafts store. The table cloths come in many colors, have great movement and texture, and can be cut into various shapes and sizes. This fabric also works great to make permanent charts for the classroom (use a permanent marker).

2. **BALLS**

Balls of all sizes and shapes are great props for movement and music. You can bounce tennis balls to the pulse and make up intricate patterns and dances with them.

3. **STICKS**

Cut these from 1/2" dowels; I suggest a hard wood like oak or maple over pine, because it splits apart. Cut 12" lengths for tossing and tapping exercises and 18" lengths for stick and Morris dances.

4. **SCARVES**

Cut desired lengths and various sizes from chiffon fabric available at fabric and costume display stores.

5. **SHAKERS**

Create great shakers from everyday items that are usually thrown away. A few favorites include aluminum cans (taped with duct tape), Parmesan cans and the cylinder-shaped three-minute plastic containers. Fill with small amounts of popcorn, rice, lentils or kidney beans for various sounds and pitches.

6. **CONTAINERS**

Save large plastic juice and milk containers and use them for pulse activities. Sticks or other odds and ends work great for mallets. Large, empty detergent boxes also have great sound. These "drums" double for objects to practice leaping and other movement concepts with.

7. **BALLOON BAGS**

Blow up several balloons and fill a large, brown garbage sack with them. Tie the bag securely. Place another bag over the first one with the opening at the opposite end. Tie securely. Students can hit the bag up in the air, keeping it off the ground for the length of a song. Use the piece *Kondo Yi* from *African Songs and Rhythms for Children* (W. K. Amoaku).

8.     BUCKETS
Ask your custodian to save 30 white wax buckets from the district for you. Using a pair of sticks for mallets, create different sounds with these buckets by striking them on the top, rim, sides, etc. Large tub or muck buckets can be found at the home supply store and make great bass drums. Match the tub pitches to the scale. Buy different sizes to create different pitches.

9.     TIMBALE STICKS
Long, slender dowels which are light in weight and timbre are good for rhythm activities and serve as mallets for a variety of instruments.

10.    WATER JUGS
These are the blue, plastic containers that offices often recycle, and they come in a variety of sizes. You might find them at the local distributing company for $1 a piece. They make fantastic congas (each has a different pitch) and can produce a variety of sounds. Water jugs make particularly good dance props as they are lightweight, durable and easy to handle.

11.    JUNK
Scour your kitchen, garage or a local sale for objects that make interesting sounds. Dustpans, brooms, utensils and assorted throwaways can be recycled to create fantastic instruments and dance props. Glasses with water make great pitch instruments.

12.    CHAIRS
Students love to drum on the plastic and metal chairs they sit on in class. Use timbale sticks or dowels for mallets. Scrape the back rungs, hit the seats and tap the legs for different sounds.

13.    BOXES
Cardboard boxes of all sizes are useful for dance props, rhythm work and creative dramatics as well as serving as storage. I like to use the 8 x 8-inch cube size in your work with children. Order these from an online paper mart to save money and use clear packing tape to seal.

14.    CUPS
Plastic cups in a variety of sizes and colors are wonderful for percussion sounds and alternative notation experiences. You can use the light-weight plastic party cups available at most grocery stores or move up to the sturdier tumbler type sold by Tupperware or other stores usually in the summer months.

15.    OBJECTS
Use everyday objects for storytelling, rhythmic explorations, passing and hiding games and alternative notation. Some favorites are thimbles, oversize buttons, wooden spoons and utensils, coins and stones.

*Music Moments To Teach Academics: Resources*

16. PAPER & MARKERS

Keep an assortment of large paper and colored markers to use in your experiences with the students. Use music to help your students visually represent concepts such as form, rhythm, shape, symmetry, repetition, story, contrast handwriting and relationships. This helps to integrate the visual, auditory and kinetic modes of learning while providing a positive outlet for expression, individuality and eye tracking skills.

17. JUMBO POST-ITS

Purchase these from an office supply store. You can write lyrics, equations, forms and other information on them and fold and keep them for other classes. These are particularly wonderful for the teacher who always misplaces the tape!

18. SPOTS

Use round mouse pads (purchased from IKEA) to create spots for the students to sit or stand on in the space. Thes help the students make circles (a difficult skill!) or find spaces around the room without colliding.

19. WHACKA-NOODLES

Make Whacka-Noodles by purchasing the long, five-foot foam swimming noodles available at many toy stores. Cut them into one-foot lengths and use them for rhythmic activities, "body" mallets, dance props and lots of fun.

20. STRETCHY BANDS

Purchase lightweight Spandex or other stretchy material from your local fabric store. The fabric usually comes in 45'' or 60'' widths. Cut strips about six inches in length (or wider if you want to make a body sock) and tie the ends together. These are good for a variety of movement and partnering experiences.

21. FOAM PADS

Available from craft stores, these brightly colored foam rectangles come in a variety of sizes. With a permanent marker, write one number (1-8) or pitch on each different color to create a visual scale that the students can walk on and sing (like steps on a pathway).

*Music Moments To Teach Academics: Resources*

## MUSICAL NAME GAMES

*RHYTHM (pulse, pattern, grouping)*

Say and clap the syllables of your name. The class echoes. Continue around the circle with all the names, then, together, clap the "rhythms" (syllables) of each name around the circle without stopping (most names have one, two, three or four syllables or claps).

Sitting in a circle, the group pats a pulse or pattern on their laps (or claps) while the names are chanted around the circle.

*MELODY (pitch, scale, interval)*

Sing your name in a rhythm with the pitches *so* and *mi* (five-three) and the group will echo you. Continue around circle.

Sing your name on any notes you want and the group echoes you. In small groups, perform four name "motives" in a sequence to create a melody.

*FORM (motive, phrase, repeat, contrast)*

Create a rondo form chant using *"Name, name, what's in a name? If you think of it, there's a game in your name"* (eight counts). The group chants together, then improvises using the first person's name with speech, singing, sounds and body percussion (eight counts). The group returns to the chant, then improvises on the next name. Continue for all names.

Create an A B A B form by having one person say or sing their name while the group echoes it exactly (A). The next person says or sings their name and the group contrasts it (B). Keep alternating around the circle.

*EXPRESSION (dynamics, articulations, pace, style)*

Say or sing your name softly, loudly, accented, staccato, legato, fast or slow. The group echoes you. Once the group knows all the names, they can choose one expression concept to perform together.

Sing your name in a particular style: reggae, opera, country, Gregorian Chant, jazz and the group echoes you, or choose one style and improvise together for eight counts.

*TIMBRE (body, voice, percussion, instruments)*

Say your name while playing the rhythm (syllables) patterns with body percussion (clap, stomp, pat, snap). Accentuate or change the way you enunciate your name through speech (stutter, stretch vowels, whisper).

Play your name in a repeated pattern on a small percussion instrument while a steady pulse is maintained elsewhere (feet, ceremonial drum, desks). The group echoes you. Perform the names together in a Name Orchestration.

*TEXTURE (combinations, harmony, accompaniment)*

The first person in the circle chants their name in a repetitive rhythm. The next person listens to that rhythm and chants their own name in a complementary pattern. Continue around the circle until all names are chanted.

Sing your name on a slow, melodic motive. The group repeats your name, some singing your notes and others voicing harmony.

*Music Moments To Teach Academics: Resources*

## VOCAL WARM-UPS FOR BEGINNING VOICES

I. Posture/Stance

    a. Marionettes (loose joints and spine, string pulls from top of head)
    b. Hands on the head; then fall to the sides, hanging heavily
    c. Shoulder movements, head circles, spinal roll-downs
    d. Jaw massage ("balk, balk" like a chicken!)

II. Breath Support

    a. Hip hip hip hip, hippopotamus    5   5   5   5   5 4   3 2   1
    b. Whooo-K (hold breath at the end of "whoo-"; release on "k")
    c. Single, double and triple hisses (S, SS, SSS)
    d. Press out arms, stretch up and behind the head, drop
    e. Hey hey hey, hee hee hee, ho ho ho, hoo hoo hoo

    5-3-1    5-3-1    5-3-1    5-3-1

III. Connection/Placement

    a. Vocal exploration sounds (caw, quack, meow, siren, etc.)
    b. Breath of surprise (you've just won a million dollars!)
    c. Inner humming (5 4 3 2 1) with mouth open
    d. Yawn-sighs

IV. Resonance/Vowels

    a. Pie, die, sigh - each on 1 2 3 2   1 slowly (stay on ah vowel)
    b. Hung - eeee (5----54321), staying on the *ng* sound on pitch 5
    c. Psalm, set, see, saw, soon (say or sing on one or more pitches)
    d. Ninety-nine nuns interned in an Indiana nunnery (use a different vowel).

V. Articulation/Consonants

    a. Tongue twisters
    b. The tip of the tongue, the lips and the teeth! (speak faster and faster)

        8    5    3    1    8    5    3    1
    c. We love to sing, indeed we do!
    d. Super bubble gum (5 4 3 2 1); super-duper bubble gum, (55-44-33-22-1);
        Super-duper double bubble, super-duper double bubble, (55-44-33-22) 2X
        Super-duper double bubble gum (55-44-33-22-1); YUM!

*Music Moments To Teach Academics: Resources*

## FAMILIAR TUNES FOR SINGING OR LYRIC WRITING

| | | |
|---|---|---|
| *The Ants Go Marching* | *Alphabet Song* | *Are You Sleeping?* |
| *A-Hunting We Will Go* | *Alouette* | *The Ash Grove* |
| *Auld Lang Syne* | *Bingo* | *Blowin' in the Wind* |
| *Big Rock Candy Mountain* | *Broadway Tunes* | *Beatles Tunes* |
| *The Bear Went over the Mountain* | *Christmas Carols* | *Clementine* |
| *Camptown Races* | *Dem Dry Bones* | *Day-O* |
| *Itsy Bitsy Spider* | *Erie Canal* | *Edelweiss* |
| *Famous Classical Tunes* | *Frere Jacques* | *Farmer in the Dell* |
| *Five Foot Two, Eyes of Blue* | *Glory, Glory Hallelujah* | *Go Tell Aunt Rhody* |
| *Go Tell It on the Mountain* | *Hokey Pokey* | *Hot Cross Buns* |
| *Here We Go Looby Loo* | *Hush Little Baby* | *Happy Birthday* |
| *How Much Is That Doggie?* | *Hickory Dickory Dock* | *Home on the Range* |
| *He's Got the Whole World* | *Heart and Soul* | *Nobody Home* |
| *I Know an Old Lady Who. . .* | *I'm a Little Teapot* | *It's a Small World* |
| *I'd Like to Teach the World to Sing* | *If I Had a Hammer* | *Jingle Bells* |
| *If You're Happy and You Know It* | *Jack and Jill* | *Kookaburra* |
| *I've Been Workin' on the Railroad* | *King of the Road* | *Jacob Jingleheimer* |
| *Louie, Louie* | *Let It Be* | *La Bamba* |
| *London Bridge* | *Lean on Me* | *Lullaby (Brahms)* |
| *Make New Friends* | *Musicals (Tunes from)* | *Michael Row the Boat* |
| *Muffin Man* | *Mary Had a Little Lamb* | *The Mulberry Bush* |
| *My Bonnie Lies over the Ocean* | *On Top of Spaghetti* | *The Old Grey Mare* |
| *O Danny Boy* | *Old MacDonald* | *Over the Rainbow* |
| *Patriotic Songs* | *Pop! Goes the Weasel* | *Puttin' on the Ritz* |
| *Paw Paw Patch* | *Pat-A-Cake* | *Peas Porridge Hot* |
| *Popular Tunes* | *Ring Around the Rosy* | *Rockabye, Baby* |
| *R.E.S.P.E.C.T.* | *Swing on a Star* | *Row Your Boat* |
| *Shoo Fly* | *Skip to My Lou* | *Simple Gifts* |
| *She'll Be Comin' Round the Mountain* | *Twinkle Twinkle* | *Little White Duck* |
| *This Old Man* | *This Little Light* | *This Land* |
| *Twist and Shout* | *That's Amore!* | *Three Blind Mice* |
| *Where, Oh Where?* | *Where Is Thumbkin?* | *Wheels on the Bus* |
| *The Water Is Wide* | *Weavily Wheat* | *Waltzing Matilda* |
| *You Are My Sunshine* | *Yellow Submarine* | *Yankee Doodle* |

*Music Moments To Teach Academics: Resources*

## FORMS AND STRUCTURES FOR MUSIC MAKING

| | | |
|---|---|---|
| 1. | *Tunes We Know* | Take a familiar tune and write new lyrics to it using an academic concept (piggyback song). |
| 2. | *Chanting* | Use a steady pulse or pattern to chant various words, concepts or memorization facts. |
| 3. | *Body Percussion* | Use claps, pats, snaps, stomps and other sounds to accompany chanting, practice math or spelling facts, enliven a lesson or to add a tactile brain activity. |
| 4. | *Voice* | Use the four voices (sing, speak, whisper, shout) and a variety of vocal sounds for chanting or singing facts, patterns, adding interest to a lesson, to resonate cells and to activate different parts of the brain. |
| 5. | *Percussion* | Use small percussion instruments for punctuation, accompaniment, accents, question/answer and to play rhythmic patterns for a variety of topics. |
| 6. | *Choral Speaking* | Use combinations of voices (solo, duet, trio, quartet, etc.) to add interest to oral reading, poetry, multiplication tables and other academic concepts. |
| 7. | *Echo* | Echo chants of facts and figures through repetition. |
| 8. | *Call/Response (Q/A)* | Chant or sing a question and the students chant or sing an answer. Chant an equation and the students chant the answer. |
| 9. | *Rondo* | Create a repeated chant, rhythm or melody using an academic concept that forms the A section. Students can create B, C, D sections on a related theme, with the whole class performing A between every section. |
| 10. | *So-mi (5-3) Melodies* | Use the so-mi (high-low) pitches to make up easy song/chants about various academic concepts. To get fancy, add so-la-so-mi (5-6-5-3) to your tune. |

11. *Contrast* — Use contrasting musical concepts (high-low, loud-soft, sharp-smooth, short-sustained, pulse-pattern, voice sounds-body percussion, up-down, repeat-contrast, rhythm-melody, sing-speak) to make up academic games/explorations in class.

12. *16 Counts* — In two groups (teacher/students, partners or half and half), use 16 pulses to pose a question or problem and 16 pulses to answer or solve it. Great for math and spelling chants, history and science facts. Chant an academic concept or topic for 16 counts, then improvise and "play with" the idea for 16 counts with voice, body percussion and other found sounds.

13. *Improvisation* — Improvise short sections between chants or songs to enliven a lesson and provide brain recuperation.

14. *Soundscapes* — With or without visual representation, create a variety of soundscapes focusing on different academic concepts: person, place or thing; math or spelling; historical date or figure; ocean, desert, marsh or city.

## "City Scape"

| vehicles | sirens | trash cans |
|---|---|---|
| voices | industries | crosswalk lights |
| children playing | dog & cat sounds | doors |

15. *Block Charts* — Use block charts to create rhythmic patterns of sound using math equations, spelling words or other facts. Mark an X or a letter or other sound in each box to be played. Change the format to add parts or develop a longer sequence. (See grids on the next page.)

*Music Moments To Teach Academics: Resources*

## SAMPLE BLOCK CHARTS

| **1** | 2 | **3** | 4 |
|---|---|---|---|
|  |  |  |  |
|  |  |  |  |

| **1** | 2 | **1** | 2 | 3 |
|---|---|---|---|---|
|  |  |  |  |  |
|  |  |  |  |  |

| **1** | 2 | **3** | 4 | **5** | 6 | **7** | 8 |
|---|---|---|---|---|---|---|---|
|  |  |  |  |  |  |  |  |
|  |  |  |  |  |  |  |  |
|  |  |  |  |  |  |  |  |
|  |  |  |  |  |  |  |  |

| **1** | 2 | 3 | **4** | 5 | 6 | **7** | 8 | 9 | **10** | 11 | 12 |
|---|---|---|---|---|---|---|---|---|---|---|---|
|  |  |  |  |  |  |  |  |  |  |  |  |
|  |  |  |  |  |  |  |  |  |  |  |  |
|  |  |  |  |  |  |  |  |  |  |  |  |
|  |  |  |  |  |  |  |  |  |  |  |  |
|  |  |  |  |  |  |  |  |  |  |  |  |

| **1** | 2 | 3 | **4** | 5 | 6 | **7** | 8 | 9 | **10** | 11 | 12 |
|---|---|---|---|---|---|---|---|---|---|---|---|
|  |  |  |  |  |  |  |  |  |  |  |  |
|  |  |  |  |  |  |  |  |  |  |  |  |
|  |  |  |  |  |  |  |  |  |  |  |  |
|  |  |  |  |  |  |  |  |  |  |  |  |
|  |  |  |  |  |  |  |  |  |  |  |  |

Permission granted to photocopy.

*Music Moments To Teach Academics: Resources*

## SIMPLE RHYTHMIC NOTATION

| | | |
|---|---|---|
| Whole Note (four pulse counts) | 𝅝 | movement words: *rise* or *fall* |
| Whole Rest (four pulse counts) | 𝄻 | (silently think the words above) |
| Half Note (two pulse counts) | 𝅗𝅥 | movement word: *stretch* |
| Half Rest (two pulse counts) | 𝄼 | (silently think the word above) |
| Quarter Note (one pulse count) | ♩ | movement word: *walk* |
| Quarter Rest (one pulse count) | 𝄽 | (silently think the word above) |
| Eighth Notes (1/2 pulse count) | ♫ | movement word: *tip(toe)* |
| Eighth Rest (1/2 pulse count) | 𝄾 𝄾 | (silently think the word above) |
| Sixteenth Notes (1/4 pulse count) | ♬ | movement words: *wig(gle) jig(gle)* |
| Sixteenth Rest (1/4 pulse count) | 𝄿 𝄿 𝄿 𝄿 | (silently think the word(s) above |

*Example One*
   In 4/4 time

*Example Two*
   In 4/4 time:

# MELODY CHART

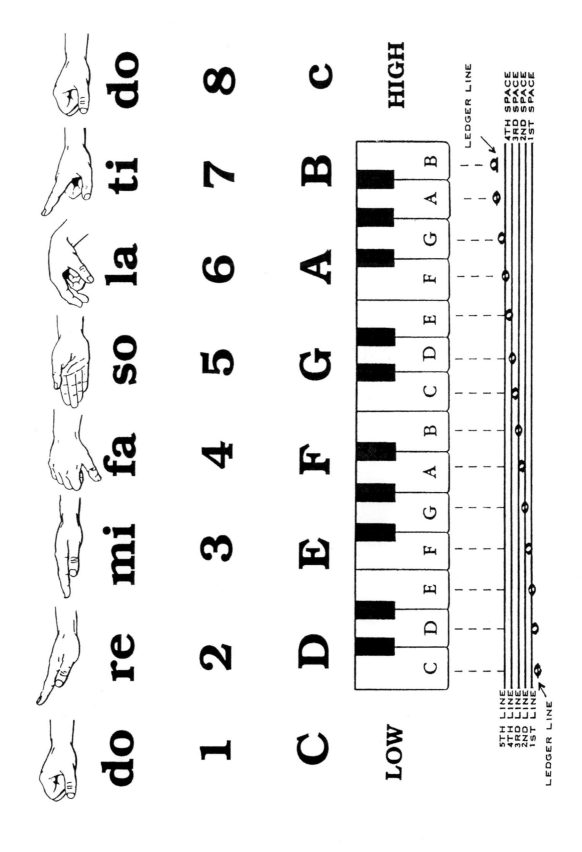

## GLOSSARY OF MUSICAL TERMS

| | |
|---|---|
| **a cappella** | *Traditionally, vocal music without instrumental accompaniment.* |
| **accellerando** | *Gradually becoming faster.* |
| **accent** | *Emphasis or stress placed on a given note.* |
| **accompaniment** | *Usually the parts of the music that go with or support the melody.* |
| **adagio** | *Slowly; leisurely.* |
| **additive form** | *A form created by layering repeated parts into the music.* |
| **Aeolian** | *A modal scale that may begin on A (using the white keys on a piano); melancholy in nature.* |
| **allegretto** | *Moderately fast; slower than allegro.* |
| **allegro** | *Lively; brisk; quick.* |
| **alto** | *The lowest female vocal part.* |
| **andante** | *Moderately slow.* |
| **arpeggio** | *The notes of a chord played in a consecutive, broken pattern rather than simultaneously.* |
| **articulation** | *The specific manner in which a note is performed.* |
| **bass** | *The lowest part; also refers to the lowest male singing voice.* |
| **beat** | *A steady, continuous pulse.* |
| **binary form** | *A two-part song form; AB.* |
| **block chart** | *A system for writing out polyrhythms using pulse groups.* |
| **body percussion** | *The practice of creating rhythm using the body (claps, snaps, pats and stomps).* |
| **bridge** | *A section in a musical composition that connects two other sections.* |
| **cadence** | *The end of a musical phrase, period or section.* |
| **canon** | *A compositional form in which one part is strictly imitated in at least one other part at a given time interval.* |
| **chaconne** | *A variation form based on a continuous, repeated baseline and harmonic progression.* |
| **chord** | *Three or more tones sounded simultaneously.* |
| **chorus** | *The primary, repeated theme (section) in a song; also refers to a large group of singers.* |
| **coda** | *A musical supplement to the end of a composition.* |

| | |
|---|---|
| **complementary** | *In rhythm, two patterns which fit together and complete each other.* |
| **contour** | *Shape; usually the shape of the melody (melodic contour).* |
| **contrast** | *A change; something different; opposite or contrary.* |
| **crescendo** | *Increasing in loudness.* |
| **decrescendo** | *Decreasing in loudness.* |
| **descant** | *A melody sung or played above the principal melody.* |
| **development** | *A section of the music where the composer elaborates upon the theme.* |
| **Dorian** | *A modal scale beginning on D; noble or serene in nature.* |
| **duet** | *A composition for two performers.* |
| **dynamics** | *A term applying to the varying degrees of volume.* |
| **echo process** | *An approach to learning a composition by rote; the leader plays or sings a phrase of music and the group repeats it.* |
| **ensemble** | *A group of musicians instrumentalists or vocalists) who perform together.* |
| **expression** | *Refers to the way in which the music is performed or interpreted; techniques used to communicate the message or emotion of the music.* |
| **fermata** | *Hold; pause.* |
| **fine** | *End; close.* |
| **form** | *The manner in which a piece of music is put together; the design or overall shape of a composition.* |
| **forte** | *Loud.* |
| **glockenspiel** | *A small, percussion instrument with metal bars.* |
| **grouping** | *The practice of organizing music into sets of two or three pulses; also called meter.* |
| **harmony** | *The quality of sound produced when two or more pitches are sounded simultaneously.* |
| **heel-toe** | *Also called a fishtail, this conga stroke is produced by striking the heel of the hand on the drum skin first and then letting the fingertips fall onto the skin.* |
| **home tone** | *The first note of a given scale; the pitch (key) a musical composition is based on.* |
| **improvisation** | *Creating music spontaneously; most closely associated with jazz and rock performances although practiced by musicians from all periods.* |
| **interval** | *The distance between two pitches.* |

| | |
|---|---|
| **intro** | *An opening section of a composition.* |
| **inversion** | *The transferring of a lower pitch of an interval or chord an octave higher or a higher pitch an octave lower.* |
| **Ionian** | *A modal scale beginning on C; open and joyful in nature.* |
| **jump** | *The distance between two, consecutive pitches that are not next to each other on the keyboard or other instrument.* |
| **key** | *The tonal center or main pitch of a composition; also refers to the part of an instrument that is pressed to create a tone.* |
| **largo** | *Very slowly.* |
| **legato** | *Smoothly connected.* |
| **lento** | *Slowly; between andante and largo.* |
| **Locrean** | *A modal scale beginning on B; rarely used; no tonal center.* |
| **Lydian** | *A modal scale beginning on F; unusual in nature.* |
| **lyrics** | *Words set to a piece of vocal music.* |
| **mapping** | *The practice of notating music using pictures and symbols.* |
| **marcato** | *Marked; emphasized.* |
| **melody** | *A series of related pitches played consecutively; usually the lead part.* |
| **metallophone** | *A medium sized percussion instrument with alloy bars.* |
| **meter** | *A practice which measures the music by grouping the pulses into groups of two or three.* |
| **metronome** | *A clock-like mechanism that clicks pulses; adjusts to any tempo, slow through fast.* |
| **mezzo** | *Medium; halfway.* |
| **Mixolydian** | *A modal scale beginning on G; extroverted in nature.* |
| **mode** | *Notes arranged in a scale that form the basic tonal material of a composition.* |
| **moderato** | *Moderate speed; between allegro and andante.* |
| **motive** | *A short melodic, rhythmic or harmonic theme or pattern.* |
| **note** | *A pitch or tone; the visual representation of a pitch or tone.* |
| **octet** | *A group of eight performers; a composition written for eight performers.* |
| **opera** | *A drama sung with an orchestral accompaniment and staged with scenery, costumes and blocking.* |

| | |
|---|---|
| **opus** | Used in conjunction with numbers to indicate the chronological position of a composition within the entire output of a composer. |
| **oratorio** | A drama of a religious nature performed by solo voices, chorus and orchestra without staging. |
| **ostinato** | A continuously repeated melodic or rhythmic pattern. |
| **overture** | An instrumental introduction to a larger work. |
| **pace** | The speed of the music; also called tempo. |
| **paraphony** | Music that has two or more simultaneous and parallel parts, usually in intervals of thirds or sixths. |
| **passacaglia** | Similar to a chaconne, but often without a harmonic progression. |
| **pattern** | A rhythm created by combining pulses of different speeds. |
| **percussion** | Instruments that are sounded by a striking motion. |
| **period** | A way of categorizing music by the time it was written in history; a unit of music consisting of two contrasting phrases. |
| **phrase** | A natural division of the rhythmic or melodic line, comparable to a sentence in speech. |
| **Phrygian** | A modal scale beginning on E; sad or intense in nature. |
| **piano** | Soft; also, a musical instrument. |
| **piggyback song** | New words are written for a known melody/song. |
| **pitch** | Also called note, refers to the highness or lowness of a tone. |
| **polyphony** | Music that has two or more simultaneous parts that are contrasting. |
| **polyrhythm** | Simultaneous use of contrasting rhythms in various parts. |
| **prelude** | A piece of music that is an introduction to a larger work. |
| **psychology** | The psychology of music refers to the emotional and interpretive aspects inferred in a given piece. |
| **pulse** | A steady, continuous beat in the music. |
| **quartet** | A piece of music written for four performers; a group of four performers. |
| **question-answer** | A binary form consisting of two contrasting but related phrases. |
| **range** | Related to voices or instruments, the notes playable or singable from the lowest to the highest. |
| **repeat signs** | Two vertical lines and two dots that indicate playing the music again. |
| **resolution** | The progression of chords or dissonances to a resting place. |

*Music Moments To Teach Academics: Resources*

| | |
|---|---|
| **rest** | *A pulse of silence.* |
| **retrograde** | *Backward.* |
| **rhythm** | *Patterns of movement and sound in time and space.* |
| **riff** | *A slang term used in drumming or other instrumental music referring to a short, improvisation.* |
| **ritardando** | *Gradually slower.* |
| **rondo** | *A musical form resulting from the alternation of a main theme and contrasting themes; A B A C A.* |
| **round** | *Also called canon, a musical form in which the melody is repeated at various time intervals.* |
| **scale** | *A ladder of notes within a specific tonal setting.* |
| **section** | *One part of a musical composition.* |
| **sequence** | *Immediate repetition of a tonal pattern at a higher or lower pitch.* |
| **sforzando** | *A sudden, strong accent.* |
| **slap** | *A sharp, quick stroke on the conga drum.* |
| **solfege** | *The study of reading music by assigning a syllable to each note, sometimes with corresponding hand signs; do, re, mi, fa, so, la, ti, do.* |
| **solo** | *A composition written for one performer; a performance by one person.* |
| **soprano** | *The highest female vocal part.* |
| **staccato** | *Detached; separate.* |
| **step** | *The distance between two, consecutive notes that are next to each other on the keyboard or other instrument.* |
| **strophic** | *A song in which all stanzas of the lyrics are sung to the same music.* |
| **style** | *A characteristic language with reference to melody, rhythm, form, expression, timbre and texture.* |
| **suite** | *A group of related compositions, usually contrasting.* |
| **syncopation** | *Rhythm that is not based on the regular strong and weak beat concept but on the up beat, most prevalent in jazz.* |
| **tempo** | *The speed or pace of the music.* |
| **tenor** | *The highest male vocal part.* |
| **ternary** | *A three part form; A B C.* |
| **texture** | *The layers of the music; simultaneous parts.* |

| | |
|---|---|
| **theme** | *A main idea or motive in a composition.* |
| **through-composed** | *A song that has new music composed for each stanza.* |
| **timbre** | *Various qualities of sound; the unique and contrasting voices of instruments, singing and speech.* |
| **tone** | *The quality of a sound, note or pitch.* |
| **tremolo** | *The rapid repetition of a single note.* |
| **trill** | *The rapid repetition of two adjacent notes.* |
| **trio** | *A composition written for three performers; a group of three performers.* |
| **tutti** | *All; everyone plays or sings together.* |
| **unison** | *Everyone playing or singing the same part; the interval created by sounding two of the same pitches.* |
| **variation** | *Changes or modifications of a musical theme.* |
| **verse** | *The changing section of the text that tells the story, followed by the chorus.* |
| **vibrato** | *A rapid fluctuation of pitch slightly above or below the main pitch.* |
| **vivace** | *Quick.* |
| **volume** | *The loudness or softness of sound or music.* |
| **xylophone** | *A percussion instrument with wooden bars.* |
| **zipper song** | *A repetitive song-form where most of the lyrics remain the same with one or more word substitutions, e.g. "Old MacDonald Had A Farm".* |

*Music Moments To Teach Academics: Resources*

## GENERAL DISCOGRAPHY

**Dance**

| | |
|---|---|
| Kerri Lynn Nichols | "I Am the Song"* |
| | "Music for Dancers"* |
| | "Music for Dancers, Too!"* |
| | "Music & Movement for Munchkins" |
| Eric Chappelle | "Music for Creative Dance: Volumes 1-4"* |
| Gemini with Phyllis Weikart | "Rhythmically Moving: Volumes 1-9"* |
| Gabrielle Roth & the Mirrors | "Bones" and "Initiation"* (and other titles) |
| Peter Jones | "Gradual Motion" |
| Brent Lewis | "The Primitive Truth" |
| Samite | "Tunula Eno"* |
| Shenanigans | "Best of Shenanigans, Volumes 1-3"* |
| Small Village Ensemble | "Dancers Journey" |

**Classical**

| | |
|---|---|
| American Boychoir | "Fast Cats and Mysterious Cows" |
| Marion Anderson (vocalist) | "Great Voices of the Century" |
| Johann Sebastian Bach (Baroque) | "Brandenburg Concertos" |
| | "Greatest Hits"* |
| | "Orchestral Suites 1-4" |
| | "Prelude No.1, BWV 846" |
| Samuel Barber (20th Century) | "Adagio for Strings"* |
| | "Secrets of Old: The Songs of Samuel Barber" |
| Bela Bartok (20th Century) | "10 Easy Pieces for Piano" and other titles |
| Kathleen Battle (vocalist) | "Opera Selections" |
| Ludwig van Beethoven | "Fur Elise" |
| (Classical/Romantic) | "Moonlight Sonata" |
| | "Symphony No. 5 in C minor"* |
| The Benedictine Monks (Medieval) | "Chant" |
| Berliner Philharmoniker | "Webern/Schoenberg/Berg: Orchestral Works" |
| Leonard Bernstein (20th Century) | "Greatest Hits" |
| Georges Bizet (Romantic) | "Carmen" (opera) |
| Sarah Brightman (vocalist) | "La Luna" and other titles |
| Benjamin Britten (20th Century) | "Ceremony of Carols" |
| John Cage (20th Century) | "Music for Percussion Quartet" and others |
| Frederic Chopin (Romantic) | "Nocturnes, Preludes and Impromptus" |
| Charlotte Church (vocalist) | "Voice of an Angel"* |
| Aaron Copland (20th Century) | "Greatest Hits" |
| Claude Debussy (Romantic/20th C.) | "Afternoon of a Faun" |
| | "Preludes and Nocturnes"* and other titles |

\* highly recommended

*Music Moments To Teach Academics: Resources*

| | |
|---|---|
| *Antonin Dvorak (Romantic)* | *"New World Symphony"* |
| *George Gershwin (20th Century)* | *"Porgy and Bess" (opera)* |
| *George Frideric Handel (Baroque)* | *"Greatest Hits"* |
| *Joseph Haydn* | *"Surprise Symphony" and other titles* |
| *Los Angeles Philharmonic (Holst/Strauss)* | *"Planets/Star Wars/Zarathustra"* |
| *Bobby McFerrin* | *"Hush" and "Paper Music"* |
| *W. A. Mozart (Classical)* | *"The Marriage of Figaro"\* (opera)* |
| *Modest Mussorgsky (Romantic)* | *"Pictures at an Exhibition"* |
| *Jessye Norman (vocalist)* | *"Brava, Jessye!"* |
| *Oregon Shakespeare Festival (Renaissance)* | *"In the Midst of Woods" and other titles* |
| *Carl Orff (20th Century)* | *"Carmina Burana"\** |
| *Johann Pachelbel (Baroque)* | *"Canon in D Major"\** |
| *Giacomo Puccini (Romantic/Twentieth)* | *"La Boheme"\* (opera)* |
| | *"Madame Butterfly"\* (opera)* |
| *Sergei Rachmaninov (Romantic/Twentieth)* | *"Piano Selections"* |
| *Gioacchino Rossini (Romantic)* | *"The Barber of Seville"\* (opera)* |
| | *"William Tell Overture"* |
| *Camille Saint-Saens (Romantic/Twentieth)* | *"Carnival of Animals"\** |
| *Dmitri Shostakovich* | *"Puppet Dances"\** |
| *Igor Stravinsky (Twentieth Century)* | *"The Firebird Suite"* |
| | *"Octet for Wind Instruments"\** |
| | *"The Rite of Spring"\** |
| *Pyotr Ilich Tchaikovsy (Romantic)* | *"The Nutcracker"* |
| | *"Sleeping Beauty"* |
| | *"Swan Lake"* |
| *Kiri Te Kanawa (vocalist)* | *"Classics"* |
| *Antonio Vivaldi (Baroque)* | *"The Four Seasons"* |
| *Windham Hill Sampler (contemporary arr.)* | *"The Bach Variations" (Baroque origin)* |

**New Age/Relaxation/Meditational**

| | |
|---|---|
| *William Ackerman* | *"A Windham Hill Retrospective"* |
| *Aria* | *"Aria"* |
| *Sarah Brightman* | *"Eden" and other titles* |
| *Cirque du Soleil* | *"Collection"* |
| *Alex de Grassi* | *"Slow Circle" and other titles* |
| *Enya* | *"A Day Without Rain"\** |
| | *"Shepherd Moons"\** |
| | *"Watermark"\** |
| *Singh Kaur and Kim Robertson* | *"Mender of Hearts"* |
| *Ray Lynch* | *"Deep Breakfast"* |
| *Rocky Mountain Learning Systems* | *"Sound Health Series"* |

\* highly recommended

*Music Moments To Teach Academics: Resources*

| | |
|---|---|
| *Magical Strings* | *"Above the Tower" and other titles* |
| *Loreena McKennitt* | *"Visit" and other titles* |
| *Music for People* | *"Improvising Chamber Music"* |
| *Narada* | *"The Wilderness Collection" and others* |
| *NorthSound* | *"Chopin Naturally"* |
| | *"Mozart Naturally" and other titles* |
| | *"The Natural Harp"* |
| | *"Songbird Symphony"* |
| | *"Spirit Winds"* |
| | *"Tranquility"* |
| *Roger Payne* | *"Songs of the Humpback Whale"* |
| *Secret Garden* | *"Dawn of a New Century" and others* |
| *Liz Story* | *"Speechless" and other titles* |
| *George Winston* | *"December" and other titles\** |
| *Yanni* | *"In My Time"* |
| | *"In the Mirror"* |
| | *"Live at the Acropolis" (CD and DVD)* |
| | *"Tribute" (CD and DVD)* |

**Ethnic/World Music**

| | |
|---|---|
| *Obo Addy* | *"Okropong"\** |
| | *"Rhythm of Which a Chief Walks Gracefully"* |
| *Erykah Badu* | *"Baduizm"\* (soul)* |
| *Harry Belafonte* | *"Island in the Sun"* |
| *Baka Beyond* | *"Spirit of the Forest"\* and other titles* |
| *Bulgarian Women's Choir* | *"Tour '93: Melody, Rhythm & Harmony"* |
| *Bryan Burton* | *"Moving Within the Circle"\** |
| *Sheila Chandra* | *"The Zen Kiss"\** |
| | *"Weaving My Ancestors' Voices"\** |
| *The Chieftains* | *"The Bells of Dublin" and other titles* |
| *Ellipsis Arts* | *"China: Time to Listen"\** |
| | *"Global Celebration Series"\** |
| | *"Global Meditation Series"\** |
| *Scott Fitzgerald* | *"All One Tribe: Thunderdrums II"* |
| *Mickey Hart* | *"At the Edge" and "Planet Drum"* |
| *Bart Hopkin* | *"Gravikords, Whirlies and Pyrophones"\** |
| | *"Orbitones: Spoons, Harps, Bellowphones"\** |
| *Inkuyo* | *"Music of the Andes: Double-Headed Serpent"* |
| *Bessie Jones* | *"Step It Down"\** |
| *Jesse Kalu* | *"One in Spirit"\* (Native flute)* |

\* highly recommended

*Music Moments To Teach Academics: Resources*

| | |
|---|---|
| *Best of Kodo* | "The Best of Kodo Drumming" |
| *Joanie Madden* | "Songs of the Irish Tin Whistle," V.1 and 2 |
| *Miriam Makeba* | "Welela" and other titles |
| *Bob Marley* | "The Complete Wailers" (reggae) |
| *Kohachiro Miyata* | "Japan: Shakuhachi - The Japanese Flute" |
| *Foday Musa Suso* | "Dreamtime" |
| *Carlos Nakai* | "Journeys" (Native American flute) |
| *Narada* | "Alma del Sur" and "Celtic Odyssey"* |
| *Narada/Various Artists* | "Faire Celts: A Woman's Voice" |
| *Baba Olatunji* | "Drums of Passion"* |
| *Samite* | "Dance My Children"* |
| | "Stars to Share"* and other titles* |
| *Sing for Freedom* | "Civil Rights Movement Songs"* |
| *T.H.E. Percussion Choir* | "A Call to Drum" |
| *Various Artists* | "Best of China" |
| *Wentz, Brooke (compilation)* | "Voices of Forgotten Worlds" |

## Children's

| | |
|---|---|
| *Adzinyah, Maraire and Tucker* | "Let Your Voice Be Heard"* |
| *William Amoaku* | "African Songs and Rhythms for Children"* |
| *Don Campbell* | "Mozart Effect: Music for Children" |
| *Classics for Children* | "Carnival of Animals and Other Selections"* |
| *Shawn Colvin* | "Holiday Songs and Lullabies"* |
| *Disney* | "For Our Children," V.1 and 2 |
| *Gemini* | "Lullabies for Our Children" |
| *Ella Jenkins* | "Multi-cultural Children's Songs" and others |
| *Ladysmith Black Mambazo* | "The Gift of the Tortoise"* |
| *Kenny Loggins* | "Return to Pooh Corner"* |
| *Bobby McFerrin & Jack Nicholson* | "The Elephant's Child"* |
| *Music for Little People* | "Peace is the World Smiling"* |
| *Narada* | "A Childhood Remembered" |
| *Kerri Lynn Nichols* | "I Am the Song"* |
| | "Music & Movement for Munchkins"* |
| *Carl Orff and Gunild Keetman* | "Orff-Schulwerk Volumes One, Two and Three" |
| *Putamayo* | "World Playground" and other titles |
| *Rock-a-bye Baby* | "Soft Hits for Little Rockers" |
| *Rosenshontz* | "It's the Truth" |
| | "Rock-n-Roll Teddy Bear" |
| | "Share It!" |
| | "Tickles You" |

* highly recommended

*Music Moments To Teach Academics: Resources*

Schoolhouse Rock — "Grammar Rock" and other titles
Moses Serwadda — "Songs and Stories from Uganda"
Shel Silverstein — "A Light in the Attic"
"Where the Sidewalk Ends"

Simply Mad About the Mouse — "A Musical Celebration of Imagination"
Songs From the Singing Sack Judith — "35 Songs/Stories from Around the World"*
Steinbergh & Victor Cockburn Sting/ — "Where I Come From: Poems and Songs"*
Claudio Abbado — "Peter and the Wolf" (Prokofiev)
Sweet Dreams — "Classical Themes"
Taj Mahal — "Shake Sugaree"
Take My Hand — "Songs from the Hundred Acre Wood"
Marlo Thomas and Friends — "Free to Be...You and Me"*
"Free to Be...A Family"

Troika — "Faeries: Realm Of Magic & Enchantment" Series
Wee Sing and Play — "Authentic Lullabies From Around the World"
World Music for Little Ears

### Folk
Joan Baez — "Classics: Volume Eight: Joan Baez"*
John Denver — "The Very Best of John Denver"*
Indigo Girls — "Rites of Passage"
Joni Mitchell — "Miles of Aisles"
The Kingston Trio — "Greatest Hits"
Laura Nyro — "The Best of Laura Nyro"
Odetta — "The Essential Odetta"
Pete Seeger — "The Essential Pete Seeger"*
Shenanigans — "International Bush Dancing"
Simon & Garfunkel — "Greatest Hits"
Sweet Honey In the Rock — "Selections: 1976-1988"*

### Jazz
Count Basie Kathleen — "One O'Clock Jump"
Battle Tony Bennet — "So Many Stars"
Big Band Fever — "MTV Unplugged" and other titles
Brian Setzer Orchestra — "Collection: Volumes 1 and 2"
Cherry Poppin' Daddies — "The Dirty Boogie"
Harry Connick, Jr. — "Zoot Suit Riot"*
"Blue Light, Red Light"

* highly recommended

*Music Moments To Teach Academics: Resources*

| | |
|---|---|
| *Duke Ellington* | *"Greatest Hits"* |
| | *"Mood Indigo"* |
| *Ella Fitzgerald* | *"The Cole Porter Songbook"** |
| | *"Oh Lady, Be Good!"* |
| *Kenny G* | *"Breathless"* |
| *George Gershwin* | *"An American in Paris"** (CD and video) |
| | *"Rhapsody in Blue"* |
| *Harry James* | *"Two O'Clock Jump"* |
| *The Manhattan Transfer* | *"Tonin'"* |
| *Audra McDonald* | *"Way Back to Paradise"* |
| *Bobby McFerrin* | *"The Best of Bobby McFerrin"* |
| | *"Circlesongs"* |
| | *"Medicine Man"** |
| *Glenn Miller* | *"Moonlight Serenade"* |
| *Diane Schuur* | *"Collection"* |
| *Shaman* | *"Toby Twining Music"* |
| *Sarah Vaughan* | *"16 Most Requested Songs"* |
| *George Winston* | *"Linus & Lucy: The Music of Vince Guaraldi"** |
| *Paul Winter* | *"Greatest Hits"** |

**Broadway/Soundtracks/Musical Theater**

| | |
|---|---|
| *Gilbert & Sullivan* | *"The Mikado"* |
| | *"Pirates of Penzance"* |
| *Original Broadway Cast Recording* | *"Bring in Da Noise, Bring in Da Funk"* |
| | *"Guys and Dolls"* |
| | *"The King and I"* |
| | *"Les Miserables"* |
| | *"The Lion King"* |
| | *"Oklahoma"* |
| | *"Once On This Island"* |
| | *"Ragtime"* |
| | *"Rent"* |
| | *"The Secret Garden"* |
| | *"Showboat"* |
| | *"Singin' in the Rain"* |
| | *"Westside Story"* |
| *Soundtracks* | *"Godspell"* |
| | *"Nell"* |
| | *"The Lion King"* |
| | *"A River Runs Through It"* |

* highly recommended

*Music Moments To Teach Academics: Resources*

|  |  |
|---|---|
|  | "Schindler's List" |
|  | "Star Wars" |
|  | "Swing Kids"* |
| Andrew Lloyd Webber | "Jesus Christ Superstar" |
|  | "Phantom of the Opera" |
|  | "The Premiere Collection"* |

**Gospel/Sacred**

| | |
|---|---|
| Marion Anderson | "Spirituals" |
| Sounds of Blackness | "Africa to America"* |
|  | "Children of the World" |
|  | "Evolution of Gospel" |
| Andre Crouch | "Pray" |
| Mahalia Jackson | "The Essence of Mahalia Jackson"* |
| Take 6 | "Take 6"* |
| Kiri Te Kanawa | "Spirituals" |
| Winans | "All Out" |

**Blues**

| | |
|---|---|
| B.B. King | "How Blue Can You Get?"* |
| Bessie Smith | "The Collection" |
| Taj Mahal | "Senor Blues" |

**A Cappella (Vocal)**

| | |
|---|---|
| A Cappella | "Best of the Vocal Bands" |
| The Heebie Jeebies | "Standards" and other titles |
| M-Pact | "2"* and other titles |
| The Nylons | "Fabric of Life" and other titles |
| SoVoSo | "Truth & Other Stories" and other titles |
| Take 6 | "Take 6" and other titles |
| The Trenchcoats | "The Trenchcoats"* and other titles |

**Country**

| | |
|---|---|
| Garth Brooks | "No Fences" and other titles |
| Johnny Cash | All titles |
| Vince Gill | "The Key" |
| The Judds | "Greatest Hits"* |
| Reba McIntyre | "Greatest Hits" |

\* highly recommended

*LeAnn Rimes*                                "Blue"
*Shania Twain*                               "Come On Over"*

**Contemporary (pop, rock, rap, techno, R & B)**

| Artist | Album |
|---|---|
| *Babyface* | "The Day"* |
| *Brian Setzer Orchestra* | "The Dirty Boogie" |
| *Tracy Chapman* | "A New Beginning" |
| *Arrested Development* | "3 Years, 5 Months and 2 Days in the Life Of" |
| *Boys II Men* | "Cooleyhighharmony"* |
| *Aretha Franklin* | "The Best of Aretha Franklin" |
| *Elton John* | "Two Rooms" |
| *Heavy D and the Boys* | "Peaceful Journey" |
| *Lauryn Hill* | "The Miseducation of Lauryn Hill"* |
| *KD Lang* | "Ingenue" |
| *Madonna* | "Ray of Light" |
| *Ricky Martin* | "Ricky Martin" |
| *Sarah McLachlan* | "Surfacing"* |
| *Salt & Pepa* | "Very Necessary" (rap) |
| *Seal* | "Seal" |
| *Paul Simon* | "The Rhythm of the Saints" |
| *Will Smith* | "Big Willie Style" |
| *Sting* | "Ten Summoner's Tales"* |
| *Real McCoy* | "Another Night" |

\* highly recommended

## CONCEPTUAL DISCOGRAPHY

**RHYTHM**
**Pulse**

<u>I Am the Song</u> by Kerri Lynn Nichols
 "Can You Feel the Happy Rhythm?"
 "Samba"
 "Listen to the Rain"
 "Tribute to Theodore Geisel"
 "Sticky Finger Suite"
 "Walkin' Now in Beauty"
 "Sansa Kroma"
 "Music is Our Common Ground"
 "Leaves That Fall"
 "Everybody Needs a Drum"
 "I Am Powerful"

<u>Music for Dancers</u> by Kerri Lynn Nichols
 "Pulsation"
 "Blocks"
 "Twos & Threes"
 "Rondo ala Copland"
 "Quiet in the Library!"
 "Staccato Legato"
 "Ching, Clop, Boom!"
 "Bolivia"
 "Three Paces"
 "Mango Walk"
 "Joyful Noyz"

<u>Music for Dancers, Too!</u> by Kerri Lynn Nichols
 "One Bent Tulip"         "Jazz'up"
 "Strong & Light"         "Technotronica"
 "Jammin' in De Jungle"
 "Ups & Downs"
 "Questions & Answers"
 "Locomotion"
 "Fee Fie Fo Fum"
 "Circles & Squares"
 "Kiyakiya"
 "Hands & Feet"
 "Percussion Discussion"
 "Consonance & Dissonance"

<u>Music & Movement for Munchkins</u> by Kerri Lynn Nichols
Disc One/Two "Button, You Must Wander"
 "Deedle, Deedle Dumpling"
 "The Elephant Rhyme"
 "Engine No. 9"
 "Head & Shoulders, Knees & Toes""
 "Hickory Dickory Dock"
 "Hot Cross Buns"
 "How Do You Do Today?"
 "Humpty Dumpty"
 "Jack B Nimble"
 "Monkey See, Monkey Do"
 "Pease Porridge Hot"
 "Shake My Hands"
 "Shoo Fly"
 "Strawberry Shortcake"
 "Tue Tue"
 "Wan Two Dwa"
 "Wee Willie Winkie"
Disc Two only "Clothesline Dance"
 "Fast and Slow"
 "La Raspa"
 "On the Spot"
 "Walk & Rock"

<u>Music for Creative Dance</u> by Eric Chappelle
Volume One   "The Add-On Machine"
             "Chirpa Chirpa"
             "A Tale of Two Villages"
Volume Two   "Bee Beat"
             "Weavers"
             "Skippy Ska"
             "Ski Reel"
             "Caribbean Leaps"
             "Andean Altitude"
             "Balinese Mask"
             "Celtic Knot"

*Music for Creative Dance by Eric Chappelle* (Continued)
Volume Three   "Dakota Dawn"
                "Rock'n Stop"
                "The Bayou Both-Step"
                "Fiesta"
                "Morning Fours"
                "Variations in Three"
                "Skip the Jig"
                "Spootiskerry"
Volume Four   "TV Dinner"
                "Islands"
                "Celtic Groove"
                "Back at Ya"
                "Skippity Jig"
                "Up & at 'Em"
                "Totem Pole"

*Rhythmically Moving*, Volumes 1-9 by Gemini/Phyllis Weikart
Various selections

## Grouping

### Duple (twos)

*I Am the Song* by Kerri Lynn Nichols
- "Samba"
- "Listen to the Rain"
- "Tribute to Theodore Geisel"
- "The Lucky Song"
- "Sticky Finger Suite"
- "Walkin' Now in Beauty"
- "Sansa Kroma"
- "Music Is Our Common Ground"
- "Leaves That Fall"
- "Shine Your Light"
- "Everybody Needs a Drum"
- "Follow Me, Moon"
- "I Am Powerful"

*Music for Dancers* by Kerri Lynn Nichols
- "Pulsation"
- "Motivation"
- "Blocks"
- "Twos & Threes"
- "Ladders"
- "Rondo ala Copland"
- "Quiet in the Library!"
- "Ching, Clop, Boom!"
- "Mango Walk"
- "Joyful Noyz"
- "Bolivia"
- "Echoes & Shadows"
- "Three Paces"
- "Snap Clapple Stomp"
- "Voices"
- "Funky Klunky"
- "Paraphony & Polyphony"

*Music Moments To Teach Academics: Resources*

<u>Music for Dancers, Too!</u> and
"One Bent Tulip"
"Jammin in De Jungle"
"Ups & Downs"
"Shape, Wiggle & Go!"
"Questions & Answers"
"Locomotion"
"Gravity"
"Fee Fie Fo Fum"
"Kiyakiya"
"Percussion Discussion"
"Jazz'up"
"Consonance & Dissonance"
"Technotronica"

<u>Music for Creative Dance</u> by Eric Chappelle
Volume One   "The Add-On Machine"
                 "Chirpa Chirpa"
                 "A Tale of Two Villages"
Volume Two   "Bee Beat"
                 "Weavers"
                 "Pathway Puzzle"
                 "Skippy Ska"
                 "Ski Reel"
                 "Caribbean Leaps"
                 "American Fiddler"
                 "Andean Altitude"
Volume Three   "Dakota Dawn"
                 "Rock'n Stop"
                 "Dancing Digits"
                 "Fiesta"
                 "Tempo Tantrum"
                 "Morning Fours"
                 "Spootiskerry"
Volume Four   "TV Dinner"
                 "Islands"
                 "Celtic Groove"
                 "Monkey Fiddle Chant"
                 "Back at Ya"
                 "Oslo Walk"

<u>Music & Movement for Munchkins</u> by Kerri Lynn Nichols
Disc One/Two "Button, You Must Wander"
"Can You Sing Your Name?"
"Cape Dorset Lullaby"
"Clothesline Dance"
"The Elephant Rhyme"
"Engine No. 9"
"Fast and Slow"
"Georgie Porgie"
"Good Night, Sleep Tight"
"Head & Shoulders, Knees & Toes"
"Hickory Dickory Dock
"Hot Cross Buns"
"How Do You Do?
"How Do You Do Today?"
"Jack B Nimble"
"Mary Mack"
"Mary Quite Contrary"
"Monkey See, Monkey Do"
"Pease "Porridge Hot"
"The Sea Song"
"Shake My Hands"
"Little Piggy"
"Tue Tue"
"Wan Two Dwa"
"Wee Willie Winkie"

"Up & at 'Em"
"Totem Pole"

## Triple (threes)

*I Am the Song* by Kerri Lynn Nichols
"Can You Feel the Happy Rhythm?"
"Melody"
"Sticky Finger Suite: Had Matter"
"I Am the Song"
"Waltz of the Toys"

*Music for Dancers* by Kerri Lynn Nichols
"Twos & Threes"
"The Hi-Lo Waltz"
"Staccato Legato"

*Music for Creative Dance* by Eric Chappelle
Volume Two    "Pharoah's Waltz"
              "Pastorale"
              "Balinese Mask"
Volume Three  "Variations in Three"
              "Planxty Irwin"
Volume Four   "Walt's Waltz"

*Rhythmically Moving*, Volumes 1-9 by Gemini/Phyllis Weikart
Volume Four   "Hole in the Wall" (England)

*Music & Movement for Munchkins* by Kerri Lynn Nichols
Disc Two    "Walk & Rock"
            "Humpty Dumpty"

*Music for Dancers, Too!* by Kerri Lynn Nichols
"Strong & Light"
"Purcell Canon"
"Circles & Squares"
"Hands & Feet"

## Compound

*Music for Dancers* by Kerri Lynn Nichols
"Snap Clapple Stomp" (12/8)

*Music for Dancers, Too!* by Kerri Lynn Nichols
"Jigalig" (6/8)
"The Return" (12/8)

*Music & Movement for Munchkins* by Kerri Lynn Nichols
Disc One/Two "Hickory Dickory Dock"

"Humpty Dumpty
"La Raspa"

*Music for Creative Dance* by Eric Chappelle
Volume One    "Fiddlers Three" (6/8)
              "Skippy" (6/8)
Volume Two    "Celtic Knot" (12/8)
Volume Three  "Skip the Jig" (6/8)

*Music Moments To Teach Academics: Resources*

*Volume Four "Skippity Jig" (6/8)*

<u>Rhythmically Moving</u>, *Volumes 1-9 by Gemini/Phyllis Weikart*
*Volume One "O'Keefe Slide/Kerry Slide" (Ireland) (12/8)*
*"Les Saluts" (French Canadian) (12/8)*

**Changing**

<u>Music for Dancers</u> *by Kerri Lynn Nichols*
"Twos & Threes"            "Motivation"
"The Space Between Your Ears"   "Snap Clapple Stomp"

<u>Music for Dancers, Too</u>! *by Kerri Lynn Nichols*
"Strong & Light"    "Court Jester"    "Viva la Voce"
"Circles & Squares"   "Hands & Feet"

<u>Music & Movement for Munchkins</u> *by Kerri Lynn Nichols*
Disc One/Two "Walk & Rock"
"Wan Two Dwa"

<u>Music for Creative Dance</u> *by Eric Chappelle*
Volume Three "The Bayou Both-Step"
"Raggedy March"

<u>Rhythmically Moving</u>, *Volumes 1-9 by Gemini/Phyllis Weikart*
Volume Eight       "Pravo Horo" (Bulgaria)
Volume Nine        "Chiotikos" (Greece)

**Mixed or Irregular**

<u>Music For Dancers</u> *by Kerri Lynn Nichols*       <u>Bones</u> *by Gabrielle Roth & the Mirrors*
"Fairydance" (5/4)                                     "The Calling" (7/4)
"Twos & Threes" (2 and 3 alternately)
"The Space Between Your Ears" (5/4)

<u>Rhythmically Moving</u>, *Volumes 1-9 by Gemini/Phyllis Weikart*
Volume Eight       "Pravo Horo" (7/4) (Bulgaria)
Volume Nine        "Tsakonikos" (5/4) (Greece)

**Pattern**

<u>I Am The Song</u> *by Kerri Lynn Nichols*
"Can You Feel the Happy Rhythm?"          "Sansa Kroma"
"Samba"                                    "Waltz of the Toys"
"Tribute to Theodore Geisel"               "Leaves That Fall"
"Sticky Finger Suite: Meticulous"          "Everybody Needs a Drum"
"I Am Powerful"

*Music for Dancers* by Kerri Lynn Nichols

"Pulsation"
"Blocks"
"The Hi-Lo Waltz"
"Motivation"
"Bolivia"
"Rondo ala Copland"
"Snap Clapple Stomp"

"Voices"
"Ching Clop Boom!"
"Mango Walk"
"Joyful Noyz"
"Three Paces"
"Quiet in the Library!"

*Music for Dancers, Too!* by Kerri Lynn Nichols

"One Bent Tulip"
"Jammin' in De Jungle"
"Jigalig"
"Questions & Answers"
"Gravity"
"Circles & Squares"
"Hands & Feet"
"Jazz'up"
"Consonance & Dissonance"

"Strong & Light"
"Ups & Downs"
"Shape, Wiggle & Go!"
"Locomotion"
"Fee Fie Fo Fum"
"Kiyakiya"
"Percussion Discussion"
"Technotronica"

*Music for Creative Dance* by Eric Chappelle

Volume One  "The Add-On Machine"
            "A Tale of Two Villages"
            "Potpourri I"
Volume Two  "Bee Beat"
            "Skippy Ska"
            "Ski Reel"
Volume Three "Rock'n Stop"
            "Dancing Digits"
            "Fiesta"
            "Potpourri III"
Volume Four "TV Dinner"
            "Islands"
            "Celtic Groove"
            "Monkey Fiddle Chant"
            "Back at Ya"
            "Oslo Walk"
            "Up & at 'Em"
            "Totem Pole"
            "Breath Meditation"
            "Caribbean Leaps"
            "Bolero"
            "Potpourri II"

*Music & Movement for Munchkins* by Kerri Lynn Nichols

Disc One/Two "Can You Sing Your Name"
             "Deedle Deedle Dumpling"
             "The Elephant Rhyme"
             "Engine No. 9"
             "Head & Shoulders, Knees & Toes"
             "Hickory Dickory Dock"
             "Hot Cross Buns"
             "How Do You Do Today?"
             "Mary Mack"
             "Tue Tue"
             "Wan Two Dwa"
Disc Two only "Clothesline Dance"
              "La Raspa"
              "Wee Willie Winkie"

*Music Moments To Teach Academics: Resources*

<u>*Rhythmically Moving*</u>, Volumes 1-9 by Gemini/Phyllis Weikart
Volume One   "Echo"
                 "Te Ve Orez" (Israel)
Volume Two   "Limbo Rock" (USA)
Volume Three  "Alley Cat" (USA)
                 "Bele Kawe" (West Africa)
                 "La Raspa" (Mexico)
Volume Five   "Carnavalito" (Bolivia)
Volume Nine  "Armenian Misirlou" (Armenia)
                 "Tanko Bushi" (Japan)
                 "Makedonikos Horos" (Greece)
                 "The Hustle" (USA)

**MELODY**

**Pitch**

<u>*I Am The Song*</u> by Kerri Lynn Nichols
"Melody"
"Journey to the Moon"
"Sticky Finger Suite: Ma-ching"
"I Am the Song"
"Music is Our Common Ground"

<u>Music for Dancers</u> by Kerri Lynn Nichols
"The Hi-Lo Waltz"
"Ladders"
"The Space Between Your Ears"
"Motivation"
"Bolivia"
"Paraphony & Polyphony"
"Twos & Threes"
"Echoes & Shadows"
"Three Paces"
"Fairydance"
"Voices"

<u>Music & Movement for Munchkins</u>
    by Kerri Lynn Nichols
Disc One/Two "The Elephant Rhyme"
              "Cape Dorset Melody"
              "Georgie Porgie"
              "Good Night, Sleep Tight"
              "Head & Shoulders, Knees & Toes"
              "Humpty Dumpty"
              "Mary Mack"
              "Shake My Hands"
              "Strawberry Shortcake"
              "There's Music in a Hammer"
              "This Little Piggy"
Disc Two only "Clothesline Dance"
              "Fast & Slow"
              "On the Spot"
              "Walk & Rock"

<u>Music for Dancers, Too!</u> by Kerri Lynn Nichols
"Strong & Light"     "Ups & Downs"
"Court Jester"       "Jigalig"
"Questions and Answers"  "Purcell Canon"
"Locomotion"        "Fee Fie Fo Fum"
"Viva la Voce"       "Jazz'up"
"Consonance & Dissonance"  "Technotronica"
"The Return"

*Music for Creative Dance* by Eric Chappelle
Volume One   "Whales"
             "All In One"
             "Levelance"
Volume Two   "Pizz Ah!"
             "Pathway Puzzle"
Volume Three "Dakota Dawn"
Volume Four  "Amphibious"
             "Back at Ya"
             "Quarks"
             "Pathways"
             "Focus"

## Scale

*I Am the Song* by Kerri Lynn Nichols
"Journey to the Moon"
"Sansa Kroma"
"Sticky Finger Suite: Metronome"
"I Am the Song"

*Music for Dancers* by Kerri Lynn Nichols
"The Hi-Lo Waltz"          "Motivation"
"Ladders"                  "Three Paces"
"Twos & Threes"            "Mango Walk"
"Paraphony & Polyphony"

*Music for Dancers, Too!* by Kerri Lynn Nichols
"One Bent Tulip"           "Strong & Light"
"Jammin' in De Jungle"     "Court Jester"
"Jigalig"                  "Shape, Wiggle & Go!"
"Questions and Answers"    "Purcell Canon"
"Locomotion"               "Viva la Voce"
"Jazz'up"                  "The Return"

*Canon in D Major* by Johann Pachelbel

*The Sound of Music* by Rodgers and Hammerstein
"Do-Re-Mi"

## Interval

### Steps and Jumps (within a melody)

*I Am the Song* by Kerri Lynn Nichols
"Can You Feel the Happy Rhythm?"
"Listen to the Rain"
"Sticky Finger Suite"
"Music is Our Common Ground"
"Waltz of the Toys"
"Samba"
"Melody"
"I Am the Song" "Sansa Kroma"
"Leaves That Fall"

*Music & Movement for Munchkins*
       by Kerri Lynn Nichols
Disc One/Two "Button, You Must Wander" (3rds)
             "Can You Sing Your Name?" (3rds)
             "Cape Dorset Lullaby" (2nds)
             "Engine No. 9" (2nds and 3rds)
             "The Elephant Rhyme" (various)
             "Georgie Porgie" (3rds)
             "Good Night, Sleep Tight" (2nds)
             "Head & Shoulders, Knees & Toes" (3rds)
             "How Do You Do?"

"How Do You Do Today? (3rds)
"Hot Cross Buns (various)
"Humpty Dumpty (3rds and 4ths)
"Jack B Nimble (2nds)
"Mary Mack (2nds, 3rds and 4ths)
"Mary, Quite Contrary (3rds)
"Monkey See, Monkey (2nds, 3rds and 6ths)
"Pease Porridge Hot (2nds)
"The Sea Song (various)
"Shake My Hands (2nds, 3rds and 5ths)
"Shoo Fly (2nds and 3rds)
"Strawberry Shortcake (2nds and 3rds)
"There's Music in a Hammer (5ths)
"This Little Piggy (3rds)
"Tue Tue (3rds)
"Wan Two Dwa (2nds and 3rds)
"Wee Willie Winkie (3rds)

Disc Two only

"Clothesline Dance (2nds and 3rds)
"Fast and Slow (various)
"La Raspa (3rds and 4ths)
"On the Spot (octaves)
"Walk & Rock (various)

**Major Melodies (keys)**

*I Am the Song* by Kerri Lynn Nichols
"Can You Feel the Happy Rhythm?"
"Listen to the Rain"
"Melody"
"The Lucky Song"
"Walkin' Now in Beauty"
"Sansa Kroma"
"I Am the Song"
"Waltz of the Toys" "Shine Your Light" "I Am Powerful"

*Music for Dancers, Too!*
  by Kerri Lynn Nichols
"Strong & Light"
"Shape, Wiggle & Go!"
"Purcell Canon"
"Jigalig"
"Questions and Answers"
"Kiyakiya"

*Music For Dancers* by Kerri Lynn Nichols
"Pulsation"                 "Rondo ala Copland"
"Blocks"                    "Quiet in the Library"
"Twos & Threes"             "Staccato Legato"
"The Hi-Lo Waltz"           "Fairydance"
"Ladders"                   "Voices"
"Bolivia"                   "Funky Klunky"
"Motivation"                "Mango Walk"
"Paraphony & Polyphony"     "Joyful Noyz"
"The Space Between Your Ears"

*Music for Dancers, Too!* by Kerri Lynn Nichols
"One Bent Tulip"            "Strong & Light"
"Ups & Downs"               "Court Jester"
"Jigalig"                   "Shape, Wiggle & Go!"
"Purcell Canon"             "Locomotion"
"Fee Fie Fo Fum"            "Circles & Squares"
"Consonance & Dissonance"   "Technotronica"

*Music for Creative Dance* by Eric Chappelle
Volumes One, Two, Three And Four: various selections

*Rhythmically Moving*, Volumes 1-9 by Gemini/Phyllis Weikart
Various selections

*Music for Dancers* by Kerri Lynn Nichols
"Blocks"
"Twos & Threes"
"The Hi-Lo Waltz"
"Motivation"
"Paraphony & Polyphony"
"Rondo ala Copland"
"Quiet in the Library"
"Staccato Legato"
"Mango Walk"

*Music for Creative Dance* by Eric Chappelle
Volume One    "Chirpa Chirpa"
Volume Two    "Caribbean Leaps"    "American Fiddler"
              "Celtic Knot"
Volume Three  "The Bayou Both-Step"    "Fiesta"
              "Skip the Jig"            "Spootiskerry"
Volume Four   "Islands"                 "Skippity Jig"
              "Pathways"                "Energy"

*Rhythmically Moving,* Volumes 1-9 by Gemini/Phyllis Weikart
Volume One   "Arkansas Traveler/Turkey In the Straw"
Volume Two   "Rakes of Mallow"
             "Yankee Doodle" (USA)
Volume Three "La Raspa" (Mexico)
Volume Five  "Carnavalito" (Bolivia)
Volume Eight "Hot Pretzels" (USA)
Volume Nine  "Tsakonikos" (Greece)

**Minor Melodies (keys)**

*I Am the Song* by Kerri Lynn Nichols
Sticky Finger Suite "Meticulous"
"Music is Our Common Ground"

*Music & Movement for Munchkins* by Kerri Lynn Nichols
  Disc One/Two "Jack B Nimble"
  Disc Two only "Clothesline Dance"

*Music for Dancers* by Kerri Lynn Nichols
"Ladders"              "Voices"
"Echoes & Shadows"     "Funky Klunky"
"Three Paces"

*Music for Dancers, Too!* by Kerri Lynn Nichols
"One Bent Tulip"        "Jazz'up"
"Ups & Downs" (Blues)   "The Return"

*Music for Creative Dance* by Eric Chappelle
Volume One   "Fiddlers Three"
             "Lucky Stiff"
             "Adagio for Two Violins"
             "Stone Soup"
Volume Two   "Weavers"
             "Pharoah's Waltz"
             "Little Bolero"
Volume Three "Rock'n Stop"
             "Tambourine"
             "Variations In Three"
             "Mr. E"

*Music Moments To Teach Academics: Resources*

<u>*Rhythmically Moving*</u>, *Volumes 1-9 by Gemini/Phyllis Weikart*
Volume One    "Brian Boru's March"

               "O'Keefe Slide/Kerry Slide" (Ireland)
Volume Two    "Troika" (Russia)
Volume Four    "Zemer Atik" (Israel)

               "Hineh Ma Tov" (Israel)
Volume Eight    "Leor Chiyuchech" (Israel)
Volume Nine    "Makedonikos Horos" (Greece)

## FORM
### Motive

<u>*Symphony No. 5 in C minor*</u>, *Movement One, by Beethoven*
<u>*Fur Elise*</u> *by Ludwig van Beethoven*
<u>*Inventions and Preludes*</u> *by Johann Sebastian Bach*
<u>*Toccata in G Minor*</u> *by Johann Sebastian Bach*
<u>*The Star-Spangled Banner*</u> *by Francis Scott Key*
<u>*Dona Nobis Pacem*</u> *by Palestrina*
<u>*Carnival of Animals*</u> *(various selections) by Camille Saint-Saens*
<u>*William Tell Overture*</u> *by Gioacchino Rossini*

<u>*Music & Movement for Munchkins*</u> *by Kerri Lynn Nichols*

Disc One/Two
- "Can You Sing Your Name?"
- "Engine No. 9"
- "Georgie Porgie"
- "Good Night, Sleep Tight"
- "Head & Shoulders, Knees & Toes"
- "Hot Cross Buns"
- "How Do You Do Today?"
- "Humpty Dumpty"
- "Jack B Nimble"
- "Mary Mack"
- "Mary, Quite Contrary"
- "Pease Porridge Hot"
- "The Sea Song"
- "Shake My Hands"
- "Shoo Fly Medley"
- "Strawberry Shortcake"
- "There's Music in a Hammer"
- "This Little Piggy"
- "Tue Tue"
- "Wan Two Dwa"
- "Wee Willie Winkie"

Disc Two only
- "Fast and Slow"
- "La Raspa"
- "On the Spot"
- "Walk and Rock"

<u>*I Am The Song*</u> *by Kerri Lynn Nichols*
- "Can You Feel the Happy Rhythm?"
- "Tribute to Theodore Geisel"
- "The Lucky Song"
- "Sticky Finger Suite: Had Matter, Meticulous"
- "Walkin' Now in Beauty"
- "Samba"
- "Melody"
- "Sansa Kroma"
- "Leaves That Fall"

*Music Moments To Teach Academics: Resources*

<u>Music for Dancers</u> *by Kerri Lynn Nichols*
"Pulsation"
"The Space Between Your Ears"
"Twos & Threes"
"The Hi-Lo Waltz"
"Quiet in the Library!"
"Fairydance"
"Ching Clop Boom!"
"Mango Walk"
"Joyful Noyz"
"Blocks"
"Motivation"
"Bolivia"
"Three Paces"
"Staccato Legato"
"Voices"
"Funky Klunky"
"Paraphony & Polyphony"

<u>Music for Dancers, Too</u>! *by Kerri Lynn Nichols*
"Strong & Light"
"Ups & Downs"
"Jigalig"
"Questions and Answers"
"Viva la Voce"
"Consonance & Dissonance"
"Jammin' in De Jungle"
"Court Jester"
"Shape, Wiggle & Go!"
"Kiyakiya"
"Jazz'up"
"Technotronica"

**Phrase**

<u>I Am the Song</u> *by Kerri Lynn Nichols*
"Can You Feel The Happy Rhythm?"
"Melody"
"Tribute to Theodore Geisel"
"Walkin' Now in Beauty"
"I Am the Song"
"Music is Our Common Ground"
"I Am Powerful"
"Samba"
"Listen to the Rain"
"The Lucky Song"
"Sansa Kroma"
"Leaves That Fall"
"Shine Your Light"

<u>Music for Dancers</u> *by Kerri Lynn Nichols*
"Blocks"
"Twos & Threes"
"The Hi-Lo Waltz"
"Ladders"
"The Space Between Your Ears"
"Motivation"
"Paraphony & Polyphony"
"Bolivia"
"Echoes & Shadows"
"Rondo ala Copland"
"Three Paces"
"Quiet in the Library!"
"Voices"
"Mango Walk"

<u>Music for Dancers, Too</u>! *by Kerri Lynn Nichols*
"One Bent Tulip"
"Jammin' in De Jungle"
"Strong & Light"
"Ups & Downs"

*Music Moments To Teach Academics: Resources*

"Court Jester"  "Jigalig"
"Shape, Wiggle & Go!"  "Questions and Answers"
"Purcell Canon"  "Locomotion"
"Fee Fie Fo Fum"  "Circles & Squares"
"Kiyakiya"  "Hands & Feet"
"Viva la Voce"  "Jazz'up"
"Consonance & Dissonance"  "Technotronica"
"The Return"

<u>Music & Movement for Munchkins</u> by Kerri Lynn Nichols
Disc One/Two "All titles"
Disc Two only "Clothesline Dance"
"Fast and Slow"
"La Raspa"
"On the Spot"

<u>Rhythmically Moving</u>, Volumes 1-9 by Gemini/Phyllis Weikart
Volume One  "Oh How Lovely"
            "Gaelic Waltz" (Ireland)
            "Echo"
            "The Sally Gardens"
Volume Two  "Haya Ze Basadeh" (Israel)
            "Limbo Rock" (USA)
            "Yankee Doodle" (USA)
Volume Three  "La Raspa" (Mexico)
Volume Four  "Zemer Atik" (Israel)
            "Hineh Ma Tov" (Israel)
Volume Five  "Carnavalito" (Bolivia)
Volume Eight  "Leor Chiyuchech" (Israel)
Volume Nine  "Tanko Bushi"

<u>One in Spirit</u> by Jesse Kalu
"Sweat Song"

<u>Watermark</u> by Enya
"On Your Shore"

*The Zen Kiss* by Sheila Chandra
*Various selections*

*Journeys* by Carlos Nakai (Native American flute)
*Various selections*

*Japan: Shakuhachi - The Japanese Flute* by Kohachiro Miyata
*(various selections)*

**Repeat**

*I Am the Song* by Kerri Lynn Nichols
"Can You Feel the Happy Rhythm?" (repeated sections)
"Samba" (repeated phrases)
"Listen to the Rain" (repeated sections)

Sticky Finger Suite:   "Ma-ching" (repeated notes/phrases)
"Had Matter" (modified rep. of phrases)
"Metronome" (repeated bass line)
"Meticulous" (repeated phrases)
"Motet" (bass line ostinato)

"Walkin' Now in Beauty" (repeated phrases and sections)
"Sansa Kroma" (modified repetition (phrase), rep. sections)
"Music is Our Common Ground" (melodic canon)
"Waltz of the Toys" (repeated phrases/sections; additive form)
"Leaves That Fall" (repeated sections)
"Shine Your Light" (repetitive, canon form)
"Follow Me, Moon" (repeated phrases and sections)
"I Am Powerful" (repeated phrases and sections)

*Music for Dancers* by Kerri Lynn Nichols

"Pulsation" (repeated pulse durations)
"Blocks" (repeated patterns/phrases)
"Twos And Threes" (repeated phrase/sections)
"Ladders" (repeated scales/phrases)
"Rondo ala Copland" (repeated A section, rondo form)
"Three Paces" (repeated patterns/phrases/sections)
"Staccato Legato" (repeated sections)
"The Hi-Lo Waltz" (repeated phrases/sections)
"Motivation" (repeated phrases/sections)
"Mango Walk" (modified repetition; percussion ostinati)
"Joyful Noyz" (repeated motives, phrases and sections)
"Bolivia" (repeated patterns/phrases/sections)

*Music Moments To Teach Academics: Resources*

*"Echoes & Shadows" (repeated patterns/phrases/sections)*
*"Quiet in the Library!" (repeated phrases/sections)*
*"Staccato Legato" (repeated phrases/sections)*
*"Fairydance" (repeated motives/phrases/sections)*
*"Snap Clapple Stomp" (repeated patterns/sections)*
*"Voices" (repeated motives/patterns/phrases)*
*"Ching Clop Boom!" (repeated patterns/sections)*
*"Funky Klunky" (repeated bass line/phrases/sections)*
*"Mango Walk" (repeated patterns/phrases/sections)*
*"Paraphony & Polyphony" (repeated phrases/sections)*
*"Joyful Noyz" (repeated bass line/patterns/phrases/sections)*

<u>Music For Dancers, Too</u>*! by Kerri Lynn Nichols*

*"One Bent Tulip" (repeated bass line, patterns, phrases and sections)*
*"Strong & Light" (repeated bass line, melodic phrases and sections)*
*"Jammin' in De Jungle" (repeated bass line, A section, melody)*
*"Ups & Downs" (repeated accompaniment, motives and A section)*
*"Court Jester" (repeated patterns, phrases and sections)*
*"Jigalig" (repeated patterns, phrases and sections)*
*"Shape, Wiggle & Go!" (ABC repeated form)*
*"Questions and Answers" (repeated phrases and sections)*
*"Purcell Canon" (repeated melodic phrases and sections)*
*"Locomotion" (repeated bass line, A section, melody)*
*"Gravity" (repeated A section)*
*"Fee Fie Fo Fum" (repeated, layered patterns, phrases and sections)*
*"Circles & Squares" (repeated bass line, patterns, phrases, sections)*
*"Kiyakiya" (repeated patterns, accompaniment, melodic phrases)*
*"Hands & Feet" (repeated rhythmic patterns)*
*"Viva la Voce" (repeated melodic phrases)*
*"Percussion Discussion" (repeated rhythmic patterns)*
*"Jazz'up" (repeated patterns, phrases and sections)*
*"Consonance & Dissonance" (repeated motives, phrases and sections)*
*"Technotronica" (repeated patterns, phrases and sections)*
*"The Return" (repeated descending scale, arpeggio-progression)*

<u>Music & Movement for Munchkins</u> *by Kerri Lynn Nichols*
*Disc One/Two "All titles"*

*Music Moments To Teach Academics: Resources*

**Contrast**

<u>I Am the Song</u> by Kerri Lynn Nichols
"Can You Feel the Happy Rhythm?" (ABC form, repeated)
"Samba" (AB form)
"Listen to the Rain" (AB form)
"Melody" (through-composed)
"Tribute to Theodore Geisel (intro/AB form)
"The Lucky Song" (AB form)
"Sticky Finger Suite" (suite form; contrast within each melody)
"Walkin' Now in Beauty" (AB form)
"Sansa Kroma" (AB form, repeated)
"I Am the Song" (intro ABABCABB coda)
"Waltz of Toys" (contrasting timbres and rhythmic patterns)
"Leaves That Fall" (AB form)
"Everybody Needs a Drum" (ABCD repeated form)
"Follow Me, Moon" (AB form)
"I Am Powerful" (intro AABAABAABCCAA)

<u>Music for Dancers</u> by Kerri Lynn Nichols
"Pulsation" (contrasting note values)
"Twos & Threes" (contrasting meter and sections)
"The Hi-Lo Waltz" (contrasting pitches)
"Ladders" (contrasting scales/modes)
"The Space Between Your Ears" (contrasting intervals)
"Bolivia" (question/answer form)
"Three Paces" (contrasting speeds)
"Rondo ala Copland" (contrasting sections to A)
"Three Paces" (contrasting speeds)
"Quiet in the Library!" (contrasting dynamics)
"Staccato Legato" (contrasting articulations)
"Fairydance" (AB form repeated)
"Blocks" (contrasting sections)
"Voices" (contrasting timbres)
"Paraphony & Polyphony" (contrasting harmonizations)
"Joyful Noyz" (contrasting sections)
"Motivation" (contrasting styles, meter and sections)
"Snap Clapple Stomp" (contrasting meter)
"Ching Clop Boom!" (contrasting timbres)
"Funky Klunky" (contrasting sections)

*Music Moments To Teach Academics: Resources*

<u>Music & Movement for Munchkins</u> *by Kerri Lynn Nichols*
Disc One/Two "All titles"

<u>Music For Dancers, Too</u>*! by Kerri Lynn Nichols*
"One Bent Tulip" *(ABCD form, repeated)*
"Strong & Light" *(AB form, repeated)*
"Jammin' in De Jungle" *(AB form, repeated)*
"Ups And Downs" *(AB form, repeated)*
"Court Jester" *(AABB form, repeated)*
"Jigalig" *(AABB form repeated with a break)*
"Shape, Wiggle & Go!" *(ABC form, repeated)*
"Questions and Answers" *(ABCB form, repeated)*
"Purcell Canon" *(AB form, repeated)*
"Locomotion" *(ABACADAEAFAGA form - Rondo)*
"Gravity" *(ABACADAEAFA form - Rondo)*
"Fee Fie Fo Fum" *(ABABACBC form)*
"Circles & Squares" *(ABACACAB form)*
"Kiyakiya" *(AB form repeated with a break)*
"Hands & Feet" *(AB form)*
"Viva la Voce" *(Additive form)*
"Percussion Discussion" *(Through-composed ABA form)*
"Jazz'up" *(ABACADBA form)*
"Consonance & Dissonance" *(AB form repeated)*
"Technotronica" *(AABCABCAB coda)*
"The Return" *(ABACADAEAA form)*

<u>Music for Creative Dance</u> *by Eric Chappelle*
Volume One    "All In One" *(AB form, repeated)*
                "Western East" *(AB form, repeated)*
                "Levelance" *(contrasting pitches and timbres)*
                "Road To Neah Bay" *(broken form/three themes)*
                "A Tale of Two Villages" *(AB form, repeated)*
                "Potpourri I" *(contrasting examples of music)*
Volume Two    "Checkerboard" *(theme and variations)*
                "Pathway Puzzle" *(contrasting melodies and timbres)*
                "Travel Notes: A Suite" *(contrasting pieces)*
                "Circular Journey" *(narrative form)*
                "Potpourri II" *(contrasting examples of music)*

*Music Moments To Teach Academics: Resources*

*Volume Three* "The Bayou Both-Step" *(AB form, contrasting meter)*
"Tempo Tantrum" *(theme & variations)*
"Fairytale" *(suite or narrative form; ABCDCBA form)*
"Celtic Suite" *(contrasting pieces)*
*Volume Four* "Amphibious" *(contrasting speeds and styles ABC)*
"Bottle Rocket" *(AB repeated form)*
"Back at Ya" *(question/answer form)*
"Pathways" *(three contrasting themes)*
"Focus" *(AB form)*
"Energy *(AB form)*
"Potpourri IV" *(contrasting examples of music)*

<u>*Rhythmically Moving*</u>*, Volumes 1-9 by Gemini/Phyllis Weikart*
*Volume Two* "Yankee Doodle" *(AB form, repeated)*
*Volume Three* "Alley Cat" *(AB form, repeated)*
"La Raspa" *(AB form, repeated)*
*Volume Four* "Ersko Kolo" *(contrasting paces)*
"Zemer Atik" *(contrasting combinations)*
"Carnavalito" *(ABC form; contrasting melodies)*
*Volume Seven* "D'Hammerschmiedsgsell'n" *(AB form, repeated)*

## EXPRESSION
### Pace

<u>*I Am the Song*</u> *by Kerri Lynn Nichols*
"Can You Feel the Happy Rhythm?" *(medium pace)*
"Journey to the Moon" *(slow pace)*
"Sticky Finger Suite"

<u>*Music for Dancers*</u> *by Kerri Lynn Nichols*
"Pulsation"                         "Ladders"
"Three Paces"                  "Rondo ala Copland"

<u>*Music for Dancers, Too!*</u> *by Kerri Lynn Nichols*
"One Bent Tulip" *(layered paces)*     "Jigalig"
"Shape, Wiggle & Go!"                        "Purcell Canon" *(slow pace)*
"Locomotion" *(variety of paces)*        "Gravity" *(variety of paces)*
"Kiyakiya" *(fast pace)*                          "Technotronica" *(fast pace)*
"The Return" *(slow pace)*

*Music Moments To Teach Academics: Resources*

<u>Music & Movement for Munchkins</u> by Kerri Lynn Nichols
Disc One/Two
"Button, You Must Wander" (medium)
"Can You Sing Your Name?" (medium)
"Cape Dorset Lullaby" (slow)
"Deedle Deedle Dumpling" (medium)
"Elephant Rhyme" (medium slow)
"Engine No.9" (medium)
"Georgie Porgie" (medium slow)
"Good Night, Sleep Tight" (medium)
"Head & Shoulders, Knees & Toes" (medium fast)
"Hickory Dickory" (medium)
"Hot Cross Buns" (medium)
"How Do You Do?" (medium slow)
"How Do You Do Today?" (fast)
"Humpty Dumpty" (medium)
"Jack B Nimble" (medium slow)
"Mary Mack" (medium)
"Mary, Quite Contrary" (medium)
"Monkey See, Monkey Do" (medium)
"Pease Porridge" (medium)
"The Sea Song" (medium)
"I Shake My Hands" (medium fast)
"Shoe Fly Medley" (medium fast)
"Strawberry Shortcake" (medium)
"There's Music in a Hammer" (medium fast)
"This Little Piggy" (medium)
"Tue Tue" (medium)
"Wan Two Dwa" (medium)
"Wee Willie Winkie" (medium)

Disc Two only
"Clothesline Dance" (medium fast)
"Fast and Slow" (fast and slow)
"La Raspa" (medium)
"On the Spot" (medium slow)
"Walk and Rock" (medium)

## Dynamics

<u>Music For Dancers</u> by Kerri Lynn Nichols
"Quiet in the Library!" (piano/soft and forte/loud)
"Rondo ala Copland" (forte/loud and mezzo/medium)
"Fairydance" (piano/soft to mezzo/medium)

<u>Music for Dancers, Too</u>! by Kerri Lynn Nichols
"Ups & Downs"
"Fee Fie Fo Fum"
"Percussion Discussion"
"Consonance & Dissonance"
"Technotronica"

<u>Musica Poetica</u>, Orff-Schulwerk Volume One by Orff and Keetman
*Four Pieces for Xylophone:* "Allegro" and "Allegretto" (crescendo)

<u>I Am the Song</u> by Kerri Lynn Nichols
"Journey to the Moon" (soft to loud)
"Waltz of the Toys" (soft to loud)
"Shine Your Light" (soft to loud)
"Everybody Needs a Drum" (soft, medium, loud)

*Music & Movement for Munchkins* by Kerri Lynn Nichols
Disc One/Two "Cape Dorset Lullaby" (soft)
"Deedle Deedle Dumpling" (soft to loud)
"How Do You Do?" (soft)
"How Do You Do Today?" (loud)
"Mary Mack" (medium to loud)
"There's Music in a Hammer" (medium and loud)
"This Little Piggy" (soft)
"Tue Tue" (medium and crescendo)
Disc Two only "Clothesline Dance" (soft to loud)
"Fast and Slow" (medium and soft)

## Articulate

*I Am the Song* by Kerri Lynn Nichols
"Can You Feel the Happy Rhythm?" (accents)
"Melody" (legato)
"Tribute to Theodore Geisel" (various articulations)
Sticky Finger Suite: "Meticulous" (staccato)
"Metronome" (legato)
"Waltz of the Toys" (accents, legato and staccato)
"Music is Our Common Ground" (legato)
"Everybody Needs a Drum" (accents)

*Music for Dancers* by Kerri Lynn Nichols
"Staccato Legato" (staccato and legato)
"Paraphony & Polyphony" (legato and staccato)
"The Hi-Lo Waltz" (accents)
"Funky Klunky" (accents)

*Music for Dancers, Too!* Kerri Lynn Nichols
"One Bent Tulip" (accents)
"Strong & Light" (pizzicato, legato)
"Ups & Downs" (accents)
"Court Jester" (accents)
"Shape, Wiggle & Go!" (accents)
"Questions and Answers" (staccato)
"Purcell Canon" (legato)
"Locomotion" (variety)
"Fee Fie Fo Fum" (marcato, staccato)
"Circles & Squares" (accents)
"Viva la Voce" (legato)
"Consonance & Dissonance" (legato, shifting accents)
"Technotronica" (accents)
"The Return" (legato)

*Music & Movement for Munchkins* by Kerri Lynn Nichols
Disc One/Two
"Cape Dorset Lullaby" (legato)
"Georgie Porgie" (accents)
"How Do You Do Today?" (accents)
"Mary Mack" (accents)
"Mary, Quite Contrary" (accents)
"Pease Porridge Hot" (legato and accents)
"Shoo Fly Medley" (accents)
"Tue Tue" (sforzando)

Disc Two only
"Clothesline Dance" (staccato, accent and sforzando)
"Fast and Slow" (staccato and legato)
"La Raspa" (accents)
"On the Spot" (legato and staccato)
"Walk and Rock" (staccato and legato)

*Music Moments To Teach Academics: Resources*

<u>Surprise Symphony</u> *by Joseph Haydn (staccato, legato, accents)*

<u>Carmina Burana</u> *by Carl Orff (this work includes every articulation)*

**Interpret**

  **Lyrics**

<u>I Am the Song</u> *by Kerri Lynn Nichols*
"Can You Feel the Happy Rhythm?"    "Listen to the Rain"
"Tribute to Theodore Geisel"    "The Lucky Song"
"Walkin' Now in Beauty"    "I Am the Song"
"Music is Our Common Ground"    "Leaves That Fall"
"Shine Your Light"    "Follow Me, Moon"
"I Am Powerful"

<u>Music & Movement for Munchkins</u> *by Kerri Lynn Nichols*
Disc One: All titles

<u>Secrets of Old: The Songs of Samuel Barber</u> *by Samuel Barber*

<u>Watermark</u> *by Enya, various selections (poetic lyrics)*

<u>The Gift of the Tortoise</u> *by Ladysmith Black Mambazo (story in song)*

<u>Songs from the Singing Sack</u> *(story songs)*

<u>Where I Come From</u> *by Steinbergh & Cockburn (poetry and song)*

*Listen to examples of songs written by Romantic period composers.*

**Psychology of Music**

  **Major and Minor Scales (keys)**

<u>Music & Movement for Munchkins</u> *by Kerri Lynn Nichols*
(see MELODY: Intervals)

  **Modes**

<u>Music & Movement for Munchkins</u> *by Kerri Lynn Nichols*
(see MELODY: Scales)

<u>I Am The Song</u> *by Kerri Lynn Nichols*
"Journey to the Moon" (Phrygian mode)
"Had Matter" (Lydian mode)

"Metronome" (Ionian mode)
"Meticulous" (Aeolian mode, modified)
"Motet" (Mixolydian mode)
"Music is Our Common Ground" (Dorian mode)
"Leaves That Fall" (Mixolydian mode)
"Follow Me, Moon" (Mixolydian mode)

*Music for Dancers* by Kerri Lynn Nichols
"Pulsation" (Mixolydian on D)
"Ladders" (various modes)
"The Space Between Your Ears"
"Echoes & Shadows" (Dorian mode)
"Three Paces" (Aeolian mode)
"Fairydance" (Lydian mode)
"Voices" (Aeolian mode)
"Joyful Noyz" (Mixolydian on E)

*Music for Dancers, Too!* by Kerri Lynn Nichols
"Jammin' in De Jungle" (Mixolydian on D)
"Court Jester" (Lydian on F)
"Shape, Wiggle & Go!" (B Section: Mixolydian on D)
"Gravity" (Mixolydian on G)
"Fee Fie Fo Fum" (Lydian on F)
"Circles & Squares" (Mixolydian on C)
"Technotronica" (Mixolydian on C)

## Intervals

*I Am the Song* by Kerri Lynn Nichols
"Can You Feel the Happy Rhythm?" (2nds)
"Samba" (2nds in the melody; 4ths/octaves in the bass)
"Meticulous" (thirds in the melody)
"Motet" (thirds)
"Ma-ching" (octaves in the echo parts/fifths in the bass line)

*Music & Movement for Munchkins* by Kerri Lynn Nichols
(see MELODY: Intervals)

*Music for Dancers* by Kerri Lynn Nichols
"Ladders" (seconds in the melody)
"Rondo ala Copland" (fourths and other intervals)
"Staccato Legato" (thirds and fourths in the melody)
"The Space Between Your Ears" (all intervals)
"Paraphony & Polyphony" (all intervals)
"Fairydance" (tri-tone/augmented fourth in the bass line)
"The Hi-Lo Waltz" (thirds and seconds in the melody)

*Music For Dancers, Too!* by Kerri Lynn Nichols
"Strong & Light" (fifths, fourths, minor thirds, seconds)
"Jammin' in De Jungle" (thirds, seconds)
"Ups & Downs" (fifths, seconds)
"Jigalig" (thirds, fourths, fifths, sixths, sevenths, octaves)
"Shape, Wiggle & Go" (seconds, thirds, fourths)
"Questions & Answers" (thirds, seconds)
"Purcell Canon" (seconds, octaves)
"Fee Fie Fo Fum" (seconds, thirds, fourths)
"Circles & Squares" (seconds, thirds, fourths, octaves)
"Viva la Voce" (seconds, thirds, fifths)
"Consonance & Dissonance" (seconds, thirds, fifths)
"Technotronica" (thirds, fourths, fifths)

*Piano Preludes*, Book One, No. 10 by Claude Debussy
"The Sunken Cathedral" (fourths in the harmony)

*Wozzeck*, Act One, Scene 4 by Alban Berg (parallel fourths)

*114 Songs* by Charles Ives
"Majority" (chords built on fourths)

*The Rite of Spring* by Igor Stravinsky (parallel fifths)

*10 Easy Piano Pieces* by Bela Bartok
"Dawn" (thirds)
"Hungarian Folk Song" (parallel fifths)

*Children's Corner* by Claude Debussy
"Serenade for the Doll" (parallel fourths and fifths)
"The Snow Is Dancing" (octaves in the echo parts)
*Piano Concerto No. 3* by Bela Bartok (seventh chords)
*Rhapsody In Blue* by George Gershwin (harmonic sevenths)
    and other examples from his work

See additional listings from the Baroque period in the general discography for examples of octaves and sevenths as well as other intervals.

## Style
See style listings in the general discography.

*Music Moments To Teach Academics: Resources*

**Period**
> *(see composers listed by period in the general discography)*

**Culture**
> *(see the Ethnic/World Music listings in the general discography and the previous references from* Rhythmically Moving*)*

<u>Music & Movement for Munchkins</u> *by Kerri Lynn Nichols*
Disc One/Two "Cape Dorset Lullaby"
          "Tue Tue"
          "Wan Two Dwa"
Disc Two only "La Raspa"

## TIMBRE

**Body Percussion**    *(add body percussion to these examples)*

<u>I Am the Song</u> *by Kerri Lynn Nichols*
"Samba"
"Can You Feel The Happy Rhythm?"
"Sansa Kroma"
"Everybody Needs a Drum"

<u>Music for Dancers</u> *by Kerri Lynn Nichols*
"Snap Clapple Stomp"
"Blocks"
"Bolivia"
"Rondo ala Copland"
"Ching, Clop, Boom!"
"Joyful Noyz"

<u>Music for Dancers, Too</u>! *by Kerri Lynn Nichols*
"Hands & Feet"
"One Bent Tulip"
"Jammin' in De Jungle"
"Ups & Downs"
"Questions and Answers"
"Kiyakiya"

<u>Stomp Out Loud</u> *by Stomp (HBO Musical)*

<u>Musica Poetica</u>, *Orff-Schulwerk Volume One by Orff and Keetman*
    Songs and Pieces: "Tun ma gehn" (clapping and stomping)

<u>African Songs and Rhythms for Children</u> *by William Amoaku (clapping)*

<u>The Best of Bobby McFerrin</u> *by Bobby McFerrin*
    "Don't Worry, Be Happy"
    "Thinkin' About Your Body"
    "Good Lovin'"

*Music Moments To Teach Academics: Resources*

<u>*Bring In 'Da Noise, Bring In 'Da Funk*</u> *by Waters, Mark and Duquesnay*
    *various selections*

**Voice**

    <u>*I Am The Song*</u> *by Kerri Lynn Nichols*
    *(see songs listed under lyrics)*

    <u>*Music for Dancers*</u> *by Kerri Lynn Nichols*
    *"Voices"*

    <u>*Music for Dancers, Too*</u>*! by Kerri Lynn Nichols*
    *"Viva la Voce"*

    <u>*Music & Movement for Munchkins*</u> *by Kerri Lynn Nichols*
    *(all selections on Disc One have singing and/or speech)*

    <u>*Music for Creative Dance*</u> *by Eric Chappelle*
    *Volume Two "Pastorale"*

    <u>*Rhythmically Moving*</u>*, Volumes 1-9 by Gemini/Phyllis Weikart*
    *Volume Four "Zemer Atik" (Israel)*

    <u>*So Many Stars*</u> *and other titles by Kathleen Battle*

    <u>*Chant*</u> *by The Benedictine Monks*

    <u>*Romanza*</u> *by Andrea Bocelli*

    <u>*Ceremony of Carols*</u> *by Benjamin Britten*

    <u>*The Three Tenors*</u> *by Carreras, Domingo and Pavarotti*

    <u>*Voice of an Angel*</u> *by Charlotte Church*

    <u>*The Elephant's Child*</u> *and* <u>*Hush*</u> *by Bobby McFerrin*

    <u>*The Marriage of Figaro*</u> *by Wolfgang Amadeus Mozart*

    <u>*Eden*</u> *by Sarah Brightman*

    <u>*Watermark*</u> *by Enya*

    <u>*Mender of Hearts*</u> *by Singh Kaur and Kim Robertson*

*Songs of the Humpback Whale* by Roger Payne

*Songbird Symphony* by NorthSound

*Spirit of the Forest* by Baka Beyond

*Weaving My Ancestors' Voices* and *The Zen Kiss* by Sheila Chandra

*Dance My Children* by Samite

*Let Your Voice Be Heard* by Adzinyah, Maraire and Tucker

*The Gift of the Tortoise* by Ladysmith Black Mambazo

*China: Time To Listen* by Ellipsis Arts

*Classics: Volume Eight, Joan Baez* by Joan Baez

*The Very Best of John Denver* by John Denver

*Rites of Passage* by the Indigo Girls

*Greatest Hits* by Simon and Garfunkel

*Selections: 1976-1988* by Sweet Honey in the Rock

*MTV Unplugged* by Tony Bennett

*16 Most Requested Songs* by Sarah Vaughan

*Tonin'* by The Manhattan Transfer

*Way Back To Paradise* by Audra McDonald

*Toby Twining Music* by Shaman

*The Best of Aretha Franklin* by Aretha Franklin

*Come On Over* by Shania Twain

*Music Moments To Teach Academics: Recources*

<u>The Trenchcoats</u> by The Trenchcoats

<u>2</u> by M-pact

<u>The Day</u> by Babyface

<u>A New Beginning</u> by Tracy Chapman

<u>The Miseducation of Lauryn Hill</u> by Lauryn Hill

<u>Surfacing</u> by Sarah McLachlan

**Percussion**

<u>I Am the Song</u> by Kerri Lynn Nichols
"Can You Feel the Happy Rhythm?" (combined)    "Waltz of the Toys"
"Samba" (xylophones, drums, small percussion)    "Leaves That Fall"
"Tribute to Theodore Geisel"    "Everybody Needs A Drum"
"Walkin' Now In Beauty" (tambourine, native drum) "I Am Powerful"
"Sansa Kroma"

<u>Music & Movement for Munchkins</u> by Kerri Lynn Nichols
Disc One/Two  "Button, You Must Wander" (woodblock, glockenspiel, metallophone)
"Can You Sing Your Name?" (metallophone, cabasa, glockenspiel)
"Cape Dorset Lullaby" (metallophone, tambourine, hand drum)
"Deedle Deedle Dumpling" (cabasa, woodblock, tambourine, drum)
"The Elephant Rhyme" (bass and alto xylophones, rototoms, woodblock,
    glockenspiel, conga drum)
"Engine No. 9" (agogo bell, cabasa, bass xylophone, glockenspiel)
"Georgie Porgie" (piano, cymbal, tambourine)
"Good Night, Sleep Tight" (piano, chime, tambourine)
"Head and Shoulders" (vibraphone, xylophone, glockenspiel, woodblock)
"Hickory Dickory Dock" (woodblock, gong)
"Hot Cross Buns (cabasa, hand drum, bass xylophone, agogo bell,
    woodblock, soprano xylophone, glockenspiel)
"How Do You Do?" (low conga, glockenspiel)
"How Do You Do Today?" (piano, cymbal, castanets)
"Humpty Dumpty" (piano, castanets, glockenspiel, alto xylophone,
    cabasa)
"Jack B Nimble" (cymbal, bass marimba, xylophone, glockenspiel,
    vibraslap, piano)
"Mary Mack" (piano, bass drum, tambourine, alto xylophone, woodblock,
    bells, finger cymbals, triangle)
"Mary, Quite Contrary" (piano, glockenspiel, rimshot, woodblock)
"Monkey See, Monkey Do" (glockenspiel, bass and soprano xylophones,
    guiro, conga, temple blocks)
"Pease Porridge Hot" (piano, alto and bass xylophones, glockenspiel,
    conga, cowbell)

*Music Moments To Teach Academics: Resources*

"Shake My Hands" (soprano, alto and bass xylophones, cabasa, hand drum, woodblock)
"Shoo Fly Medley" (drum set, chimes, piano)
"Strawberry Shortcake" (piano, alto xylophone, cowbell, castanets)
"There's Music In a Hammer" (cabasa, xylophones, glockenspiel, piano)
"This Little Piggy" (woodblock, guiro, xylophone, glockenspiel)
"Tue, Tue" (conga, xylophones, cabasa/shekere)
"Wan Two Dwa" (conga, cabasa/shekere, xylophones, gangokui, dundun)
"Wee Willie Winkie" (bass marimba, xylophone, hand drum, triangle, woodblock, maracas)

Disc Two
"Clothesline Dance" (piano)
"Fast and Slow" (piano, castanets, bass marimba)
"La Raspa" (guiro, cabasa, bass marimba, bass & soprano xylophones, quica)
"On the Spot" (vibraphone, glockenspiel)
"Walk and Rock" (woodblock, triangle, xylophone, conga)

<u>Music for Dancers</u> by Kerri Lynn Nichols
"Pulsation"                              "Quiet in the Library!"
"Blocks"                                 "Ching, Clop, Boom!"
"Motivation" (B and C sections)          "Funky Klunky"
"Bolivia" (skins, metals)                "Mango Walk"
"Rondo ala Copland"                      "Joyful Noyz"
"Three Paces"

<u>Music for Dancers, Too!</u> by Kerri Lynn Nichols
"Jammin' In De Jungle"                   "Jigalig"
"Shape, Wiggle & Go!"                    "Locomotion"
"Fee Fie Fo Fum"                         "Kiyakiya"
"Percussion Discussion"                  "Jazz'up"

<u>Music for Creative Dance</u> by Eric Chappelle
Volume One    "Chirpa Chirpa" (combined)
              "Western East" (metals and woods)
              "Stone Soup" (skins)
              "A Tale of Two Villages" (metals and skins)
Volume Two    "Skippy Ska" (combined)
              "Caribbean Leaps" (combined)
              "Andean Altitude" (combined)
              "Saharan Campsite" (combined)
              "Indian Incense" (metals and skins)
Volume Three  "Dakota Dawn" (skins and shakers)
              "Rock'n Stop" (combined with xylophone)
              "Dancing Digits" (combined)

*Music Moments To Teach Academics: Resources*

                    "Tambourine" (metals and skins)
                    "Tempo Tantrum" (woods)
                    "I Say, You Say" (skins and metals)
                    "Varations In Three" (metals and shakers)
                    "Mr. E" (metals)
                    "Spootiskerry" (woods)
Volume Four   "Monkey Fiddle Chant"
                    "Back At Ya"
                    "Skippity Jig"
                    "Totem Pole"

<u>Rhythmically Moving</u>, Volumes 1-9 by Gemini/Phyllis Weikart
Volume Two    "Limbo Rock" (USA) (combined)
Volume Three  "Alley Cat" (USA) (xylophone)
                    "Bele Kawe" (Africa) (skins)
                    "La Raspa" (Mexico) (woods)
Volume Five   "Carnavalito" (Bolivia) (skins)
Volume Nine  "Makedonikos Horos" (Greece) (skins)

<u>Carmina Burana</u> by Carl Orff (various selections)

<u>Musica Poetica</u>, Orff-Schulwerk Volume One by Orff and Keetman

<u>Music for Children</u>, Orff-Schulwerk Volume Two by Orff and Keetman

<u>Okropong</u> by Obo Addy

<u>Island In the Sun</u> by Harry Belafonte

<u>Buscando America</u> by Ruben Blades

<u>Global Meditation</u> and <u>Global Celebration</u> by Ellipsis Arts

<u>Planet Drum</u> and <u>At the Edge</u> by Mickey Hart

<u>Orbitones: Spoons, Harps and Bellowphones</u> by Bart Hopkin

<u>China: Time To Listen</u> by Ellipsis Arts

<u>The Lion's Roar: Chinese Luogu Percussion Ensembles</u> by Patricia Campbell

**Instruments**
 **Strings**

   <u>I Am the Song</u> by Kerri Lynn Nichols

*Music Moments To Teach Academics: Resources*

"Can You Feel the Happy Rhythm?" (guitars)
"Samba" (nylon guitar)
"Melody" (guitars)
"Listen to the Rain" (harp)
"Journey to the Moon" (strings)
"Motet" (harp)
"I Am the Song" (guitars)
"Shine Your Light" (strings)
"Follow Me, Moon" (guitars)

<u>Music & Movement for Munchkins</u> by Kerri Lynn Nichols
Disc One/Two  "Button, You Must Wander" (harp)
              "Can You Sing Your Name?" (harp)
              "How Do You Do?" (string bass)
              "Monkey See, Monkey Do" (harp)
              "Good Night, Sleep Tight" (string bass)
Disc Two      "Fast and Slow" (string bass)
              "On the Spot" (string bass, violin (pizzicato))
              "Walk and Rock" (guitar)

<u>Music for Dancers</u> by Kerri Lynn Nichols
"Twos & Threes" (cello/guitar)      "Funky Klunky" (strings)
"The Hi-Lo Waltz" (bassoon)         "Staccato Legato" (guitars)
"Rondo ala Copland" (violin)        "Echoes & Shadows (guitars)

<u>Music for Dancers, Too!</u> by Kerri Lynn Nichols
"Strong & Light" (harp)             "Jigalig" (nylon guitar)
"Shape, Wiggle & Go!" (guitars)     "Questions and Answers" (strings)
"Purcell Canon" (guitars)           "Locomotion" (Spanish guitar)
"Gravity" (synth strings)           "Fee Fie Fo Fum" (harp, pizzicato)
"The Return" (guitars)              "Circles & Squares" (synth strings)

<u>Music for Creative Dance</u> by Eric Chappelle
Various selections from Volumes I-IV with violin/viola/cello including
Volume Two    "Pastorale" (harp)
Volume Three  "Planxty Irwin" (guitars and violin)

<u>Rhythmically Moving</u>, Volumes 1-9 by Gemini/Phyllis Weikart
Various selections (violins, guitars and harp) including:
Volume One    "Joe Clark Mixer" (USA) (jaw harp)
Volume Two    "Djurdjevka Kolo" (Yugoslavia) (mandolin)

<u>Orchestral Suites</u> by Johann Sebastian Bach

*Music Moments To Teach Academics: Resources*

<u>The Four Seasons</u> *by Antonio Vivaldi*

<u>Celtic Odyssey</u> *by Narada*

<u>Dreamtime</u> *by Foday Musa Suso*

*Listen to additional examples listed in the general discography.*

**Winds**

<u>I Am the Song</u> *by Kerri Lynn Nichols*
*"Can You Feel the Happy Rhythm?" (recorder)*
*"Samba" (recorder)*
*"Melody" (flute)*
*"Motet" (recorder)*
*"Walkin' Now In Beauty" (ocarina)*
*"Sansa Kroma" (recorder)*
*"I Am the Song" (flute)*
*"Waltz of the Toys" (ocarina)*
*"Leaves That Fall" (flute)*

<u>Music & Movement for Munchkins</u> *by Kerri Lynn Nichols*
Disc One/Two  *"Can You Sing Your Name?" (flute)*
              *"Cape Dorset Lullaby" (flute/recorder)*
              *"Engine No. 9" (bandoneon)*
              *"Georgie Porgie" (clarinet)*
              *"How Do You Do?" (flute)*
              *"Pease Porridge Hot" (recorder/synth)*
              *"Shoo Fly Medley" (clarinet)*
              *"There's Music In a Hammer" (bandoneon)*
              *"This Little Piggy" (whistle/synth)*
Disc Two      *"La Raspa" (flute)*
              *"Walk and Rock" (flute/recorder)*

<u>Music for Dancers</u> *by Kerri Lynn Nichols*
*"Blocks" (recorder)*          *"Twos & Threes" (recorder)*
*"The Hi-Lo Waltz" (clarinet)* *"Motivation" (recorder)*
*"Bolivia" (pan flutes)*       *"Echoes & Shadows" (flute)*
*"Rondo ala Copland" (whistle)* *"Staccato Legato" (recorder)*
*"Mango Walk" (recorder)*

<u>Music for Dancers, Too!</u> *by Kerri Lynn Nichols*
*"Strong & Light" (recorder)*       *"Court Jester" (recorder)*
*"Jigalig" (recorder)*              *"Shape, Wiggle & Go!" (recorder)*
*"Purcell Canon" (flute & recorder)* *"Locomotion" (variety of winds)*
*"Gravity" (wind sounds, etc.)*     *"Circles & Squares" (flute)*
*"Kiyakiya" (flute)*                *"Jazz'up" (clarinet, etc.)*
*"Consonance & Dissonance" (flute)* *"The Return" (recorder, flute)*

*The Four Seasons* by Antonio Vivaldi

*Celtic Odyssey* by Narada

*Dreamtime* by Foday Musa Suso

Listen to additional examples listed in the general discography.

**Winds**

*I Am the Song* by Kerri Lynn Nichols
"Can You Feel the Happy Rhythm?" (recorder)
"Samba" (recorder)
"Melody" (flute)
"Motet" (recorder)
"Walkin' Now In Beauty" (ocarina)
"Sansa Kroma" (recorder)
"I Am the Song" (flute)
"Waltz of the Toys" (ocarina)
"Leaves That Fall" (flute)

*Music & Movement for Munchkins* by Kerri Lynn Nichols
Disc One/Two  "Can You Sing Your Name?" (flute)
              "Cape Dorset Lullaby" (flute/recorder)
              "Engine No. 9" (bandoneon)
              "Georgie Porgie" (clarinet)
              "How Do You Do?" (flute)
              "Pease Porridge Hot" (recorder/synth)
              "Shoo Fly Medley" (clarinet)
              "There's Music In a Hammer" (bandoneon)
              "This Little Piggy" (whistle/synth)
Disc Two      "La Raspa" (flute)
              "Walk and Rock" (flute/recorder)

*Music for Dancers* by Kerri Lynn Nichols
"Blocks" (recorder)              "Twos & Threes" (recorder)
"The Hi-Lo Waltz" (clarinet)     "Motivation" (recorder)
"Bolivia" (pan flutes)           "Echoes & Shadows" (flute)
"Rondo ala Copland" (whistle)    "Staccato Legato" (recorder)
"Mango Walk" (recorder)

*Music for Dancers, Too!* by Kerri Lynn Nichols
"Strong & Light" (recorder)           "Court Jester" (recorder)
"Jigalig" (recorder)                  "Shape, Wiggle & Go!" (recorder)
"Purcell Canon" (flute & recorder)    "Locomotion" (variety of winds)
"Gravity" (wind sounds, etc.)         "Circles & Squares" (flute)
"Kiyakiya" (flute)                    "Jazz'up" (clarinet, etc.)
"Consonance & Dissonance" (flute)     "The Return" (recorder, flute)

## TEXTURE
### Combinations
#### Solo

*I Am the Song* by Kerri Lynn Nichols
"Melody" (flute solo)

*Music & Movement for Munchkins* by Kerri Lynn Nichols
Disc One: All titles

*Music for Dancers* by Kerri Lynn Nichols
"Rondo ala Copland" (instrumental solos)

*Music for Dancers, Too!* by Kerri Lynn Nichols
"Ups & Downs" (piano solos)
"Court Jester" (recorder solo)
"Viva la Voce" (begins with vocal solo)
"Jazz'up" (instrumental solos)
"The Return" (recorder, flute solos)

*One in Spirit* by Jesse Kalu (various selections, voice & flute)

*Japan: Shakuhachi - The Japanese Flute* by K. Miyata (various selections)

*Piano Music*, Orff-Schulwerk Volume Three by Carl Orff (various selections, piano)

*Tunula Eno* by Samite (various selections, voice & Ugandan flute)

*The Zen Kiss* by Sheila Chandra (various selections, vocal)

#### Ensemble

*I Am the Song* by Kerri Lynn Nichols
All titles

*Music & Movement for Munchkins* by Kerri Lynn Nichols
Disc One: All titles
Disc Two only: La Raspa (instrumental)

*Music for Dancers* by Kerri Lynn Nichols
"Blocks" (drum and percussion ensembles)
"Bolivia" (drum ensemble)
"Rondo ala Copland" (Orff ensemble)
"Voices" (vocal ensemble)
"Ching Clop Boom!" (woods, metals, drum ensembles)

*Music for Dancers, Too!* by Kerri Lynn Nichols
"Purcell Canon" (instrumental canon)
"Locomotion" (various instrumental/percussion ensembles)
"Kiyakiya" (drum ensemble)
"Fee Fie Fo Fum" (instrumental ensemble)
"Viva la Voce" (vocal ensemble)
"Percussion Discussion" (percussion ensemble)

*Octet for Wind Instruments* by Igor Stravinsky

*Musica Poetica*, Orff-Schulwerk Volume One by Orff/Keetman (various selections)

*Take 6* by Take 6 (vocal sextet)

*Hush* by Bobby McFerrin and Yo Yo Ma (vocal/cello duets)

*Rhythmically Moving*, Volumes 1-9 by Gemini/Phyllis Weikart
    Volume Four "Zemer Atik"

## Unison

*Chant* by The Benedictine Monks

*The Three Tenors* by Carreras, Domingo and Pavarotti (various selections)

## Choir

*Ceremony of Carols* by Benjamin Britten

*Greatest Hits* by George Frideric Handel

*Greatest Hits* by Johann Sebastian Bach (choral selections)

*Africa to America* by Sounds of Blackness

## Harmony
### Tension

*I Am the Song* by Kerri Lynn Nichols
"Samba"                                    "Melody"
"Tribute to Theodore Geisel"               "Journey to the Moon"
"Sticky Finger Suite" (selections)         "Shine Your Light"

*Music & Movement for Munchkins* by Kerri Lynn Nichols
    Disc One/Two: "Georgie Porgie"
                     "Engine No. 9"
    Disc Two only: "Clothesline Dance"

*Music for Dancers* by Kerri Lynn Nichols
"Fairydance"           "Voices"
"Ching Clop Boom!"    "Funky Klunky"

*Music for Dancers, Too!* by Kerri Lynn Nichols
"Ups & Downs"       "Court Jester"
"Gravity"             "Fee Fie Fo Fum"
"Jazz'up"             "Consonance & Dissonance"
"Technotronica"

*Music for Creative Dance* by Eric Chappelle
Volume Two  "Indian Incense"
                "Balinese Mask"

*Rhythmically Moving*, Volumes 1-9 by Gemini/Phyllis Weikart
Volume Eight "Misirlou-Kritikos" (Greek-American)

*10 Easy Pieces for Piano* by Bela Bartok

*The Rite of Spring* by Igor Stravinsky

## Resolution

*I Am the Song* by Kerri Lynn Nichols
"Samba"              "Melody"
"Journey to the Moon"    "Metronome"

*Music & Movement for Munchkins* by Kerri Lynn Nichols
    Disc One/Two (all titles)
    Disc Two only (all titles)

*Music for Dancers* by Kerri Lynn Nichols
"Rondo ala Copland"     "Twos & Threes"
"Pulsation"             "Quiet in the Library"
"The Hi-Lo Waltz"      "Staccato Legato"
"Ching Clop Boom!"    "Mango Walk"
"Paraphony & Polyphony"  "Joyful Noyz"

*Music Moments To Teach Academics: Resources*

<u>*Music for Dancers, Too!*</u> *by Kerri Lynn Nichols*
"Strong & Light"          "Jigalig"
"Viva la Voce"            "Jazz' up"
"Consonance & Dissonance"

<u>*Music for Creative Dance*</u> *by Eric Chappelle*
Volume Two "Pastorale"    Volume Three "Breathe"

**Polyphony**

<u>*I Am the Song*</u> *by Kerri Lynn Nichols*
"Sticky Finger Suite" (selections)    "Sansa Kroma"
"Waltz of the Toys"                   "Everybody Needs a Drum"
"I am Powerful"

<u>*Music & Movement for Munchkins*</u> *by Kerri Lynn Nichols*
    Disc One/Two "Deedle Deedle Dumpling"
                      "Good Night, Sleep Tight
                        "Wan Two Dwa
    Disc Two only "Fast and Slow
                        "On the Spot

<u>*Music for Dancers*</u> *by Kerri Lynn Nichols*
"Blocks"                  "Twos & Threes"
"The Hi-Lo Waltz"         "Ladders"
"Motivation"              "Staccato Legato"
"Snap Clapple Stomp"      "Voices"
"Ching Clop Boom"         "Paraphony & Polyphony"
"The Space Between Your Ears"

<u>*Music for Dancers, Too!*</u> *by Kerri Lynn Nichols*
"Questions and Answers"   "Purcell Canon"
"Locomotion"              "Gravity"
"Fee Fie Fo Fum"          "Kiyakiya"
"Percussion Discussion"

<u>*Greatest Hits*</u> *by Johann Sebastian Bach*
"Fugue"

<u>*Messiah*</u> *by George Frideric Handel* (choral selections)

<u>*Madrigals*</u> *by Thomas Morley*

<u>*African Songs & Rhythms for Children*</u> *by William Amoaku* (polyrhythms)

236

*Music Moments To Teach Academics: Resources*

**Paraphony**

*I Am the Song* by Kerri Lynn Nichols
"Samba"                              "Motet"

*Music & Movement for Munchkins* by Kerri Lynn Nichols
    Disc One/Two "How Do You Do Today?"
        "The Sea Song"
        "Tue Tue"
        "Wan Two Dwa"
    Disc Two only "Strawberry Shortcake"

*Music for Dancers* by Kerri Lynn Nichols
"The Space Between Your Ears"     "Paraphony And Polyphony"

*Music for Dancers, Too!* by Kerri Lynn Nichols
"Purcell Canon"                    "Viva la Voce"

*Rhythmically Moving*, Volumes 1-9 by Gemini/Phyllis Weikart
Volume One "Southwind"
Volume Four "Hole in the Wall" (recorder harmony)
    "Hineh Ma Tov" (vocal harmony)

*Piano Preludes*, Book Two, No. 10 by Claude Debussy
"Canope" and other selections

*Nocturnes* by Claude Debussy
"Fetes" and other selections

**Accompaniment**
  **a Cappella**

*Music for Dancers* by Kerri Lynn Nichols "Voices"

*Music for Dancers, Too!* by Kerri Lynn Nichols "Viva la Voce"

*Selections: 1976-1988* by Sweet Honey In the Rock

*Take 6* by Take 6

*The Zen Kiss* by Sheila Chandra

See listings under a cappella in the general discography.

*Music Moments To Teach Academics: Resources*

**Instrumental**

*I Am the Song* by Kerri Lynn Nichols "Sansa Kroma"

*Music & Movement for Munchkins* by Kerri Lynn Nichols
    Disc One (All titles)
    Disc Two only "Walk and Rock" (ostinato)

*Music for Dancers* by Kerri Lynn Nichols
"Joyful Noyz"               "Mango Walk"
"Quiet in the Library"      "Snap Clapple Stomp"
"Bolivia"

*Music for Creative Dance* by Eric Chappelle
Volume Two: "Pastorale"

*Zoot Suit Riot* by The Cherry Poppin' Daddies

**Vocal**

*I Am the Song* by Kerri Lynn Nichols
"Everybody Needs A Drum"

*Music & Movement for Munchkins* by Kerri Lynn Nichols
Disc One "Deedle Deedle Dumpling"

*Selections: 1976-1988* by Sweet Honey In the Rock
"Breaths" and other selections

*The Medicine Man* by Bobby McFerrin with Voicestra
"Sweet in the Mornin'" and other selections

*The Trenchcoats* by The Trenchcoats (various selections)

**Nature Sounds**

*Sounds of the Humpback Whale* by Roger Payne

*Earthbeat* by Paul Winter

*Songbird Symphony* and other titles by NorthSound

*Firebird Suite* by Igor Stravinsky

*Music Moments To Teach Academics: Resources*

## Instrumental

*I Am the Song* by Kerri Lynn Nichols "Sansa Kroma"

*Music & Movement for Munchkins* by Kerri Lynn Nichols
    Disc One (All titles)
    Disc Two only "Walk and Rock" (ostinato)

*Music for Dancers* by Kerri Lynn Nichols
"Joyful Noyz"  "Mango Walk"
"Quiet in the Library"  "Snap Clapple Stomp"
"Bolivia"

*Music for Creative Dance* by Eric Chappelle
Volume Two: "Pastorale"

*Zoot Suit Riot* by The Cherry Poppin' Daddies

## Vocal

*I Am the Song* by Kerri Lynn Nichols
"Everybody Needs A Drum"

*Music & Movement for Munchkins* by Kerri Lynn Nichols
Disc One "Deedle Deedle Dumpling"

*Selections: 1976-1988* by Sweet Honey In the Rock
"Breaths" and other selections

*The Medicine Man* by Bobby McFerrin with Voicestra
"Sweet in the Mornin'" and other selections

*The Trenchcoats* by The Trenchcoats (various selections)

## Nature Sounds

*Sounds of the Humpback Whale* by Roger Payne

*Earthbeat* by Paul Winter

*Songbird Symphony* and other titles by NorthSound

*Firebird Suite* by Igor Stravinsky

## BIBLIOGRAPHY

**Music Books**

Adzinyah, A.K., Maraire, D. and Tucker, J. *Let Your Voice Be Heard! Songs From Ghana and Zimbabwe.* World Music Press, Danbury, CT. 1986.

Amoaku, W.K. *African Songs and Rhythms for Children.* Schott Publishing, New York, NY. 1971.

Anderson, William. *Integrating Music into the Elementary Classroom.* Wadsworth Publishing Company, Belmont, CA. 1998.

Barber, David. *Bach, Beethoven and the Boys: Music History As It Ought To Be Taught.* Sound and Vision, Toronto, Canada. 1986.

Barnwell, Ysaye. *Continuum: The First Songbook of Sweet Honey in the Rock.* Contemporary A Cappella Publishing, Southwest Harbor, ME. 1999.

Barrett, Janet, et al. *Sound Ways Of Knowing: Music in the Interdisciplinary Curriculum.* Schirmer Books, New York, NY. 1997.

Bernstein, Sara. *Hand Clap!* Adams Media Corporation, Avon, MA. 1994. Birkenshaw-Fleming,

Lois. *Music for All: Teaching Music to People with Special Needs.* Gordon V. Thompson Music, Toronto, Canada. 1993.

Blood, Peter and Patterson, Annie. *Rise Up Singing! The Group Singing Songbook.* The Sing Out Corporation, Bethlehem, PA. 1988, 1992.

Blumenfeld, Larry. *Voices of Forgotten Worlds: Traditional Music of Indigenous People.* Ellipsis Arts, Roslyn, NY. 1993.

Burton, Bryan. *Moving Within the Circle: Contemporary Native American Music and Dance.* World Music Press, Danbury, CT. 1993.

Campbell, Don. *Introduction to the Musical Brain.* MMB Music Inc., St. Louis, MO. 1992.

Campbell, Don. *Rhythms of Learning.* Zephyr Press, Inc., Tuscon, AZ. 1991.

Campbell, Patricia Shehan, et al. *Roots And Branches: A Legacy of Multicultural Music for Children.* World Music Press, Danbury, CT. 1994.

Chernoff, John Miller. *African Rhythm and African Sensibility.* The University of Chicago Press, Chicago, IL. 1979.

Choksy, Lois. *The Kodaly Context: Creating an Environment for Musical Learning.* Prentice-Hall, Inc., Englewood Cliffs, NJ. 1981.

Choksy, Lois. *The Kodaly Method: Comprehensive Music Education from Infant to Adult.* Prentice-Hall, Inc., Englewood Cliffs, NJ. 1974.

East, Helen. *The Singing Sack: 28 Song-Stories From Around the World.* A & C Black Publishers, Ltd., Bedford Row, London. 1989.

Findlay, Elsa. *Rhythm and Movement: Applications of Dalcroze Eurhythmics.* Summy-Birchard Music, Princeton, NJ. 1971.

Fulton, Eleanor and Smith, Pat. *Let's Slice the Ice: A Collection of Black Children's Ring Games and Chants.* MMB Music, Inc., St. Louis, MO. 1978.

Garland, Trudi Hammel and Kahn, Charity Vaughan. *Math And Music: Harmonious Connections.* Dale Seymour Publications. 1995.

Goodkin, Doug. *Now's the Time: Teaching Jazz to All Ages.* Pentatonic Press, San Francisco, CA. 2004.

Grout, Donald Jay. *A History of Western Music.* W. W. Norton & Company, Inc., New York, NY. 1996.

Habermeyer, Sharlene. *Good Music, Brighter Children.* Prima Publishing, Rocklin, CA. 1999.

Hackett, Patricia. *The Melody Book.* Prentice Hall, Inc., Englewood Cliffs, NJ. 1983.

Hart, Mickey and Lieberman, Fredric. *Planet Drum: A Celebration of Percussion and Rhythm.* HarperCollins Publishers, New York, NY. 1991.

Hart, Mickey and Lieberman, Fredric. *Spirit Into Sound: The Magic of Music.* Grateful Dead Books, Petaluma, CA. 1999.

Hughes, Langston. *The Book of Rhythms.* Oxford University Press, New York, NY. 1954.

Jacques-Dalcroze, Emile. *Rhythm, Music and Education.* The Dalcroze Society, London, England. Reprinted 1980.

Jensen, Eric. *Music With The Brain in Mind.* The Brain Store, Inc. San Diego, CA. 2000.

Jessup, Lynne. *Afro-Ensemble: A Beginning Book.* Harris Music Publications, Ft. Worth, TX. 1975.

Johnston, Richard. *Folk Songs of North America: A Source Book for All Teachers.* Caveat Music Publishers, Ltd., Toronto, Canada. 1984.

Jones, Bessie and Hawes, Bess Lomax. *Step It Down: Games, Plays, Songs and Stories from the Afro-American Heritage.* University of Georgia Press, Athens, GA. 1972.

Jourdain, Robert. *Music, The Brain, And Ecstacy.* Avon Books, Inc., New York, NY. 1997.

Keetman, Gunild. *Elementaria: First Acquaintance with Orff-Schulwerk.* Schott Publishing. 1969.

Kennedy, Maureen. *Circle Round the Zero: Play Chants and Singing Games of City Children.* Beatin' Path Publications LLC, Bridgewater, VA. 2014.

Kerlee, Paul. *Welcome in the Spring: Morris & Sword Dances for Children.* World Music Press, Danbury, CT. 1994.

Kuo-Huang, Han and Campbell, Patricia. *The Lion's Roar: Chinese Luogu Percussion Ensembles.* World Music Press, Danbury, CT. 1992.

Madin, Jon. *Make Your Own Wacky Instruments.* Beatin' Path Publications LLC, Bridgewater, VA. 2012.

Mandell, Muriel and Wood, Robert E. *Make Your Own Musical Instruments.* Sterling Publishing Co., Inc., New York, NY. 1957.

Marks, Kate. *Circle Of Song: Songs, Chants, and Dances for Ritual and Celebration.* Full Circle Press, Amhurst, MA. 1993.

Mathieu, W.A. *The Listening Book: Discovering Your Own Music.* Shambala Publications, Inc., Boston, MA. 1991.

Mathieu, W.A. *The Musical Life.* Shambhala Publications, Inc., Boston, MA. 1994.

Medina, John. *Brain Rules: 12 Principles for Surviving and Thriving at Work, Home and School.* Pear Press. Reprint Edition, 2009.

Melick, Brian. *Percussion Instruments Made Out of Found Objects.* Brian M. Melick, Ravena, NY. 1994.

Middleton, Julie Forest. *Songs For Earthlings: A Green Spirituality Songbook.* Emerald Earth Publishing, Philadelphia, PA. 1998.

Miles, Elizabeth. *Tune Your Brain. Using Music to Manage Your Mind, Body, and Mood.* Berkley Books, New York, NY. 1997.

Mitchell, Kevin M. *Songwriter's Rhyming Dictionary.* Alfred Publishing Company, Inc., Van Nuys, CA. 1995.

Nash, Grace. *Do It My Way: A Handbook for Building Creative Teaching Experiences.* Alfred Publishing Company, Inc., Sherman Oaks, CA. 1977.

National Arts Education Association. *National Standards for Arts Education: What Every Young American Should Know and Be Able To Do In the Arts.* Music Educators National Conference, Reston, VA. 1994.

Nguyen, Phong and Campbell, Patricia. *From Rice Paddies and Temple Yards: Traditional Music of Vietnam.* World Music Press, Danbury, CT. 1990.

Nichols, Kerri Lynn. *Inspirations.* Beatin' Path Publications LLC, Bridgewater, VA. 2014.

Nichols, Kerri Lynn. *Music & Movement For Munchkins.* Beatin' Path Publications LLC Bridgewater, VA. 2014.

Nichols, Kerri Lynn. *Music for Dancers.* Beatin' Path Publications LLC, Bridgewater, VA. 1999.

Orff, Carl and Keetman, Gunild. *Music for Children: Volumes I-V.* Schott and Co., Thetford, London England. 1954.

Orff, Gertrud. *Key Concepts in the Orff Music Therapy.* Schott, London, England. 1968.

Ortiz, John M. *The Tao of Music: Sound Psychology.* Samuel Weiser, Inc. York Beach, ME. 1997.

Page, Nick. *Music As a Way of Knowing.* Stenhouse Publishers, York, MN. 1995.

Page, Nick. *Sing and Shine On!* World Music Press, Danbury, CT. 2001.

Paynter, Elizabeth and John. *The Dance and the Drum: Integrated projects in music, dance and drama for schools.* Universal Edition (London) Ltd., London, England. 1974.

Perkins, William. *Droppin' Science: Critical Essays On Rap Music and Hip Hop Culture.* Temple University Press, Philadelphia, PA. 1996.

Randel, Don Michael. *The New Harvard Dictionary of Music.* Harvard University Press, Cambridge, MA. 1986.

*Movement.* Schott Musik International, Mainz. 2004.

Regner, Hermann. *Music for Children: Orff-Schulwerk American Edition, Volumes One, Two and Three.* Schott Music Corporation, New York, NY. 1977, 1980, 1982.

Reimer, Bennett. *World Musics and Music Education: Facing the Issues.* MENC, Reston, VA. 2002.

Richards, Mary Helen. *Aesthetic Foundations For Thinking: Part Three-The ETM Process.* Richards Institute, Portola Valley, CA. 1980.

Schafer, R. Murray. *The Thinking Ear.* Arcana Editions, Toronto, Canada. 1986.

Schnelby-Black, Julin and Moore, Stephen. *The Rhythm Inside: Connecting Body, Mind and Spirit Through Music.* Alred Publishing. Van Nuys, CA. 2003.

Seeger, Pete. *Where Have All the Flowers Gone?* Sing Out Corporation, Bethlehem, PA. 1993.

Stevens, Christine. *The Art and Heart of Drum Circles.* Hal Leonard Corporation, Milwaukee, WI. 2003.

Suzuki, Waltraud. *Nurtured by Love.* Warner Bros. Publications, Inc., Miami, FL. 1983.

Thomas, Marlo. *Free to Be. . .You and Me.* McGraw-Hill Book Company, New York, NY. 1974.

Wade, Bonnie. *Thinking Musically.* Oxford University Press, New York, NY. 2004

Walther, Tom. *Make Mine Music!* Yolla Bolly Press, Covelo, CA. 1980.

*Music Moments To Teach Academics: Resources*

Weber, Sol. *Rounds Galore! Captivating Rounds Old nad New.* Astoria Press, Astoria, NY. 1994.

Weikart, Phyllis. *Movement Plus Music: Activities for Children Ages Three to Seven.* High/Scope Press, Ypsilanti, MI. 1989.

Wilson, Frank and Roehmann, F. *Music and Child Development.* MMB Music, St. Louis, MO. 1990.

Wuytack, Jos. *Musica Activa: An Approach to Music Education.* Schott Music Corporation, New York, NY. 1994.

**Dance/Movement Books**

Barlin, Anne. *Teaching Your Wings to Fly: The Nonspecialists Guide To Movement Activities for Young Children.* Goodyear, Santa Monica, CA. 1979.

Blom, Lynne and Chaplin L. Tarin. *The Moment of Movement: Dance Improvisation.* University of Pittsburgh Press, Pittsburgh, PA. 1988.

Blythe, Sally Goddard. *The Well Balanced Child: Movement and Early Learning.* Hawthorn Press, Gloucestershire, UK. 2004.

Clayman, Charles. *The Human Body.* Dorling Kindersley Ltd., London, England. 1995. Gilbert,

Anne Green. *Brain-Compatible Dance Education.* NDA/AAHPERD, Reston, VA. 2006. Gilbert,

Anne Green. *Creative Dance for All Ages.* American Alliance For Health, Physical Education, Reston, VA. 1992.

Gilbert, Anne Green. *Teaching the Three R's Through Movement Experiences.* Anne Green Gilbert, Publisher (www.creativedance.org), Seattle, WA. 2000.

Goddard, Sally. *Reflexes, Learning and Behavior: A Window Into the Child's Mind.* Fern Ridge Press, Eugene, OR. 2002.

Hackney, Peggy. *Making Connections: Total Body Integration Through Bartenieff Fundamentals.* Gordon And Breach Publishers, Amsterdam, The Netherlands. 1998.

Hannaford, Carla. *Smart Moves.* Great Ocean Publishers, Arlington, VA. 1995.

Joyce, Mary. *First Steps in Teaching Creative Dance to Children* (3rd ed.). Mayfield Publishing Company, Mt. View, CA. 1994.

Kindersley, Barnabas and Anabel. *Celebrations!* Dorling Kindersley Ltd., London, England. 1997.

Laban, Rudolf, and Lawrence, F.C. *Effort.* Hollen Street Press, Ltd., Slough, Berkshire. 1974.

Nash, Grace. *More Verses and Movement: For the Classroom.* NASH, Scottsdale, AZ. 1975.

Nash, Grace. *Verses and Movement: For the Classroom.* NASH, Scottsdale, AZ. 1967.

Porter, Phil. *Having It All.* Wing It! Press, Oakland, CA. 1997.

Sivananda Yoga Vedanta Center. *Yoga Mind and Body.* Dorling Kindersley Ltd., London, England. 1996.

Stinson, Sue. *Dance For Young Children: Finding the Magic in Movement.* American Alliance for Health, Physical Education, Recreation and Dance, Reston, VA. 1988.

Weikart, Phyllis. *Teaching Movement and Dance.* High/Scope Press, Ypsilanti, MI. 1982.

**Education Resources**

Britz-Crecelius, Heidi. *Children at Play: Using Waldorf Principles to Foster Childhood Development.* Park Street Press, Rochester, VT. 1972/1996.

Gardner, Howard. *Frames Of Mind: The Theory of Multiple Intelligences.* Basic Books, New York, NY. 1983.

Goodkin, Doug. *The ABC's of Education: A Primer for Schools To Come.* Pentatonic Press, San Francisco, CA. 2006.

**Poetry and Storytelling**

Cockburn, Victor and Steinbergh, Judith. *Where I Come From! Songs and Poems From Many Cultures.* Talking Stone Press, Boston, MA. 1991.

Forest, Heather. *Wisdom Tales from Around the World.* August House Publishers, Inc. Little Rock, AK. 1996.

Forest, Heather. *Wonder Tales from Around the World.* August House Publishers, Inc. Little Rock, AK. 1995.

Hughes, Langston. *The Dreamkeeper and Other Poems.* Alfred A. Knopf, Inc., New York, NY. 1994.

**Children's Books With Music**

Adoff, Arnold. *Street Music*. HarperCollins Publishers, 1995.

Auch, Mary Jane. *Bantam of the Opera*. Holiday House, Inc., 1997.

Baer, Gene. *Rat-A-Tat-Tat*. HarperCollins Publishers, 1989.

Barner, Bob. *Dem Bones*. Chronicle Books, 1996.

Bryan, Ashley. *All Night, All Day*. Simon & Schuster, 1991.

Davol, Marguerite W. *The Heart of the Wood*. Simon & Schuster, 1992.

de Vos, Philip. *Carnival of the Animals*. Front Street Books, Inc., 1998.

Fleischman, Paul. *I Am the Phoenix: Poems for Two Voices*. HarperCollins, 1998.
    *Joyful Noise: Poems For Two Voices*. HarperCollins, 1995.

Fleming, Candace. *Gabriella's Song*. Simon & Schuster, 1997.

Hopkins, Lee Bennett. *Song and Dance*. Simon & Schuster, 1997.

Igus, Toyomi and Wood, Michele. *I See the Rhythm*. Children's Book Press, 1998.

London, Jonathan. *Hip Cat*. Chronicle Books, 1993.

McDermott, Gerald. *Musicians of the Sun*. Simon & Schuster, 1997.

Mutchnick, Brenda and Casden, Ron. *A Noteworthy Tale*. Harry N. Abrams, Inc., 1997.

Ober, Hal and Carol. *How Music Came to the World*. Houghton Mifflin Company, 1994.

Pinkney, Brian. *Max Found Two Sticks*. Simon & Schuster, 1997.

Sendak, Maurice. *Nutcracker.* Crown Publishers, Inc., 1984.

Sikundar, Sylvia. *Forest Singer.* Barefoot Books, 1999.

Spagnoli, Cathy. *Nine-In-One Grr! Grr!* Children's Book Press, 1989.

Staines, Bill. *All God's Critters Got a Place in the Choir.* Dutton Children's Books, 1989.

## WEBSITES

| | |
|---|---|
| *www.acda.org* | *American Choral Directors Association* |
| *www.amazon.com* | *Amazon (for music books, CDs, videos)* |
| *www.amc-music.com* | *American Music Conference* |
| *www.amshq.org* | *American Montessori Society* |
| *www.aosa.org* | *American Orff-Schulwerk Association* |
| *www.awsna.org* | *Association Of Waldorf Schools Of North America* |
| *www.bobbymcferrin.com* | *Bobby McFerrin's website* |
| *www.interplay.org* | *InterPlay (Body Wisdom)* |
| *www.barnesandnobel.com* | *Borders Books And Music* |
| *www.brainrules.net* | *Dr. John Medina's site for the book, DVD and info* |
| *www.creativedance.org* | *Creative Dance Center (Anne Gilbert, Director)* |
| *www.dalcrozeusa.org* | *American Dalcroze Society* |
| *richardsinstitute.org* | *Education Through Music (Mary Helen Richards)* |
| *www.folkways.si.edu* | *Smithsonian Folkways - nonprofit record label* |
| *www.madrobinmusic.com* | *Mad Robin Music & Dance* |
| *www.beatinpathpublications.com* | *Beatin' Path Publications LLC* |
| *www.jwpepper.com* | *JW Pepper (sheet music and books)* |
| *www.trinitylaban.ac.uk* | *Laban/Bartenieff Institute Of Movement Studies* |
| *www.ladyslipper.org* | *Ladyslipper Catalog (music by women)* |
| *www.livingmusic.com* | *Paul Winter's site for music and earth healing* |
| *nafme.org* | *Music Educator's National Conference* |
| *www.musicforlittlepeople.com* | *Music for Little People* |
| *musicforpeople.org/my/* | *Music for People* |
| *www.nickmusic.com* | *Nick Page's website (Choral Family Newsletter)* |
| *www.oake.org* | *Organization Of American Kodaly Educators* |
| *pbskids.org* | *Public Broadcasting System (Sesame Street, etc.)* |
| *www.singout.org* | *SING OUT! Corporation* |
| *www.stepafrika.org* | *Step Afrika* |
| *www.suzukiassociation.org* | *Suzuki Association Of The Americas, Inc.* |
| *www.sweethoney.com* | *Sweet Honey in the Rock* |
| *www.treefrogpro.com* | *Tree Frog Productions/Kerri-oke Publications* |
| *www.westmusic.com* | *West Music Company* |
| *www.worldmusicpress.com* | *World Music Press* |

## VIDEOGRAPHY/DVD

*The 5000 Fingers Of Dr. T.* Columbia Pictures, Culver City, CA. 1952, 1980.

*Amazing Grace: With Bill Moyers.* Newbridge Communications, Inc. 1999.

*Beethoven Lives Upstairs.* The Children's Group, Inc., Toronto, Ontario. 1992.

*Celtic Tides: A Musical Odyssey.* Putamayo World Music, Cottonpourt Holdings, Inc./Nashmount Productions, Inc., New York, NY. 1998.

*BLAST!* PBS Home DVD. Distributed by Warner Home Video. Burbank, CA. 2001.

*Body Music With Keith Terry.* Crosspulse Records & DVD, Berkeley, CA. 2002.

*Body Tjak.* Crosspulse Records & DVD, Berkeley, CA. 2001.

*BrainDance.* AGG Productions, Seattle, WA. 2005.

*Cirque du Soleil: We Reinvent the Circus.* Telemagik Productions/Island Visual Arts, New York, NY. 1989, 1992.

*Creating Music: Orff-Schulwerk in Action.* The American Orff-Schulwerk Association, Cincinnati, OH.

*Dances of the 7 Continents.* FolkStyle Productions, Evanston, IL. 2006.

*Dancing: Series.* Kultur, West Long Branch, NJ. 1993.

*Falling Down Stairs: Yo-Yo Ma Inspired by Bach With Mark Morris.* Rhoumus Media, New York, NY. 1995.

*The Very Hungry Caterpillar and Other Stories by Eric Carle (I See A Song).* Buena Vista Home Entertainment/Disney, 1995/2006.

*Into the Circle: An Introduction To the Powwow.* Full Circle Communications, 2004. Scott Swearingen and Sandy Rhoades, producers. 1.800.940.8849

*John Cage.* Kultur, West Long Branch, NJ. 1990.

*Kodo: Live At Acropolis, Athens, Greece.* Sony Music Entertainment, Inc., Japan. 1995, 1997.

*Music Moments To Teach Academics: Resources*

*Music and the Mind.* NAMM/VH 1. 1999.

*The Nature of Music.* Kultur, West Long Branch, NJ. 1988.

*Notes Alive! Dr. Seuss's My Many Colored Days.* Minnesota Orchestral Association, Minneapolis, MN. 1999.

*Notes Alive! On the Day You Were Born.* Minnesota Orchestral Association, Minneapolis, MN. 1996.

*Nursery Tap, Hip to Toe: Volumes One and Two.* Juleen Murray Shaw, Nursery Tap, LLC. Gig Harbor, WA. 2005, 2006.

*Odetta: Exploring Life, Music and Song.* Homespun Video, Woodstock, NY. 1999.

*Peter and the Wolf.* Walt Disney Home Video, Burbank, CA.

*River of Song: A Musical Journey Down the Mississippi.* AcornMedia.

*Roots of Rhythm: With Harry Belafonte.* Cultural Research And Communication, Inc., Los Angeles, CA. 1994.

*Say Amen, Somebody.* First Run Features, New York, NY.

*Schoolhouse Rock: Series.* Capital Cities/ABC Video Publishing, Inc., Stamford, CT. 1995.

*Spirit: A Journey in Dance, Drums And Song.* Back Row Productions, New York, NY. 1998.

*Stomp Out Loud.* Yes/No Productions, Ltd., New York, NY. 1997.

*Tickle Tune Typhoon: Let's Be Friends.* Celebrity Home Entertainment, Inc., Woodland Hills, CA. 1990.

*Travel the World with Putumayo.* Putumayo World Music, New York, NY. 2004. *Victor Borge in London.* Kultur, Long Branch, NJ. 1972.

*Young People's Concerts with Leonard Bernstein: What Does Music Mean?* Video Music Education, Inc., New York, NY. 1958 (Television release), 1990, 1993.

*Zimbabwe Children's Singing Games.* ITS Video Production Center, University of Idaho. 2003.